Preface – Ch. 3

American Populism

The Golden Bottle
pg. 94

Democrats ~~Socofoco~~ – who were a secretive
group, ~~when asked to~~ working class
reminent – refers to matches instead
of lighting your cigarette by the fire
urban, northern

PROBLEMS IN AMERICAN CIVILIZATION

American Populism

Edited and with an introduction by

William F. Holmes
University of Georgia

D. C. HEATH AND COMPANY
Lexington, Massachusetts   Toronto

Address editorial correspondence to:

D. C. Heath and Company
125 Spring Street
Lexington, MA 02173

Acquisitions Editor: James Miller
Production Editor: Melissa Ray
Designer: Kenneth Hollman
Photo Researcher: Martha Shethar
Production Coordinator: Charles Dutton
Permissions Editor: Margaret Roll

Cover: Minnesota Historical Society

Published simultaneously in Canada.

Printed in the United States of America.

International Standard Book Number: 0–669–33495–2

Library of Congress Catalog Number: 93–78317

10 9 8 7 6 5 4 3 2 1

To my daughter, Catherine, and my son, William

The Editor

William F. Holmes grew up in Yazoo City, Mississippi. He received his B.A. from the University of Notre Dame, his M.A. from the University of Delaware, and his Ph.D. from Rice University. Since 1968 he has taught American history at the University of Georgia, where he currently serves as Professor of History and Secretary/Treasurer of the Southern Historical Association.

His publications include *The White Chief: James Kimble Vardaman* (1970); *A History of Georgia* (1977, 1991); and articles in *Agricultural History, Alabama Review, American Jewish Historical Quarterly, Arkansas Historical Quarterly, Delaware History, Georgia Historical Quarterly, Journal of American History, Journal of Mississippi History, Journal of Southern History, Mid-America, Mississippi Quarterly, Phylon,* and *South Atlantic Quarterly.* His articles include pieces on the Colored Farmers' Alliance, the Southern Farmers' Alliance, and Populism.

Preface

A quarter of a century ago, Raymond J. Cunningham edited *The Populists in Historical Perspective* (1968) for D. C. Heath's Problems in American Civilization series. Its publication coincided closely with that of two other anthologies: Theodore Saloutos, *Populism: Reaction or Reform?* (1968) and Sheldon Hackney, *Populism: The Critical Issues* (1971). Although each of the three volumes differed significantly from the others, they all devoted considerable attention to Richard Hofstadter's critique of Populism in *The Age of Reform* (1955) and to some of the responses to his interpretation.

None of these volumes is now available, at least in a form accessible to the undergraduate reader. Moreover, the focus of Populist scholarship has shifted significantly since the 1960s. Over the past two decades a wide variety of able studies have appeared on many aspects of the movement, and this volume concentrates primarily on that body of work. It also includes three older pieces, one of which was published in a modified form in Cunningham's anthology. Populism's continuing attraction for scholars underscores the importance of the movement in American history. Appearing near the end of the nineteenth century, Populism reflected the transition from an agrarian order dominated by small proprietors to an urban order controlled by corporations. The movement addressed many central issues, including the role of the individual in an economy increasingly dominated by big business, relations between black and white Americans, and the role of an insurgent movement in challenging the established political parties. Those issues remain relevant a century after Populism's initial poularity.

I would like to thank the following historians who reviewed the proposal for this anthology: Paula Baker, University of Pittsburgh; Gene Clanton, Washington State University; David Danbom, North Dakota State University; Wayne Flynt, Auburn University; Lewis Gould, University of Texas—Austin; Gerald McFarland, University of Massachusetts—Amherst; H. Wayne Morgan, University of Oklahoma; and Ronald Petrin, Oklahoma State University. Marguerite Gahagan Holmes, my wife, and John

C. Inscoe, a friend and colleague, read the introduction and suggested ways to improve it. James Miller, Melissa Ray, and Margaret
Roll of D. C. Heath provided valuable assistance in bringing this
project to completion. I am deeply grateful for the help given by
each person listed above.

W. H.

Contents

Introduction

The 1890s was a turbulent decade characterized by the closing of the frontier, the great strikes at Homestead and Pullman, a major depression, the pivotal presidential election of 1896, and the Spanish-American War and its imperialistic aftermath. Populism flourished during that decade, becoming the largest grass roots political insurgence in American history. Appearing initially at the state level in 1890, it quickly developed into a national movement that spread through the South, the Western Plains, and the Rocky Mountains. The new party's platform offered a bold reform program that included government ownership of railroads, a flexible currency free from control by private bankers, a graduated income tax, the free and unlimited coinage of silver, and the opportunity for settlers to acquire lands owned by American corporations and foreigners.

Although easterners perceived the new party as having exploded on the scene from out of nowhere in the 1890s, the forces that generated Populism had been at work for twenty years and involved developments that threatened the security of family farms. During the quarter century following the Civil War, the American economy experienced one of the most profound periods of change in its history. Industrial expansion and the rise of big business changed the faces of the nation's cities, but the countryside also underwent a fundamental transformation. The expansion of railroads throughout the South and West ended the isolation of rural communities, drawing more and more inhabitants from subsistance farming into a highly commercial agricultural system. That change brought rural people into a complex set of market relations with merchants, commodities dealers, and railroads. In the new system, farmers confronted rising operating costs, falling commodity prices, high railroad rates, and inadequate credit facilities. The persistence of these problems eroded the farmers' status as every year a growing number of them lost ownership of their lands and became farm laborers and tenants.

The difficulties confronting commercialized farmers gave rise to a variety of agricultural organizations during the 1870s and 1880s including the Patrons of Husbandry, the Agricultural Wheel, the Farmers' Mutual Benefit Association, the Northern Farmers' Alliance, and the Colored Farmers' Alliance. However, the organization that played the strongest role in shaping Populism originaed in Texas and eventually became known as the Southern Farmers' Alliance. Through its cooperatives the Southern Farmers' Alliance united small, land-owning farmers in a campaign to free themselves from the exploitative interest rates charged by merchants. Enjoying its greatest strength in the cotton belt, the Southern Farmers' Alliance also became a powerful force in the West. Populism derived much of its ideology and many of its members from that Alliance.

The agrarian uprising occasionally intersected with third parties and industrial working class organizations. For example, the Greenback party persuaded many farmers of the need for a flexible currency independent of gold or silver. During the strikes against Jay Gould's southwestern railroad system in 1885 and 1886, the Southern Alliance also cooperated with the Knights of Labor. This interaction between rural people and non-farm organizations influenced the agrarian crusade and broadened its appeal.

Developing in response to problems that threatened the farmer's very existence, Populism reflected a deep strain of anger in its members. The preamble to the party's 1892 platform declared:

> We meet in the midst of a nation brought to the verge of moral, political, and material ruin. Corruption dominates the ballot-box, the legislatures, the Congress, and touches even the ermine of the bench. . . . The fruits of the toil of millions are boldly stolen to build up colossal fortunes for the few, unprecedented in the history of mankind; and the possessors of those, in turn, despise the republic and endanger liberty. From the same prolific womb of governmental injustice we breed the two great classes—tramps and millionaires.

Additionally, Populist challenges alarmed members of the older parties. Georgia Democrats perceived a distinct threat when Tom Watson, a Populist congressman, urged blacks *and* whites to unite in the new party. The appearance of Mary Lease, a dynamic female spokesperson for the Kansas Populists, offered little comfort to the commercial classes when she announced that it "is no longer a government of the people, for the people, and by the people, but a government of Wall Street, for Wall Street and by Wall Street." Colorado Republicans were deeply troubled by their state's Populist governor, Davis Waite, who announced that the People's party wanted to return the nation to a bimetallic standard by means of the ballot. But, he went on to warn that "if the money power shall attempt to sustain its usurpations by the 'strong hand,' we will meet that issue when it is forced upon us, for it is better, infinitely better that blood should flow to the horses' bridles than our national liberties should be destroyed."

Despite the passions that it generated, Populism proved to be a short-lived movement. By 1896 the Democrats seized the most popular issue in the Populist platform—free silver—and nominated William Jennings Bryan for president. Believing that silver could serve as a catalyst for additional reforms and that they did not have a candidate with Bryan's appeal, the Populists also selected him as their nominee. In doing that they undermined their party's existence as an entity distinct from the Democrats and Republicans. Although the People's party persisted into the early twentieth century, the movement had become an empty shell.

Though of brief duration, Populism played a significant role in the nineteenth century's final years. In addition to challenging the older parties, it contributed to a fundamental change in the Democratic party by elevating silver to the central place in the 1896 platform and by transferring leadership from the conservative Grover Cleveland to the progressive Bryan. More importantly, Populism reflected a fundamental transition in the nation's political economy from a system characterized by small-town culture dominated by proprietary capitalism to a system typified by an industrial, urban culture where corporate capitalism ruled.

Historians have long recognized that Populism represented an important point in American history. Constructive scholarly work actually began in the midst of the movement. In 1893 Arthur F. Bentley, who had a distinguished career as a political scientist, provided insight into the origins of the movement in his study of a Nebraska township. In the early decades of the twentieth century, historians such as Alex Mathews Arnett, John Buyan Clark, and Raymond Curtis Miller wrote able monographs that further advanced understanding of the movement. More significant historical studies appeared in the 1930s and 1940s with the works of John D. Hicks, C. Vann Woodward, and Chester McArthur Destler. They presented Populism as a movement of hard-working farmers victimized by bankers, railroads, and merchants. Populism represented a positive response to those problems and marked the beginning of modern liberalism, which would later find expression in Progressivism and the New Deal.

The positive image enjoyed by Populism in the 1930s and 1940s received a major challenge in the 1950s when a more critical view emerged, especially in the writings of Richard Hofstadter. While not completely abandoning the older view of Populism, Hofstadter argued that it contained serious flaws that found expression in repressive right-wing movements of the twentieth century. Hofstadter's critique of Populism sparked fresh interest in the subject, and during the 1960s scholars examined many aspects of the movement, some continuing the critical appraisals that were fashionable in the 1950s, others adhering to the far more positive image that dominated works of the 1930s and 1940s.

The debate between the two schools of critical analysis essentially had run its course by the close of the 1960s, but interest in Populism did not abate. Historians published more studies on the Populist movement during the 1970s and 1980s than in any comparable period. However, the new body of literature did not lend itself to the clear division that characterized earlier scholarship. For one thing, no single work served as a point of departure as did Hofstadter's *Age of Reform* during the 1950s and 1960s and Hicks's *Populist Revolt* during the 1930s and 1940s. Nor has Populist scholarship taken on the outlines of a distinct school like the new labor history. Instead, Populist historiography has consisted primarily of regional monographs and has addressed issues and employed methodologies common to the broader field of American history. Scholars have, for example, relied increasingly on quantification to determine more precisely the pockets of Populist strength and to understand more clearly voting patterns in legislative bodies; sociologists have employed mobilization theory in examining class divisions within the movement; and Marxist modes of analysis have helped to illuminate the relationship between Populism and the modern capitalist system. The most prominent subjects of Populist studies since the 1960s include the origins of the movement in the Southern Farmers' Alliance, Populism's relation to capitalism and the class structure, the ordeal of establishing a viable third party in a two-party system, Populism's influence on southern race relations, and the movement's place in the American reform tradition.

The readings in this volume consist primarily of studies that appeared during the 1970s and 1980s, although I have also included selections from the 1930s, 1940s, and 1950s. Two of the earlier pieces appearing in the first section address the origins and causes of the movement. In 1931 John D. Hicks explained western Populism as a response to the closing of the frontier. A decade later Chester McArthur Destler kept the focus on the West but did so by tracing Populism's origins to a series of reform causes that stretched back into the early nineteenth century and emanated from eastern cities. More recent works by Lawrence Goodwyn, Steven Hahn, and James Turner focus on the South. Goodwyn traced the origins of Populist radicalism to the cooperative programs that the Southern Alliance sponsored during the 1880s. While their works differ in many ways, Hahn and Turner both found that Populism provided the more rural and less developed areas a way to protest the modernizing forces that began rapidly transforming the countryside. Collectively, the five selections in the first section provide rich insights into the ideas and developments that gave rise to Populism while also reflecting major historiographical trends from as early as 1931.

The pieces included in the second section appeared relatively recently and address a variety of subjects that contribute to a clearer understanding of the movement. In examining public education, Theodore Mitchell illustrated the strong sense of localism that pervaded the Southern Farmers' Alliance and Populism. The Southern Alliance embodied a grass roots movement that wanted to empower its members and that distrusted attempts to centralize authority in bureaucracies at the county and state levels. Although they each addressed quite different issues, Michael Schwartz and Peter H. Argersinger explored weaknesses that contributed to the demise of the Alliance and People's party. Schwartz discovered a serious class division that undermined relations between Alliance leaders and the rank-and-file membership. Argersinger found that Kansas Populism suffered from a monumental case of political indigestion because the new party could not ameliorate the rivalries that its members brought with them from the Republican, Democratic, and Union Labor parties. Mari Jo Buhle is one of the few historians who considered how gender influenced the movement. It clearly did, because the Southern Alliance opened its membership to women, and in the West women were very active in the People's party. Robert Larson challenged the long-time assumption that free silver alone fueled Rocky Mountain Populism by tracing its origins to a variety of issues. Finally, Gene Clanton addressed the question of what kind of reform movement Populism was by examining the voting records of the people who represented the party in Congress. Although small in number, these Congressmen had the opportunity to apply the movement's principles by supporting measures designed to help the small farmer class.

Section three focuses on the relationship between white Populists and African Americans. The birth of Populism coincided with a pivotal time in southern race relations because it was in the 1890s that southern states began enacting segregation statutes and adding disfranchisement provisions to their constitutions. Although the status of African Americans had declined since the close of Reconstruction, it took a decided turn for the worse in the 1890s. Historians have long debated whether the Populists contributed to that deterioration. One group, represented by Carl Degler, contended that white Populists recognized the right of blacks to vote and to have their votes counted honestly. They realized that the Populists did not condone social equality between the races, but they argued that African Americans would have enjoyed fairer treatment if the Populists had dominated public offices in the South. Since the 1960s a rival group of historians has challenged this view, but the work from that side became stronger in the 1980s as the pieces by Barton C. Shaw, Gregg Cantrell, and D. Scott Barton illustrate.

The selections in the final section discuss Populism's place in American history and how it compared to movements that came before and after it. As noted earlier, Richard Hofstadter wrote one of the more critical appraisals of Populism in the 1950s, and it still warrants consideration. Two decades after Hofstadter's work was published, Lawrence Goodwyn advanced what remains the most positive view of the movement to date. Because Populism did not prevail, Goodwyn contended, twentieth-century America has become a poorer place in which to live. While Bruce Palmer appreciated Populism, he found that the movement clung to an older republican outlook that prevented it from effectively addressing the problems of its era. Robert Cherny did not present as exalted a view of Populism as Goodwyn did, but he saw it as an important grass roots movement that had a positive influence on Nebraska politics persisting well into the twentieth century. Like a number of other recent scholars, including Theodore Mitchell and Gene Clanton, Cherny found that Populism differed in important ways from Progressivism and other manifestations of twentieth-century liberalism. Worth Robert Miller also perceived these differences and presented Populism within the context of nineteenth-century republican movements.

For many years historians have debated over what Populism represented. This debate remains relevant because the Populists addressed issues that still affect us. By critically reading and discussing the selections in this volume, students can come to their own understanding of the movement and its place in history.

Chronology

1867	Founding of the Patrons of Husbandry.
1869	Founding of the Knights of Labor
1873	Coinage Act—"Crime of '73".
1876–1882	Greenback party is active.
1877	*March:* Founding of New York Farmers' Alliance; *July:* Great Railroad Strike; *September:* Founding of Texas Farmers' Alliance.
1878	Bland–Allison Act.
1879	Farmers' Alliance is organized in Parker County, Texas.
1880	Milton George establishes the Northern Farmers' Alliance in Cook County, Illinois.
1884	S. O. Daws becomes a traveling lecturer for the Texas Alliance.
1885	Strike against Jay Gould's southwestern railroad system results in victory for the Knights of Labor.
1886	Second strike against the Gould system results in a victory for the railroad; *May 4:* Haymarket Square Riot in Chicago; *August:* Texas Alliance adopts the Cleburne Platform; Colored Farmers' Alliance is organized in Texas.
1887	The Texas Alliance spreads through the South and becomes popularly known as the Southern Farmers' Alliance.

1888   *June:* There is an unsuccessful attempt to save the Texas Alliance's State Exchange; *August:* Jute Cartel doubles the price of its product and the Southern Alliance initiates a boycott against it; *November:* Union Labor party runs candidates in state elections.

1889   Southern Alliance boycott forces the Jute Cartel to lower its price; *December:* The Southern Alliance renames itself the National Farmers' Alliance and Industrial Union at its national meeting in St. Louis, adopts a reform platform, introduces the subtreasury plan, and elects Leonidas Polk as its president.

1890   Congress enacts the Sherman Silver Purchase Act; *November:* Through the Democratic party in the South and independent parties in the West, Alliance candidates win impressive victories in state elections; *December:* The National Farmers' Alliance and Industrial Union meets at Ocala, Florida and adopts a major reform platform.

1891   *January:* The Northern Alliance meets at Omaha and adopts demands similar to those in the Ocala platform; *May:* Delegates representing the alliances, other farm organizations, and a variety of reform groups meet in Cincinnati to make plans for the formation of the People's party; *Summer:* Third party advocates from the West address large Alliance rallies in the South; *November:* National Farmers' Alliance and Industrial Union meets in Indianapolis; *December:* Congressional Populists hold their first caucus and nominate Tom Watson for House Speaker.

1892   *February:* Conference of Industrial Organizations meets in St. Louis and organizes the People's party; *April:* Johnson County Range War in Wyoming;

June: Death of Leonidas Polk; *July:* Populist convention nominates James B. Weaver for president and James G. Field for vice president; *November:* Grover Cleveland wins the presidential election.

1893 *May:* Onset of the depression; *August:* Congress repeals the Sherman Silver Purchase Act.

1894 *March–August:* Industrial armies (including Jacob Coxey's) march on Washington; *July:* Federal troops break the Pullman strike; American Bimetallic League intensifies its campaign for the free and unlimited coinage of silver; William Jennings Bryan becomes a major spokesman for free silver; *November:* In the mid-term elections, the western Populists suffer setbacks, but southern Populists make gains.

1896 *January:* Populist leaders decide to postpone their national nominating convention until after the Democrats and Republicans complete their conventions; *June:* Republicans nominate William McKinley for president; *July:* Democrats nominate William Jennings Bryan for president and Arthur Sewall for vice president; Populists nominate Bryan for president and Tom Watson for vice president; *November:* McKinley wins the election.

American Populism

I

Origins and Causes of the Movement

John D. Hicks

THE FRONTIER BACKGROUND

When John D. Hicks published the first major history of Populism in 1931, he accounted for the rise of the movement in the western plains as a response to the sudden closing of the frontier. The rapid migration of people into Kansas, Nebraska, and the Dakotas that had swelled into a boom by the 1880s, suddenly collapsed in 1887, when a drought destroyed the crops and rainfall remained below normal over the next decade. By 1890, Hicks concluded, flight "to a new frontier could no longer avail, for the era of free lands was over. **The various agrarian movements, particularly the [Farmers'] Alliance and the Populist revolts, were but the inevitable attempts of a bewildered people to find relief from a state of economic distress made certain by the unprecedented size and suddenness of their assault upon the West and by the finality with which they had conquered it."** Hicks, who was strongly influenced by Frederick Jackson Turner's frontier thesis, published extensively on agrarian movements. He also wrote *Republican Ascendancy, 1921–1933* (1960).

To the nineteenth century American . . . it probably never occurred that the rapid expansion of the West was perhaps not an unmixed good. The land, he assumed, was there to be conquered, and the sooner the conquest could be completed the better. Whatever helped to further that end was wise and good and right. Whatever held it back was an obstacle in the way of "progress." The railways had doubtless accelerated the conquest of the continent quite as much as he believed, and they were therefore of the very essence of all that was best. The suggestion of a foreigner, Lord Bryce, that perhaps the American West had grown too fast and that if development had been slower "it might have moved upon better lines," would have filled him with amazement and disgust.

But Bryce was doubtless right. Certainly when the railways assumed command of the westward movement, they pushed it forward with unseemly haste. Never deliberate, the advance of the

From *The Populist Revolt: A History of the Farmers' Alliance and the People's Party* by John D. Hicks, pp. 1–5, 7, 15–16, 18–21, 23–25, 29–32, 34–35. Copyright 1961, originally published by the University of Minnesota Press, 1931. Reprinted by permission of the publisher.

frontier now became a headlong rush. It took a century and a half for the frontier to reach the Appalachians; it took a good half century for it to move from the Appalachians to the Mississippi, even though in this second West the rivers generally solved the problem of transportation by flowing the right way; but it took only another half century to annihilate the frontier altogether, in spite of the vast mountain and desert spaces that blocked the way in the trans-Mississippi West. Under railway leadership the population came in too rapidly to permit the thoughtful and deliberate readjustments. A society at once so new and so numerous was immediately confronted with problems that it could not comprehend, much less hope to solve. Flight to a new frontier could no longer avail, for the era of free lands was over. The various agrarian movements, particularly the [Farmer's] Alliance and the Populist revolts, were but the inevitable attempts of a bewildered people to find relief from a state of economic distress made certain by the unprecedented size and suddenness of their assault upon the West and by the finality with which they had conquered it.

The building of the transcontinental railways marked the beginning of the end for the last American frontier. These lines were projected before the Civil War, and most of the available routes were surveyed during the decade of the fifties, but the impending struggle between North and South prevented immediate action. Only when the war was on and the objections of "state righters" and strict constructionists were no longer heard in Congress was the nationalistic North free to go ahead with what was essentially a nationalistic policy. Then one Pacific railway bill after another was enacted into law. The Union Pacific received its original charter in 1862, the Northern Pacific in 1864, the Atlantic and Pacific, whose charter rights were later enjoyed mainly by the Santa Fe, in 1866, and the Texas Pacific in 1871.

These laws carried the practice of governmental assistance to railways a step further than it had ever gone before. Grants of government land to states in aid of internal improvements had been common since 1850, and great quantities of land thus given to the states had been handed on to the railways. But the Pacific railways received their lands directly from the national government. . . . In the meantime the policy of land grants to the states for railway purposes enabled some of the newly created western commonwealths to

Cripple Creek Miners. In 1894 Colorado's Populist governor, Davis H. Waite, helped resolve a strike at Cripple Creek in a way the miners judged to be fair. This photograph illustrates Populism's appeal to industrial laborers in the West. (*Colorado Historical Society*)

vie with the national government in the generosity of their gifts. Altogether no less than 129,000,000 acres of the public lands were distributed, directly or indirectly, to the railways. . . .

It was quite as much the business of the roads to people this West as to penetrate it. Only by so doing could they hope to build up the thriving local business upon which their future prosperity would depend. Handsome dividends could come only from local freight rates, and local freight rates could be paid only by actual settlers. The transcontinental lines had, of course, a certain secure through business, but no one was sanguine enough to believe that this business alone, divided up as it must be among four or five competitors, would supply much revenue. The new frontier must be advertised and settled—the sooner the better. Naturally enough, this duty was assumed in the main by the land-grant roads, each of which speedily organized a land department and began to boom its wares. The land departments, ably managed, made it their chief concern to collect and disseminate by every known method such information about the territory adjacent to their roads as might induce people to come there to live.

This task was not altogether an easy one, in spite of the normal proneness of the American farmer to go West, for the old fiction of the Great American Desert was not yet fully discredited. Many people knew better, but for the multitudes the tradition that the country to the west of the Missouri River was good only for the Indians and of no value to the whites was still sound doctrine. Political necessities rather than the pressure of population had forced the organization of Kansas and Nebraska, and the sparseness of their settlements in the sixties testified eloquently to the common belief in the worthlessness of their soil and climate. The average man who had heard of these and neighboring regions was afraid of them. He might concede that agriculture would have a chance for a few miles beyond the Missouri River, but he solemnly warned the prospective emigrant that to adventure farther was to enter a region where "nothing would grow." Some placed the dead line as close as ten miles to the west of the river; the most optimistic made it less than a hundred; there was general agreement that agricultural settlement beyond that distance was impossible. . . .

As the illusion of the Great American Desert gradually disappeared, the tremendous attractiveness of this new West became more and more apparent. The terms offered by the railways were clearly designed to bring in settlers rather than to produce a revenue. The prices asked were uniformly low. The average price at which the Burlington sold its entire Nebraska grant was $5.14 an acre, but it disposed of enormous tracts of land at as low a price as twenty-five cents an acre. The usual government minimum of $1.25 an acre and "double minimum" of $2.50 an acre were prices very commonly asked and obtained. . . .

It was not until well along in the seventies that settlers began to pour into the new West in satisfactory numbers. The few who came first were not entirely contented with their lot. In addition to the usual hard times of the frontier the early venturers were confronted with grasshopper plagues of such appalling severity that many of the fainter-hearted gave up and returned to their eastern homes. The period of hard times following the panic of 1873, however, caused considerable unemployment and unrest in the eastern portion of the United States and created a class who were not unwilling to listen to the blandishments of the railway advertisers. By the late seventies a tremendous westward migration had set in, the magnitude of which was fully attested by the census reports of

1880. In the decade of the seventies Kansas had advanced from a third of a million to a million inhabitants; Nebraska, from a quarter of a million to a half million; Dakota Territory, from fourteen thousand to nearly ten times that number. The neighboring states of Iowa and Minnesota, in the western portions of which there was still much vacant land in 1870, were similarly affected, although to a smaller degree. In this decade Iowa added nearly half a million to her population and jumped from twentieth to eleventh place among the states with respect to number of inhabitants. Minnesota gained nearly three hundred thousand, an increase of about seventy-five percent over the figures for 1870. . . .

. . . The frontier expansion reflected by the census of 1880 gained such momentum in the succeeding years that by the middle eighties it had attained the full proportions of a boom. According to Senator Peffer, who did not exaggerate greatly, "a territory larger than that of the thirteen original states was populated in half a dozen years." Whereas the movement of the seventies had resulted mainly in the settlement of the eastern third of the trans-Missouri states, that of the eighties pushed beyond into the central portions. In Kansas, Nebraska, and Dakota Territory each new legislature created new counties in this central region literally by the dozen, and new villages, new towns, and new cities sprang up by the hundreds. Each little town became a boom town, foolishly optimistic about its future and ready enough to believe the rhetorical absurdities of its pamphleteers.

Indeed, settlers pushed on into the arid zone of western Kansas and Nebraska and even farther. Eastern Colorado, where the "only crop for years was bankrupts," now became the scene of a lively boom. Here land that had an elevation of thirty-five hundred feet was seized upon as eagerly as land along the Missouri River where the elevation was only seven hundred and fifty feet. The Colorado boomers claimed that in a single year fifty thousand people had entered the eastern portion of the state. These newcomers shared with the settlers in western Kansas and Nebraska a conviction, duly fostered by the advertisers, that the rain belt had lately moved so far to the westward that the high table-lands of the plains could now no longer properly be classified as arid. The fact was that in the eight years preceding 1887 there had been an unusual amount of rainfall in this area, and the belief was common that the plowing of ground, the planting of trees, and the introduction of irrigation were the causes:

"These vast extents of plowed land not only create a rainfall by their evaporation, but invite rains by their contrasts of temperature."

Whatever the causes, people were soon persuaded that the change had taken place, and they seemed not to question its permanence. Even a professor of natural science at the University of Nebraska appears to have shared the common delusion. He seemed to think that ultimately rainfall in the western part of the state would equal the rainfall in the eastern portions. . . .

This rapid movement of population to the West was accompanied by an equally extraordinary movement of capital in the same direction. Not much of this capital, however, was brought in by the settlers. Especially in the earlier years of the migration the men who went West were poor, and sometimes, in spite of the warning of the railway advertisers that disappointment, homesickness, and discontent might be the lot of those who came entirely destitute of means, they were penniless. Even those who had some savings to depend upon rarely had enough to tide them through the first hard year, for it took several hundred dollars at the very least to pay the cost of living until a crop could be harvested, to erect farm buildings and fences, and to buy seed grain and machinery. Those who had no money when they came and were unable to obtain it from interested friends or relatives often worked as farm hands until they had saved the necessary minimum upon which to make a start. Almost all the newcomers were potential borrowers. Loans upon "the possible products of wild, unfenced, uncleared, or unbroken lands" were indeed hard to get, but when the pioneers had built their houses and barns and had broken up a few acres of land, they might confidently expect such help. In fact, outside capital by the millions of dollars was necessary if these men were to succeed.

It chanced that the money needed by the western farmers could be supplied without much difficulty by eastern investors, who, as the hard times of the seventies gave way to the prosperity of the eighties, found their savings increasing by leaps and bounds. The man who had only a small sum to invest was especially attracted by western mortgages on which he could easily obtain high interest rates—from six to eight per cent on real estate and from ten to eighteen per cent on chattels. Such an investment seemed the more attractive because of the well-advertised rise in western land values. The competition of free lands, always before this time a potent cause of the low price of land, was now nearly at an end. Moreover, crop yields in the West over a period of years had averaged high, prices were good, and collections were easily made. The mortgage notes themselves, "gorgeous with gold and green ink," looked the part of stability, and the idea spread throughout the East that savings placed in this class of investments were as safe as they were remunerative. Small wonder that money descended like a flood upon those who made it their business to place loans in the West! . . .

It was inevitable that this avalanche of credit, which far outran the real needs of the situation, should tempt the new West to extravagance, overinvestment, and speculation. Farmers could rarely resist the funds proffered them. With bumper crops, high prices, and rising land values, it appeared, indeed, the part of wisdom to borrow money for enlarging holdings, improving breeds of stock, and purchasing the latest and best machinery. The federal census figures of 1890 relating to real estate mortgages furnish convincing evidence of what went on. They show that Kansas, Nebraska, North and South Dakota, and Minnesota, in spite of the comparative poverty of their inhabitants, ranked well toward the top of the list of states in the amount of per capita mortgage debt. The ratio of the real estate mortgage debt to the true value of all taxed real estate was higher in Kansas than in any other state except New York, and none of the other states mentioned ranked lower than ninth. In Kansas, also, where the amount of speculation was greatest and the figures were always most extreme, the new mortgage debt incurred per capita in the year 1885 was more than double and in 1887 more than treble, the amount of 1880; but some of the other frontier states were not far behind. In Kansas and North Dakota there was in 1890 a mortgage for every two persons, and in Nebraska, South Dakota, and Minnesota, one for every three persons—more than one to a family in all five states. In certain counties where seventy-five per cent of the farms occupied by their owners were mortgaged and where the total mortgage debt was about three-fourths of the true valuation of all the land taxed, it is not an unfair inference that most of the mortgaged farms were mortgaged literally for all they were worth. The census statistics show, in short, that Minnesota, the Dakotas, and Nebraska were all appreciably better off than Kansas, approximately in the order named, but that throughout this region mortgages had multiplied in number and amount far beyond any reasonable limits.

It is not surprising that land values rose to unprecedented heights. In a block of six counties in southeastern Nebraska the price of land doubled in the years 1881 to 1887, achieving by the latter year a price of about $17.50 an acre. This may be regarded as a typical nonspeculative gain, inasmuch as that region was as little affected by the boom as any and experienced no material decline in land prices in the period of hard times that followed. Extravagant figures, however, became a commonplace, particularly in or near the boom towns. Near Clifton, Kansas, a quarter section of land, once thought worthless, brought $6,000. A farm near Abilene in the same state that had cost $6.25 an acre in 1867 sold twenty years later for $270 an acre. Wild and unimproved land in eastern Colorado was held at from $3 to $10 an acre and when slightly cultivated, at from $8 to $20 an acre. If newspaper advertisements are to be trusted, increases in value of from 400 to 600 per cent from 1881 to 1887 were by no means unusual. . . .

That the boom could not continue indefinitely, sensible people should have foreseen, but few of them apparently had any premonition of what was to come. The process of deflation began in 1887. In Kansas the end came with dramatic suddenness; elsewhere it arrived more slowly but with disheartening certainty. The immediate cause of the slump was the lack of rainfall during the season of 1887 and, with a few exceptions, each succeeding season for a period of ten years. With the year 1886 the era of abundant rainfall on the frontier ended more or less abruptly, and the attractive stories that had circulated concerning the westward migration of the rain belt were soon demonstrated to be false. About eighteen or twenty inches of rainfall annually coming at the proper time of year is regarded by agriculturists as sufficient to produce a good crop. For a considerable period prior to 1887 these conditions had been fulfilled throughout the eastern and central portions of Kansas, Nebraska, and Dakota, and even well into the western regions. But from 1887 to 1897 there were only two years in which the central and western areas had enough rainfall to insure a full crop, and for five seasons out of the ten they had practically no crops at all. To the distress that resulted from lack of moisture were added heavy losses due to the hot winds that persisted throughout the summer months and burned the already suffering crops to a crisp. "Week after week," wrote H. W. Foght in his *History of the Loup River Region,* "the hot burning sun glared down from a cloudless steel-blue sky. The dread hot winds blew in from the south. Day after day they continued. All fodder, small grain, and corn were cut short. Where farming had been carried on extensively rather than intensively the yield amounted to preciously near nothing. The careful expert got some returns for his work, though small." Other losses came from the chinch bugs, whose depredations are worst in a period of drought, and from early frosts, especially in Dakota.

The summer of 1887, giving evidence of impending crop failure, called a halt to the boom. As the hot weeks wore on the number of real estate transfers and the prices paid for land and lots declined precipitately. The boom towns were no less affected than was the country, for their future depended quite as completely upon a continuing agricultural prosperity. It was in these towns, indeed, that the collapse was most complete, for with popular confidence shaken, there was a rush to sell out, and this speedily brought prices to a minimum. Eastern investors, learning of the turn of events in the West, no longer clamored for western securities; while countless numbers of real estate men, mortgage vendors, railway promoters, and bankers went out of business altogether, many of them hopelessly bankrupt. The cattle industry on the northwestern plains was all but destroyed. The hot summer of 1886 had left the range in poor condition, and the winter of 1886–87 had been merciless. When spring came at last only a few pitiful remnants of the great herds remained. Speculative live-stock companies lost all they had invested; "cattle barons" and "bovine kings" ceased to exist; the ranges were almost stripped of cattle in a vain effort to satisfy the demands of creditors. Hard times settled down upon the whole frontier, not to be shaken off for a decade.

Convinced by bitter experience that they had pushed too far into the arid West, people who had moved hopefully into western Kansas, Nebraska, Dakota, or beyond before 1887 now began to retrace their steps. Within a few years whole districts in this region were almost totally depopulated except for the older cattlemen who had been there before the boom began and did not depend for success upon a heavy rainfall. Covered wagons, sometimes bearing such legends as "Going back to the wife's folks," or "In God we trusted, in Kansas we busted," streamed toward the East. Fully half the people of western Kansas left the country between 1888 and

1892. Twenty well-built towns in that part of the state were reputed to have been left without a single inhabitant, and in one of them an opera house worth thirty thousand dollars, a schoolhouse worth twenty thousand dollars, and a number of fine business houses were abandoned. In the single year of 1891 no less than eighteen thousand prairie schooners crossed from the Nebraska to the Iowa side of the Missouri River in full retreat from the hopeless hard times. Twenty-six counties in South Dakota lost thirty thousand people during the nineties. Disappointed pioneers handed over their farms to the loan companies by which they had been mortgaged or abandoned them outright. Some of the more courageous may have headed for Oklahoma, where other frontier lands were being opened to settlement, but doubtless the rank and file had had enough of pioneering. . . .

Throughout the frontier region the exodus from the boom towns was appalling. Statistics are not available for all the frontier states, but for Kansas the biennial report of the state board of agriculture furnishes convincing proof of what occurred. In the two years covered by the report some sixteen cities in the eastern half of the state lost a total of more than forty-five thousand people. Leavenworth lost fifteen thousand; Wichita, thirteen thousand; and some of the smaller towns were almost wiped out. Although the figures are not available, it is clear that much the same thing happened in Nebraska and the Dakotas. Census statistics for the decade of the nineties are obviously of no great value in estimating the immediate effect of the collapse of the boom, for generally the most striking loss of population was before 1890, and there was a compensating increase after 1897, when prosperity returned. Furthermore, in nearly every western community that had been hard hit by the collapse of the boom, census statistics in 1890 were deliberately falsified to conceal as completely as possible what had happened. But it is perhaps worth noting that, according to census statistics, from one-third to one-half of the counties in Kansas, Nebraska, and South Dakota had a smaller population in 1900 than in 1890.

Aside from the fact that they may have carried the seeds of agricultural discontent back with them, the later fortunes of those who left the frontier in the period of hard times are of no interest here. The history of the West was made not by those who moved out but by those who stayed on. The withdrawal of practically all the newcomers from the arid region in the extreme western part of the frontier states left there a class accustomed to the environment and not inordinately dissatisfied. The flight of the floating and speculating element from the boom towns and cities placed control in the hands of the more substantial and conservative citizens. Nor did the eastern counties have the necessary economic basis or radicalism. But in the rural portions of the central regions, where farmers stayed and struggled with failing crops and low prices, with unyielding debts and relentless taxes, where they fought a battle, now successful, now unavailing, to retain the land they had bought and to redeem the high hopes with which they had come to the West—in this region unrest and discontent prevailed, and the grievances that later found statement in the Populist creed smouldered for a season, finally to break forth in a program of open revolt.

Chester McArthur Destler

WESTERN RADICALISM, 1865–1900: CONCEPTS AND ORIGINS

Writing in the 1940s, Chester McArthur Destler found the roots of Populist reforms in American cities. Some of the reforms extended back to the antebellum era, where they had found expression in the Locofoco movement and Edward Kellogg's monetary policy. After the Civil War, Henry Demarest Lloyd and Henry George's ideas influenced western radicals. By placing Populism in the context of other reform movements that had emanated from cities during the previous half-century, Destler provided a valuable dimension to the understanding of Populist thought. Destler taught for many years at Connecticut College, and his publications include *Henry Demarest Lloyd and the Empire of Reform* (1963) and *Roger Sherman and the Independent Oil Men* (1967).

From *American Radicalism, 1865–1901*, pp. 3–4, 6–12, 14–17, by Chester McArthur Destler pp. 3–4, 6–12, 14–17, Quadrangle Books, 1966, originally published by Connecticut College, 1946. Reprinted by permission.

The existence in the Upper Mississippi Valley, in 1865, of a system of democratic thought derived from an earlier integration of urban radicalism with the coonskin democracy of the hardwood frontier, suggests that subsequent intercourse between urban and agrarian radicals occurred within a conceptual pattern common to both. William Trimble has shown how the working-class Locofocoism of the Jacksonian era was transplanted by the westward movement to the rich soil of the Middle West in the forties and fifties. There it fused with the similar but less well-defined conceptions of the Benton Democracy in neighboring upland southern areas of settlement. It was reproduced so completely by wheat farmers on the prairies and oak openings farther to the north that insistence upon "equal rights" and intense hostility to monopoly, chartered corporations, banks, and the "money power" are to this day frequently regarded as peculiar to the rural mind. The great emphasis placed upon natural rights and the social compact by the Locofocos served in the North Central States only to re-emphasize the still dominant Lockean psychology and political theory that the region had received with its population from the Atlantic seaboard. Insistence that "Democracy is the cause of Humanity" quickened there and in the Old Northwest alike the humanitarian impulse that Charles Grandison Finney and the Second Great Awakening had aroused in American Protestantism. Although much of the older liberal heritage had been institutionalized by the establishment of constitutional democracy and the development of democratic churches, it had been vitalized anew by the evangelical movement, the temperance and anti-slavery agitations, the homestead movement, and the continuous struggle against chartered banks and special privilege in the prairie states until the appeal to arms imposed an ill-kept truce upon domestic quarrels. Shared by western farmers and the laborers of East and West alike, the radical democracy of the Locofocos and Free Democrats was Abraham Lincoln's mainstay in 1860.

The revival of the democratic movement in the trans-Allegheny states after the Civil War was more than the resurgence of ante-bellum quarrels provoked by exclusively western impulses. It offers the first clear illustrations in this period of the effect of intercourse and co-operation between eastern and western, urban-born and agrarian movements upon the development of western radical thought and action. This is notably true of the antimonopoly sentiment that flourished in the western states in the half dozen years before the panic of 1873. Although rural grievances against a railroad and steamboat combination in the Upper Mississippi Valley furnished the initial impetus, and the Locofoco heritage supplied the intellectual foundation, the continuing antimonopoly movement of these years cannot be fully understood without reference to mercantile interests, the National Labor Union, and the activities of several propaganda organizations that operated from central offices on the eastern seaboard. Resentment against the extortions and monopolistic practices of the railroads was not peculiar to western farmers. It was shared by western merchants, eastern importers and shippers, the producers and refiners of the Pennsylvania oil region, and laboring men as well. . . .

The central role of the tariff reformers in the Liberal Republican movement illustrates both the intersectional character of the anti-monopoly revival and the role of nonagrarian elements in it. At the outset the Liberal Republican revolt in Missouri was itself an urban movement, initiated and sustained as it was by the liberals of St. Louis of whom Colonel Grosvenor, then editor of the *Democrat*, was a leading figure. In the original Missouri movement, as in its larger extension to the Old Northwest, the urban free traders were the most active and influential single element. They were encouraged by the branch Free-Trade Leagues in the region and by the home office in New York, which was deliberately stimulating a widespread movement against special legislation and the corrupt, pressure politics of the period. . . .

Most students of western radicalism had overlooked the dual character of the Greenback agitation that spread so rapidly after the panic of 1873. Judged by its origins, Greenbackism was at once a western inflationist proposal and an eastern radical philosophy by means of which its urban working-class adherents sought to substitute a co-operative economy for the mercantile and industrial capitalism of the day. In its former capacity it originated with Henry Clay Dean, the bitter end Iowa "Copperhead," who urged greenback inflation upon a depressed, indebted West as a means of liquidating the war debt, overthrowing Radical rule, and emancipating the region from eastern financial and economic controls. It was taken up by the Cincinnati *Enquirer* in 1867 as a means of wresting control of the Democratic party from August Belmont and Tammany Hall. Toned down by George H. Pendleton into a currency stabilization, debt reduction scheme involving little or no inflation, it continued to attract support in the West for nearly a decade under the title of the "Ohio rag baby."

Some of the support enjoyed by the *Enquirer's* brand of Greenbackism came from the trades unions of Cincinnati. The political spokesman of this element was Congressman General Samuel F. Cary. Along with the wage earners of Cincinnati, Chicago, and the Atlantic seaboard, he adhered to a much more elaborate economic and monetary theory. This, for want of a more distinguishing name, must be termed Kelloggism. Its author, Edward Kellogg, had been a New York merchant during the Locofoco period. Forced into assignment by the panic of 1837, he had found in the usurious manipulation of currency and credit by privately owned banks the cause of periodic depressions and of the concentration of wealth. Arguing that monetary policy and banking were strictly governmental functions, he sought to supplant private and state banks with a national banking and currency system to be operated exclusively by the central government. Its outstanding features were to be a flexible currency, loans on real estate at low rates, and interchangeability of the paper currency with government bonds. Such a system with its low interest rates, Kellogg taught, would destroy money monopoly, secure to labor its just reward, lower rents, and promote the development of rural society. His book, *Labor and Other Capital*, was republished in successive editions after 1860 and became a classic of American radicalism, the "Bible" of currency reformers until shunted aside by the free-silver craze of the nineties.

Kelloggism won wide support among wage earners and western antimonopolists after the Civil War. Alexander Campbell disseminated its doctrines among the discontented farmers of the Mississippi Valley and urged them to institute the new monetary and banking system by adapting it to the greenback currency and public debt of the day. While Campbell and another Illinois Congressman seconded the efforts of General Cary in pressing Kellogg's system upon the national legislature, the Illinois Anti-Monopoly Association joined hands with noted labor leaders, A. C. Cameron of Chicago and William L. Sylvis. Together they wrote the Kellogg program into the platform adopted by the National Labor

Union at Chicago in 1867, the same year in which the "Pendleton plan" emerged from the inflationary agitation initiated by Henry Clay Dean and the Cincinnati *Enquirer.*

Space is lacking to trace in detail the interaction of the two currency agitations upon each other and of both upon the agricultural West through the next three decades. It should be noted, however, that after the failure of the Labor Party in 1872, the labor reformers secured endorsement of Kellogg's monetary system from the Illinois State Farmers Association in 1874–1875. They persuaded it and the Indiana farmers to join them in the organization of an independent political party representing both laborers and farmers, a movement that culminated in the National Greenback Party of 1876. Revived in the eighties by the Knights of Labor, Kelloggs' familiar monetary and land banking proposals were taken up by farm journals such as the Chicago *Express* and the *Western Rural*, and championed by W. D. Vincent, the future journalistic exponent of Populism in Kansas. Eventually the National Farmers' Alliance, led by Jay Burrows, a disciple of Kellogg, embodied the land loan plan in its platform while the southern Alliance advanced from this to the noted "subtreasury" scheme as an adaptation more attractive to staple farming. Government loans of greenbacks to farmers on land or crop mortgage security became the central feature in the platforms of farm organizations from 1886–1892, of the Union Labor Party in 1888, and of the Populists in 1892. Faith in the far-reaching efficacy of such a program was a common and distinguishing feature of working-class and western agrarian radicalism until the decline of the Knights of Labor and the rising free-silver crusade pushed its advocates into the "middle-of-the-road" during the "Battle of the Standards."

The co-operative movement is another example of the alacrity with which western agrarians borrowed urban formulas ready-made in their attempts to solve agricultural problems. In this case European experience was clearly drawn upon, while the influence of organized labor in America upon the farming co-operative movements seems almost indubitable. Although anti-bellum *Arbeiterbund* experiments and agitation by Horace Greeley may have suggested the feasibility of a co-operative movement, the first vigorous development of productive and distributive co-operation in the United States occurred after Appomattox in the urban centers of the East and the Ohio Valley. There workmen in all leading trades experimented with co-operative workshops and patronized co-operative stores. This movement was vigorously espoused by William L. Sylvis and the National Labor Union as "a sure and lasting remedy for the abuses of the present industrial system." The need of these co-operative experiments for adequate credit was one reason why the laborers espoused Kellogg's monetary and banking system. Western antimonopolists, whose delegates attended the congresses of the National Labor Union, learned there of the co-operative plans of the wage earners. By 1871, in the same region where Kelloggism was propagated by Alexander Campbell and the railroads and war tariff were attacked by the antimonopolists, the farmers turned also to "Co-operation" as a sovereign remedy for rural ills. Eventually the Grangers adopted the Rochdale plan of consumers' co-operation and made direct contact with the English Co-operative Union. The revival of interest in co-operation among western and southern farmers during the eighties followed hard upon the renewed agitation of the idea by the Knights of Labor who were the greatest agency then propagating knowledge of European and American co-operative experiments in the United States. Its contact with the farmers increased rather than diminished after its catastrophic defeats in 1886 since it deliberately penetrated the country towns and rural areas of the East in search of recruits. Thus, while the ideological impulse to the co-operative experiments of the Farmers' Alliance movement was partially derived from surviving Granger experiments or drawn directly from British experience, a portion at least came from the American labor movement. In this period, also, co-operative creameries were introduced into the Middle West from Scandinavia by Danish immigrants. . . .

Western cities made significant contributions to the radical movements of the rural West and urban East in the seventies and eighties. The wider antimonopoly movement that was directed against industrial combinations and speculative manipulation of commodity prices received its initial impetus from Henry Demarest Lloyd. His antimonopolism was derived from a Locofoco family background. It was confirmed by four years' work as assistant secretary of the American Free-Trade League. After this he joined the staff of the Chicago *Tribune*. First as financial editor and then as chief editorial writer, he campaigned for over a decade for reform of the Chicago Board of Trade, exposed the looting of western mining companies by rings of insiders, described the daily misdeeds and monopolistic practices of the railroads, and attacked the Standard Oil Company and other trusts as they emerged into public view. . . .

An equally notable contribution to American radicalism came from San Francisco and Oakland, California, urban centers developing within a few hundred miles of the mining and agricultural frontier of the Far West. There Henry George, another journalist, but onetime Philadelphia printer's devil, perfected the single-tax theory in the midst of a prolonged struggle with the West Coast monopolies. An admirer of Jefferson, a Jacksonian Democrat of the Locofoco tradition, he saw in land monopoly the cause of poverty. By taxing away the unearned increment in land values, or virtually confiscating ground rents, he would break up the great speculative holdings in the West, check the dissipation of the national domain, and weaken franchise monopolies of all kinds. Abolition of all other taxes would destroy the monopolies dependent upon the protective tariff. Thus a single, decisive use of taxing power would restore both liberty and equality of opportunity to American economic life while at the same time it would check the urban movement, revive agriculture, and enrich rural life. After leading a fruitless land reform movement on the West Coast during the depressed seventies, Henry George moved to New York City where he published *Progress and Poverty* in 1880. Its appeal to natural rights, its indictment of the existing business system, its moral overtones and moving appeal to the traditions of humanitarian democracy, and its utopian panacea all exerted a profound influence upon public opinion in Ireland, Great Britain, and the United States. . . .

The examples of effective intercourse between the rural West and the urban world, whether within or outside the region, could be increased still further by reference to the agitation for reform of the nation's land policy, led by George W. Julian, and the free-silver movement. They are sufficient, however, to indicate something of the diverse origins and composite character of the western radicalism that burgeoned beyond the Alleghenies in the last third of the century. Western agrarian movements were influenced by at least five schools of reform or radical agitation originating from without the region before 1890. In at least one important field the farmers' movements of the region made a major contribution to democratic thought and action in the same period, while publicists in two western cities initiated the important antitrust and single-tax movements. Such cross-fertilization between eastern and western, urban and rural movements was but one aspect of the larger development of the West, which on intellectual, technological, business, and artistic planes was subject to similar processes of acculturation. In each field the result was a mosaic of indigenous and imported elements, all adapted in greater or lesser degree to the regional *milieu.*

This analysis suggests that in Populism may be found the system of radical thought that emerged in the West from three decades of recurring unrest, agitation, and intercourse with radical and reform movements in the urban world. Although scholars have studied it as a political movement or as the product of social and economic conditions, as a school of thought Populism has been rarely, if ever, subjected to the careful analysis that Socialism, Anarchism, or Communism have received. Yet the Populists themselves regarded Populism as a faith and a creed as well as a program. They exhibited, furthermore, a clear sense of continuity with preceding radical movements. This was illustrated at the Omaha convention by the wild cheering that greeted Alexander Campbell, the aged prophet of Kelloggism to midwestern farmers in the sixties. Further continuity between Populism and its forerunners was exhibited by the leadership of the People's Party. Not only were General James B. Weaver and Ignatius Donnelly representatives of the older Greenback and Anti-Monopoly traditions in the West, but the chairman of the national executive committee, Herman E. Taubeneck, was a former Greenbacker, while the first secretary of the committee was Robert Schilling, veteran labor reformer and labor leader. As secretary of the platform committee in the Cincinnati conference of May, 1891, Schilling reported and together with Colonel S. F. Norton of the Chicago *Express* undoubtedly induced the committee to base its manifesto on Edward Kellogg's economic philosophy. Further evidence of continuity between Populism and earlier radical movements is found in the long series of conferences that began with the organization of the Union Labor Party in Cincinnati in 1887 and culminated at Omaha on July 4, 1892. There Kelloggism, Nationalism, the more limited program of government ownership proposed by the Knights, the single tax, land reform, woman suffrage, the liquor question, and the cause of organized labor were urged upon successive platform committees by reformers who had grown gray in the service of each particular "cause."

At first glance the program that emerged from this process seemed like a "crazy-quilt" of unrelated and "crackpot" proposals. Yet it produced a fairly durable synthesis, judging from the tenacity with which the Populists reiterated their Omaha platform on all and sundry occasions, until an era of unemployment, mortgage foreclosures, Coxey's armies, and industrial conflict had so heightened the emotional overtones of the movement that the least well-ballasted agrarians and the professional politicians in control of the party machinery sought quick relief and easy victory through free silver. It was this synthesis, under the name of Populism, which received such intense loyalty from its adherents and provoked an emotional opposition from conservative elements. Proclaimed in the Omaha platform as the official version of the Populist creed, it must now be analyzed in an attempt to identify the basic concepts that it shared with its progenitors and to determine the extent to which it presented a well-defined system of radical thought.

The continuing vitality of the equalitarian tradition among the radical movements that produced the Populist "revolt" will be apparent from the foregoing narrative. Examination of the Omaha platform, also, indicates beyond doubt that Populism, too, was consciously cast in the mold of "equal rights." Inherent in its thought lay the traditional Jeffersonian hostility to special privilege, to gross inequality in economic possessions, to concentrated economic power, and a preference for human rights when opposed by overshadowing property rights. All of this had motivated American democratic radicalism since the days of Thomas Paine and the Democratic Republican Clubs of 1793–1800. So oriented it is not surprising to find the preamble of the Omaha platform declaring in 1892 that the purpose of a government freed from corporate control would be to establish "equal rights and equal privileges . . . for all the men and women of this country." Coupled with this is the clearly expressed, traditional faith of American liberals in "civilization" as a liberating, elevating process, which, like human rights, must be saved from the machinations of the money power. Thus, Populism was but an extreme projection of the Jeffersonian creed.

Lawrence Goodwyn

THE ALLIANCE DEVELOPS A MOVEMENT CULTURE

Lawrence Goodwyn, who studied Populism in the 1970s, located its origins in the Southern Farmers' Alliance, which developed in Texas and then spread through the South and into the West. The Alliance sponsored cooperatives to help southern farmers escape the exploitative crop lien system, and out of these groups emerged a radical movement culture that became the basis of Populism. The Alliance also generated another fundamental ingredient of Populist radicalism, the subtreasury plan, which envisioned a democratic monetary system based on the production of nonperishable agricultural commodities. Goodwyn, a history professor at Duke University, wrote the first complete history of American Populism since Hicks's 1931 study: *Democratic Promise: The Populist Moment in America* (1976). *The Populist Moment: A Short History of the Agrarian Revolt in America* (1978) is a briefer version of this study.

The agrarian revolt first stirred on the Southern frontier, then swept eastward across Texas and the other states of the Old Confederacy and thence to the Western Plains. The gathering of democratic momentum required almost fifteen years—seven within a tier of counties along the Texas farming frontier, three more to cover the rest of the state, and another five to envelop the South and West. Yet the best way to view this process of mass radicalization of farmers is not by focusing on the farming frontier from which the doctrines of insurgency emanated, but rather by discovering the humiliating conditions of life which penetrated into every farm and hamlet of the South. These conditions really illuminated the potential support for the agrarian revolt because they caused thousands to flee to the frontier and armed those who remained with a fervent desire to join the movement when it eventually swept through their region. Further, these conditions

Excerpted from *The Populist Moment: A Short History of the Agrarian Revolt in America* by Lawrence Goodwyn, pp. 20–23, 25–35, 90–93; 1978. Copyright © 1978 by Lawrence Goodwyn. Reprinted by permission of Oxford University Press, Inc.

were so pervasive in their impact, shaping in demeaning detail the daily options of millions of Southerners, that they constituted a system that ordered life itself.

※

The "system" was the crop lien system. It defined with brutalizing finality not only the day-to-day existence of most Southerners who worked the land, but also the narrowed possibilities of their entire lives. Both the literal meaning and the ultimate dimension of the crop lien were visible in simple scenes occurring daily, year after year, decade after decade, in every village of every Southern state. Acted out at a thousand merchant counters in the South after the Civil War, these scenes were so ubiquitous that to describe one is to convey a sense of them all. The farmer, his eyes downcast, and his hat sometimes literally in his hand, approached the merchant with a list of his needs. The man behind the counter consulted a ledger, and after a mumbled exchange, moved to his shelves to select the goods that would satisfy at least a part of his customer's wants. Rarely did the farmer receive the range of items or even the quantity of one item he had requested. No money changed hands; the merchant merely made brief notations in his ledger. Two weeks or a month later, the farmer would return, the consultation would recur, the mumbled exchange and the careful selection of goods would ensue, and new additions would be noted in the ledger. From early spring to late fall the ritual would be enacted until, at "settlin'-up" time, the farmer and the merchant would meet at the local cotton gin, where the fruits of a year's toil would be ginned, bagged, tied, weighed, and sold. At that moment, the farmer would learn what his cotton had brought. The merchant, who had possessed title to the crop even before the farmer had planted it, then consulted his ledger for a final time. The accumulated debt for the year, he informed the farmer, exceeded the income received from the cotton crop. The farmer had failed in his effort to "pay out"—he still owed the merchant a remaining balance for the supplies "furnished" on credit during the year. The "furnishing merchant" would then announce his intention to carry the farmer through the winter on a new account, the latter merely having to sign a note mortgaging to the merchant the next year's crop. The lien signed, the farmer, empty-handed, climbed in his wagon and drove home, knowing that for the second or fifth or fifteenth year he had not paid out.

Such was the crop lien system. It constituted a new and debasing method of economic organization that took its specific form from the devastation of the Civil War and from the collapse of the economic structure of Southern society which had resulted from the war. In the aftermath of Appomattox, the people of the South had very little capital or the institutions dealing in it—banks. Emancipation had erased the slave system's massive investment in human capital, and surrender had not only invalidated all Confederacy currency, it had also engendered a wave of Southern bank failures. Massachusetts alone had five times as much national bank circulation as the entire South, while Bridgeport, Connecticut, had more than the states of Texas, Alabama, and North and South Carolina combined. The per capita figure for Rhode Island was $77.16; it was 13 cents for Arkansas. One hundred and twenty-three counties in the state of Georgia had no banking facilities of any kind. The South had become, in the words of one historian, a "giant pawn shop."

The furnishing merchants, able to get most of their goods on consignment from competing Northern mercantile houses, bought supplies and "furnished" them on credit to farmers, taking a lien on the farmer's crop for security. Farmers learned that the interest they were paying on everything they consumed limited their lives in a new and terrible way; the rates imposed were frequently well in excess of 100 per cent annually, sometimes over 200 per cent. The system had subtle ramifications which made this mountain of interest possible. At the heart of the process was a simple two-price system for all items—one price for cash customers and a second and higher price for credit customers. Interest of 25 to 50 per cent would then be charged on this inflated base. An item carrying a "cash price" of 10 cents would be sold on credit for 14 cents and at the end of the year would bring the merchant, after the addition of, say, 33 per cent interest, a total of 19 cents—almost double the standard purchasing price. Once a farmer had signed his first crop lien he was in bondage to his merchant as long as he failed to pay out, because "no competitor would sell the farmer so much as a side of fat back, except for cash, since the only acceptable security, his crop, had been forfeited." The farmer rarely was even aware of the disparity between cash and credit prices, for he usually had no basis for comparison; "many of the merchants did a credit business so exclusively they set no cash prices." The farmer soon learned that the prudent judgment—or whim—of his furnishing merchant was the towering reality of his life. Did his wife want some calico for her single "Sunday dress," or did his family need a slab of bacon? Whether he got them or not depended on the invisible scales on which the merchant across the counter weighed the central question—would the farmer's crop yield enough money to pay off the accumulating furnishing debt?

In ways people outside the South had difficulty perceiving, the crop lien system became for millions of Southerners, white and black, little more than slavery. "When one of these mortgages has been recorded against the Southern farmer," wrote a contemporary, "he had usually passed into a state of helpless peonage. . . . From this time until he has paid the last dollar of his indebtedness, he is subject to the constant oversight and direction of the merchant." The man with the ledger became the farmer's sole significant contact with the outside world. Across the South he was known as "the furnishing man" or "the advancing man." To black farmers he became "the Man." . . .

✳

It is not surprising that men were lured or driven west. Yet even the great migration that began in the 1870's did not alter the guiding principles of the new system. One Southern historian described the bitter logic which had made cotton a new king of poverty: "Let . . . the soil be worn out, let the people move to Texas . . . let almost anything happen provided all possible cotton is produced each year."

For simple, geographical reasons, "Going West" for most Southerners meant, in the familiar phrase of the time, "Gone to Texas." The phrase became so common that often only the initials "G. T. T." scrawled across a nailed-shut door were needed to convey the message. White and Negro farmers by the thousands drove down the plank roads and rutted trails of the rural South, westward across the Mississippi River to the Sabine and into the pine forests of East Texas. The quest for new land and a new start drove lengthening caravans of the poor—almost 100,000 every year of the 1870's—ever deeper into Texas, through and beyond the "piney woods" and on into the hill country and prairie Cross Timbers. There the men and women of the South stepped out into the world of the Great Plains. It was there that the culture of a new people's politics took form in nineteenth-century America.

In September 1877 a group of farmers gathered at the Lampasas County farm of J. R. Allen and banded together as the "Knights of Reliance." In the words of one of the founders, they were all "comparatively poor" and the farm organization was the "first enterprise of much importance undertaken." The overriding purpose, he later said, was to organize to "more speedily educate ourselves" in preparation for the day "when all the balance of labor's products become concentrated into the hands of a few, there to constitute a power that would enslave posterity." In his view, the farmers needed to organize a new institution for America, a "grand social and political palace where liberty may dwell and justice be safely domiciled." How to achieve such a useful "palace" was, of course, the problem.

The new organization soon changed its name to "The Farmers Alliance," borrowed freely from the rituals of older farm organizations, and spread to surrounding counties. In the summer of 1878, a "Grand State Farmers Alliance" was formed. The growing county and state structure was to be a rural organization of self-help, but workable models were in short supply. How to cope with the lien system? Some of the farmers decided politics was the answer and they tried to lead the order into the Greenback Party. But the Lampasas-based Alliance collapsed in 1880, sundered by the sectional loyalties of many members to "the party of the fathers."

The Alliance experience thus yielded its first lesson: immediate political insurgency was not the answer; too many of the poor had strong cultural memories that yoked them to traditional modes of political thought and behavior. Some means would have to be found to cut such ties before any kind of genuine people's politics was possible.

In the next two years, the organizational sprouts in frontier regions north of Lampasas, unhampered by internal political divisions, slowly took root as 120 alliances came into being in twelve counties. But the crop lien system, supported as it was by the entire structure of American commerce, proved an overwhelming obstacle. Though Alliancemen wanted to do something to solve the underlying problems of agricultural credit, their fledgling cooperative efforts at buying and selling were treated with contempt by merchants. In 1883, the Alliance lost what momentum it had achieved—only thirty suballiances were represented at the state meeting.

Into this situation stepped the first Populist, S. O. Daws. A thirty-six-year-old Mississippian, Daws had developed an interesting kind of personal political self-respect. Raised in the humiliating school of the crop lien system, he did not believe the inherited economic folkways were fair, and he thought he has the right to say so. Indeed, Daws, a compelling speaker, was dedicated to instilling a similar kind of political self-respect in his fellow farmers. Late in 1883 the Alliance named Daws to a newly created position, that of "Traveling Lecturer," and endowed the new chief organizer with broad executive powers to appoint suborganizers and sublecturers for every county in the state of Texas.

It proved a decisive step. Within a month, Daws had energized fifty dormant suballiances into sending delegates to a state meeting where the entire cooperative effort was put under review. If merchants practiced monopolistic techniques by refusing to deal with the Alliance, perhaps Alliance members could reply in kind. A "trade store" system was agreed upon wherein Alliance members would contract to trade exclusively with one merchant. The range of discussion was broad: it extended to the role of Alliance county business agents and Alliance joint stock companies, to the opposition of cotton buyers and the resistance of manufacturers who refused to sell to the Alliance except through middlemen, and even to the refusal of townsmen to sell farmers land for Alliance-owned cotton yards where they might store their crops while awaiting higher prices. Determined to test the trade store system, Alliance delegates dispersed from the February meeting with new hope. Daws's efforts had been so impressive that his office and his appointment powers were confirmed by the convention.

The spring of 1884 saw a rebirth of the Alliance. Daws traveled far and wide, denouncing credit merchants, railroads, trusts, the money power, and capitalists. The work-worn men and barefooted women who gathered to hear the Alliance lecturer were not impressive advertisements for the blessings of the crop lien or the gold standard. Such audiences did not require detailed proof of the evils of the two-price credit system and the other sins of the furnishing merchants. They had known "hard times" all their lives. But Daws could climax his recitation of exploitation with a call for a specific act: join the Alliance and form trade stores. Were monopolistic trusts charging exorbitant prices for fertilizers and farm implements? Join the Alliance and form cooperative buying committees. Did buyers underweigh the cotton, overcharge for sampling, inspecting, classifying, and handling? Join the Alliance and form your own cotton yard. The new urgency was evidenced not only by a steady increase in suballiances to over 200, but also in the style of the men who materialized as presidents and lecturers of the recently organized county structures—men like Daws: articulate, indignant, and capable of speaking a language the farmers understood.

※

Foremost among them was a thirty-four-year-old farmer named William Lamb. Beyond his red hair and ruggedly handsome appearance, there was at first glance little to distinguish Lamb from scores of other men who had come west to escape the post–Civil War blight of the South. A Tennessean, Lamb had arrived on the frontier at the age of sixteen, settling first near what was to become the town of Bowie in Montague County. Like most rural Southern youths, Lamb had had almost no formal education—a total of twenty-five days. After working as a hired man, he married, rented land, and began farming in Denton County. In 1876 he "preempted" a farmstead in Montague County, living alone part of the time in a rude log hut until he could clear the land and build a homestead. He farmed by day and read by night, acquiring the strengths and weaknesses of self-taught men. When he spoke publicly, his sentences were overly formal, the syntax sometimes losing its way; in the early days, when he began to write in behalf of political causes, the strength of his ideas had to overcome impediments of grammar and spelling. To Daws, who was seeking other men of energy, those faults were no liability; the younger man had strength of mind, and Daws realized it when the two men met in 1884. Lamb knew the extent of the agrarian disaster in the South, and he had an urge to do something about it. He was ripe for the missions Daws was ready to give him. By the time of the 1884 state meeting, Lamb's work in organizing suballiances in his own county had attracted enough attention that a new statewide office was created specifically for him. He was made "state lecturer" while Daws continued in the role of traveling lecturer.

William Lamb emerged in 1884–85 as a man of enormous energy and tenacity. As president of the Montague County Alliance he had organized over 100 suballiances by October 1885, a record that eclipsed even Daws's performance in his own county. Lamb soon surpassed his mentor in other ways. As a spokesman for farmers, the red-haired organizer thought in the broadest tactical terms. He early saw the value of a coalition between the Alliance and the Knights of Labor, which was then beginning to organize railroad workers in North Texas. Lamb also pushed cooperative buying and selling, eventually becoming the Alliance's most aggressive advocate of this program. And, after the business community had shown its hostility to Alliance cooperatives, he was the first of the Alliance leaders to react politically—and in the most sweeping terms. Encouraged by his association with Daws and the Alliance, Lamb demonstrated that he, too, had developed a new kind of personal political self-respect.

The increasing momentum of the idea of the Alliance cooperative inexorably shaped the lives of Daws and Lamb as they, in turn, shaped the lives of other men. They spent their lives in political reform, and in so doing became allies, exhorted their comrades, crowded them, sometimes challenged them, and performed the various acts that men in the grip of a moral idea are wont to perform. They influenced each other steadily, the impetus initially coming from Daws, as he introduced Lamb into an environment where the younger man's political horizons could be broadened, then from Lamb, as he pressed his views to the point of crisis and carried Daws along with him until the older man could use his influence and creativity to resolve the crisis and preserve the forward momentum of the organization.

In the personal relationship between William Lamb and S. O. Daws a rhythm was discernible: along the course they set toward independent political action, Daws was always a step or two behind; at the moment of triumph, when the third party was formed in the South, Lamb, not Daws, held the gavel.

*

The young organizer learned in 1884–85 that cooperative buying and selling was easier to plan at country meetings than to carry out. Town merchants opposed cooperative schemes, as did manufacturers and cotton buyers. Indeed, the entire commercial world was hostile to the concept. Cooperation was not the American way; competition was.

But if the new movement did not invariably achieve immediate economic gains, the cooperative idea spurred organizing work. The 1885 state meeting of the Alliance was the largest gathering of farmers ever held in Texas to that time. The order adopted a program calling on all members "to act together as a unit in the sale of their product" and to that end moved to have each county alliance set apart a special day for selling. Thus, Alliancemen began what they called "bulking." These mass cotton sales were widely advertised and cotton buyers contacted in advance, for the Alliance sought a representative turnout of agents who might themselves engage in a modicum of competition.

The cooperative movement clearly stirred a new kind of collective self-confidence among Alliance farmers: county trade committees amassed 500, 1000, and in some instances as many as 1500 bales of cotton at Alliance warehouses. Because of the convenience of bulking, particularly to foreign buyers, the trade committees asked for premium prices, 5 to 10 cents per 100 pounds above prevailing levels. Though results were mixed, the successful sales gave the farmers a sense of accomplishment. After one mass sale at Fort Worth had brought 5 cents per 100 above what individual farmers had received, Alliancemen were ecstatic. As one metropolitan daily reported it, their "empty wagons returned homeward bearing blue flags and other evidence of rejoicing." It did not take long for such stories to spread through the farming districts, and each success brought the Alliance thousands of new members. Cooperation worked—in more ways than one.

But though bulking helped, and was a marvelous boon to the self-respect of individual farmers and to the growing collective self-confidence represented by the Alliance movement, it did not eliminate the furnishing merchant, nor did it fundamentally alter the two-piece credit system. Alliancemen slowly discovered they needed to establish an internal method of communication which would arm the Alliance purchasing agent with hard facts so that he could inform manufacturers of the size and value of the Alliance market for their products. Late in 1885 the Alliance moved to centralize its cooperative procurement effort by naming its own purchasing agent. The Alliance state president appointed William Lamb as the official "Traveling Agent" to represent the order "for sale of farm implements and machinery through the state where the Alliance is organized."

Though the long-term effects of that decision were to change the whole direction of the Farmers Alliance, the results in the short run were disappointing. Despite zealous efforts, Lamb failed in his attempts to establish direct purchasing arrangements with commercial America. It was the credit problem again. "I can furnish wagons in car-load lots cheap for cash, but as yet I have no offer on time," Lamb reported to his Alliance brethren. The young lecturer pondered the implications of the dilemma and decided the ultimate answer had to lie in cooperative manufacturing efforts by the Alliance itself! His plan, based on his loss of faith in the good will of merchants, scarcely constituted a serious threat to the commercial world, but it represented the first public hint that his political perspective was shifting.

And he was not alone. The "Erath County Alliance Lumber Company," with 2800 Alliance members, announced "we stand united. . . . We can purchase anything we want through our agent, dry goods, and groceries, farm implements and machinery. We have a market for all of our wheat, oats and corn." Meanwhile, the Tarrant County Alliance announced the organization of its forty-sixth suballiance and claimed a total of 2000 members throughout the county.

"The Farmers Alliance is making its power felt in this state now," a country newspaper reported approvingly. And, indeed, by October 1885, the order reported that the total number of suballiances stood at 815. Each suballiance had its lecturer; each county had its county Alliance and county lecturer. The message of agrarian self-help now sounded from hundreds of platforms.

Yet the outside world knew almost nothing of the growing energy of the Alliance cooperative movement. Few in the power centers of Texas or the nation were remotely aware of the gathering impatience among the members of a rural organization calling itself the Farmers Alliance. Ironically, it was the conservatives of the Patrons of Husbandry—better known as the Grange—who became the first to sense the new mood in the rural districts of the state. The route to this perception was a painful one. Initially, Grangers had watched with equanimity the early stirrings of the Farmers Alliance and, courteously, if condescendingly, had rebuffed suggestions for cooperation. But soon complacency within the Grange leadership gave way to alarm, then to anger, and finally to helpless, private denunciation. Nothing availed. Within thirty-six months the Grange was all but obliterated in Texas. . . .

❋

It is appropriate, at the moment of Alliance ascendency, to explore the process that had produced an emerging mass movement of farmers. Tactically, the rise of the Alliance was a result of its determination to go beyond the cash stores of the Grange and make pioneering efforts in cooperative marketing as well as purchasing. The cooperative effort was helpful because it recruited farmers by the thousands. But in a deeper political sense the Alliance organization was experimenting in a new kind of mass autonomy. As such, it was engaged in a cultural struggle to redefine the form and meaning of life and politics in America. Out of the individual sense of self of leaders like S. O. Daws and William Lamb the Alliance had begun to develop a collective sense of purpose symbolized by the ambitious strivings of scores of groups who were anxious to show the world why they intended to "stand united." Inexorably, the mutually supportive dynamics inherent in these individual and collective modes of behavior began to produce something new among the huge mass that Alliancemen called "the plain people." This consisted of a new way of looking at society, a way of thinking that represented a shaking off of inherited forms of deference. The achievement was not an easy one. The farmers of the Alliance had spent much of their lives in humiliating circumstances; repeated dealings with Southern merchants had inculcated insecurity in generations of farming people. They were ridiculed for their poverty, and they knew it. They were called "hayseeds" and they knew that, too. But they had also known for decades that they could do nothing about their plight because they were locked into the fabric of the lien system and crushed by the mountain of interest they had been forced to pay. But now, in their Alliance, they had found something new. That something may be described as individual self-respect and collective self-confidence, or what some would call "class-consciousness." All are useful if imprecise terms to describe a growing political sensibility, one free of deference and ridicule. Such an intuition shared by enough people is, of course, a potentially powerful force. In whatever terminology this intuition is described, it clearly represents a seminal kind of democratic instinct; and it was this instinct that emerged in the Alliance in 1884–85.

In the succeeding eighteen months their new way of looking at things flowered into a mass expression of a new political vision. We may call it (for that is what it was) the movement culture of Populism. This culture involved more than just the bulking of cotton. It extended to frequent Alliance meetings to plan the mass sales—meetings where the whole family came, where the twilight suppers were, in the early days, laid out for ten or twenty members of the suballiance, or for hundreds at a county Alliance meeting, but which soon grew into vast spectacles; long trains of wagons, emblazoned with suballiance banners, stretching literally for miles, trekking to enormous encampments where five, ten, and twenty thousand men and women listened intently to the plans of their Alliance and talked among themselves about those plans. At those encampments speakers, with growing confidence, pioneered a new political language to describe the "money trust," the gold standard, and the private national banking system that underlay all of their troubles in the lien system.

How is a democratic culture created? Apparently in such prosaic, powerful ways. When a farm family's wagon crested a hill en route to a Fourth of July "Alliance Day" encampment and the occupants looked back to see thousands of other families trailed out behind them in wagon trains, the thought that "the Alliance is the people and the people are together" took on transforming possibilities. Such a moment—and the Alliance experience was to yield hundreds of them—instilled hope in hundreds of thousands of people who had been without it. The successes of the cooperative effort gave substance to the hope, but it was the hope itself, the sense of autonomy it encouraged and the sense of possibility it stimulated, that lay at the heart of Populism. If "the Alliance was the people and the people were together," who could not see that the people had created the means to change the circumstances of their lives? This was the soul of the Populist faith. The cooperative movement of the Alliance was its source.

In 1884–85, the Alliance began developing its own rhythm of internal "education" and its own broadening political consciousness among leaders and followers. The movement culture would develop its own mechanism of recruitment (the large-scale credit cooperative), its own theoretical analysis (the greenback interpretation of the American version of finance capitalism), its own solution (the sub-treasury land and loan system), its own symbols of politics (the Alliance "Demands" and the Omaha Platform), and its own political institution (the People's Party). Grounded in a common experience, nurtured by years of experimentation and self-education, it produced a party, a platform, a specific new democratic ideology, and a pathbreaking political agenda for the American nation. But none of these things were the essence of Populism. At bottom, Populism was, quite simply, an expression of self-respect. It was not an individual trait, but a collective one, surfacing as the shared hope of millions organized by the Alliance into its cooperative crusade. This individual and collective striving generated the movement culture that was Populism. . . .

Precisely what the Alliance movement was in the process of becoming could scarcely have been predicted by the farmers themselves from the contradictory events of 1888–89. Only one thing was certain: the Alliance was attempting to construct, within the framework of American capitalism, some variety of cooperative commonwealth. Precisely where that would lead was unclear. More than any other Allianceman, Charles Macune* had felt the power of the corporate system arrayed alongside the power of a self-help farmer coop-

*Charles W. Macune played an important role in expanding the Alliance from Texas throughout the cotton producing regions of the South. He served as president of the Southern Alliance in 1887 and 1888 and in 1889 he became editor of the organization's major publication, the *National Economist*.

erative. He had gone to the bankers and they had replied in the negative. Though his own farmer associates had said "yes," they could not marshal enough resources to defeat the crop lien system. Macune knew that an exchange of considerably reduced scope could be constructed on a sound basis within the means available to organized farmers. One could avoid the credit problem simply by operating cash stores for affluent farmers.

But while he was an orthodox, even a reactionary social philosopher, and still a political traditionalist, C. W. Macune was obsessed with the need to create a democratic monetary system. The pressure of the multiple experiences that had propelled him to leadership. . . , to fame as an organizer and national leader during the Southern expansion, to crisis and potential loss of political power over the exchange, and to constant maneuvering against his driving, exasperating, creative left wing—all, taken together, conjoined to carry Macune to a conception of the uses of democratic government that was beyond the reach of orthodox political theorists of the Gilded Age. Out of his need for personal exoneration, out of his ambition, and out of his exposure to the realities in the daily lives of the nation's farmers, Macune in 1889 came to the sub-treasury plan. Politically, his proposal was a theoretical and psychological breakthrough of considerable implication: he proposed to mobilize the monetary authority of the nation and put it to work in behalf of a sector of its poorest citizens through the creation of a system of currency designed to benefit everyone in the "producing classes," including urban workers.

120,000 papers sold

The main outlines of the sub-treasury system gradually unfolded in the pages of the *National Economist* during the summer and fall of 1889. There can be no question that Macune saved his proposal for dramatic use in achieving, finally, a national merger of all the nation's major farm and labor organizations. He now planned that event for St. Louis in December 1889, when a great "confederation of labor organizations," convened by the Alliance, would attempt to achieve a workable coalition of the rural and urban working classes, both North and South.

But the sub-treasury was more than a tactical adjunct to organizational expansion. Macune's concept was the intellectual culmination of the cooperative crusade and directly addressed its most compelling liability—inadequate credit. Through his sub-treasury system, the federal government would underwrite the cooperatives by issuing greenbacks to provide credit for the farmer's crops, creating the basis of a more flexible national currency in the process; the necessary marketing and purchasing facilities would be achieved through government-owned warehouses, or "sub-treasuries," and through federal sub-treasury certificates paid to the farmer for his produce—credit which would remove furnishing merchants, commercial banks, and chattel mortgage companies from American agriculture. The sub-treasury "certificates" would be government-issued greenbacks, "full legal tender for all debts, public and private," in the words of the Alliance platform. As outlined at St. Louis in 1889, the sub-treasury system was a slight but decisive modification of the treasury-note plan Macune had presented to the Texas Alliance the year before. Intellectually, the plan was profoundly innovative. It was to prove far too much so for Gilded Age America.

In its own time, the sub-treasury represented the political equivalent of full-scale greenbackism for farmers. This was the plan's immediate import: it defined the doctrine of fiat money in clear terms of self-interest that had unmistakable appeal to farmers desperately overburdened with debt. As the cooperative crusade made abundantly clear, the appeal extended to both West and South, to Kansas as well as to Georgia. Macune's concept went beyond the generalized greenbackism of radicals such as William Lamb to a specific practical solution that appealed directly to farmers in a context they could grasp. But more than this, the sub-treasury plan directly benefited all of the nation's "producing classes" and the nation's economy itself. For the greenback dollars for the farmers created a workable basis for a new and flexible national currency originating outside the exclusive control of Eastern commercial bankers. Beyond the benefits to the economy as a whole, Macune's system provided broad new options to the United States Treasury in giving private citizens access to reasonable credit. As Macune fully understood, the revolutionary implications of the sub-treasury system went far beyond its immediate value to farmers.

The line of nineteenth-century theorists of an irredeemable currency . . . culminated in the farmer advocate, Charles Macune. As Macune argued, the agrarian-greenbackism underlying his sub-treasury system provided organizational cohesion between Southern

1890 - Macune organizes National Reform Press

1889 - sub-treasury call for national government to build warehouses for farmers to store

and Western farmers. As he did not foresee, it also provided political cohesion for a radical third party. The People's Party was to wage a frantic campaign to wrest effective operating control of the American monetary system from the nation's commercial bankers and restore it, "in the name of the whole people," to the United States Treasury. It was a campaign that was never to be waged again.

Steven Hahn

THE TRANSFORMATION OF THE COUNTRYSIDE

Steven Hahn examined the origins of Populism in Georgia's upper piedmont. In the 1850s the yeomen there had enjoyed a high degree of self-sufficiency while engaging in a limited amount of commercial farming and subscribing to a republican ideology that encouraged resistance to the intrusion of a market society. But in the quarter century following the Civil War, railroads and towns expanded, farmers engaged in commercial relations, the crop lien system became widespread, and local notions of just prices disappeared. Between 1850 and 1890, the up-country moved from a precapitalist to a capitalist society, and the small farmer class declared its opposition to that change through Populism. In addition to his work on Populism, Hahn has edited with Jonathan Prude *Countryside in the Age of Capitalist Transformation: Essays in the Social History of Rural America* (1985).

The problems of destitution and relief remained chronic in the Upcountry through the 1860s, compounded as they were by adverse weather and increasingly widespread indebtedness. The serious droughts that plagued the area, and much of the South, during the sectional conflagration persisted into the immediate postwar years, worsening the travails of recovering from war-related destruction. "[I]t would be hard to exaggerate the disaster, or the suffering and distress which result [from the drought]," the ex-governor Joseph Brown wrote in September 1866, "the corn crop is almost an utter failure in a large part of the state embracing the upper section." One month later, citing "the short crops made in our county and the distressed condition of our people and the uncertainty of future prospects," the Carroll County grand jury urged that "our next legislature . . . use all the power with the Constitution for the relief of our people especially for the widows and orp[h]ans and the maimed and distressed soldiers. . . ." Such reports continued to flow out of the Upcountry the next year. . . .

Statistics from the 1870 federal census, despite their short-comings, bear striking testimony to the magnitude of economic tribulation. Upcountry farm values had declined by more than 25 percent from their 1860 levels, and although the population had grown by about 5 percent during this ten-year period, farmers raised 40 percent fewer bushels of corn, 45 percent fewer bales of cotton, and 35 percent fewer head of livestock. Indeed, per capita grain production dropped by almost 40 percent between 1860 and 1870. Small wonder that newspapers could express the fear that "Cherokee Georgia" might soon find "many of her valuable citizens" emigrating west to more promising locales.

As census officials tabulated their figures, however, a significant development in Upcountry agriculture was already becoming apparent. "[W]e learn that a considerable revolution has taken place in the last year or two in the productions of Carroll," the Carroll County *Times* observed in 1872. "Cotton, formerly cultivated on a very limited extent, has increased rapidly . . . so that if the ratio continues, the county will, ere long, take rank among the foremost cotton producing counties of the state." The Columbus *Sun* reported a similar trend throughout the area a year later: "We took occasion in the spring . . . to direct attention to the rapid increase in cotton planting in the counties of upper Georgia. All the statistics and newspaper accounts received from the region confirm . . . the extensive planting of cotton. . . ."

There was much to recommend the new orientation. With short crops and generally depleted resources, farmers faced a difficult enough road to recovery. But that road had also become ridden with debts—debts contracted during those dim and desperate years of war and Reconstruction (often at much inflated prices) as the purchasing of provisions, seed, and implements grew more necessary and extensive. Although grain crops could bring attractive returns and thus help families regain a stable economic footing, the advantage was undercut by the cost of hauling them to market. Cotton, on the other hand, not only brought a relatively high price in the late 1860s and early 1870s but, according to the Cartersville *Standard and Express,* did "not cost one half [of what corn costs] to carry. . . ." As a Jackson County paper put it, "The majority of the farmers are going to plant largely of cotton, as most of them are in debt, and cotton is the only thing raised on the farm that will command ready money in the fall."

Growing a cash crop traditionally had been part of the general farming practiced by Upcountry yeoman households. The need for money to pay state and local taxes, for goods that could not be made at home, and for additional productive property to maintain the independence of the family led these farmers into the market. Like peasantries in much of the world, they could respond to commercial incentives, could evince an acquisitive disposition. Yet such acquisitiveness fell within a larger "security first" framework, and even under the trying conditions that followed the war they made no radical departure from familiar patterns, as a Black Belt newspaper took care to note: "While many of our south Georgia planters have . . . failed to plant sufficient corn or raise their own meat, but have devoted most of their labor to cotton, the farmers of upper Georgia have first made sure of their grain, provender, and provisions, and then bestowed their surplus labor on cotton." Nevertheless, a survey issued by the state commissioner of agriculture in 1875 gave unmistakable evidence of cotton's burgeoning importance in the Upcountry. Of the total acreage planted in the five major crops on white-operated farms, cotton accounted for more than one-quarter, stood only second in size to corn, and nearly amounted to the acreage sown in wheat, oats, and sweet potatoes combined.

The expansion of cotton culture was sustained and accelerated by the construction of rail lines into the Upcountry and by the increasing use of commercial fertilizers. Railroad promoters, stymied during the 1850s by capital shortages, skepticism about profitability, and popular opposition, renewed their efforts within a short time after the war's end. Meetings in numerous Upcountry counties during the late 1860s and early 1870s, convened at the behest of commercially minded interests situated in or near the small market towns, pressed for the revitalization of formerly chartered projects or the establishment of new companies. . . .

The extension of rail lines coupled with falling international guano prices led to the greater availability of commercial fertilizers, which played a key role in propelling the expansion of Upcountry cotton production. Aside from a widespread penchant for general farming, north Georgia cotton cultivation was limited by late-spring and early-autumn frosts which shortened the growing season. Fertilizers not only enriched the soil and increased yields but also enabled farmers to plant "their cotton a month later than they could formerly, and have it mature fully as soon, if not sooner than it did under the old system." . . . Between the 1874–1875 and the 1880–1881 seasons, the quantity of fertilizer inspected for the entire state rose more than threefold and much of it was destined for the Upcountry, with, as one fertilizer manufacturer made plain, significant consequences. "In the region above Atlanta, prior to the introduction of commercial fertilizers, little or no cotton was raised, from the fact that the seasons were too short," he maintained, "but since the introduction of commercial fertilizers the production of cotton in this section of the state has been greatly increased. In fact, it has come to be a very considerable item of production there."

A very considerable item of production to be sure. In 1880, Upcountry counties grew roughly 180,000 bales of cotton, an almost 200-percent increase over the harvest in 1860 and a more than 200-percent increase over the harvest in 1870. Per capita cotton production doubled during the same period. Perhaps of greater importance, the place of the Upcountry in Georgia's staple agriculture changed dramatically. Whereas in 1860 the region grew less than 10 percent of the total cotton raised in the state, by 1880 it grew close to 25 percent. This shift was reflected in the composition of the overall crop mix. During the antebellum era, corn was the Upcountry's major crop. Yet, within two decades following the Civil War, corn's status relative to cotton's declined substantially. A 22-percent increase in corn production between 1860 and 1880 paled when compared with that of cotton. No figures on crop acreage are available until the mid-1870s, but the change in the five years preceding 1880 was itself highly suggestive. In 1875, cotton acreage was about two-thirds the size of the acreage planted in corn; in 1879, it was about nine-tenths. And as per capita cotton production rose by 100 percent between 1860 and 1880, per capita corn production dropped by 20 percent. These patterns were evident in Jackson and Carroll counties, as well as in the Upcountry at large. . . .

✳

The Upcountry had never been dominated by plantations. During the antebellum period, yeoman farms composed the overwhelming majority of agricultural units and embraced most of the land under cultivation. By 1880, large farms and plantations were even fewer in number and had even less economic importance. They constituted under 5 percent of all agricultural units and embraced under 15 percent of the cropland. Yet the further predominance of small farms did not reflect a redistribution of wealth. As before the war, substantial landowners held a disproportionate share of Upcountry real estate. In 1870 the richest tenth of real-property holders in Jackson and Carroll counties owned 37 percent and 45 percent of the real wealth respectively, much the same proportions as had prevailed ten years earlier. While the 1880 census did not record the value of individual real-estate holdings, there is no reason to believe that the structure of wealth became less concentrated during the 1870s. If anything, the expansion of commercial agriculture, the construction of railroads, and the attendant rise in land values led to greater concentrations.

The paradox of proliferating small farms and persisting, if not increasing, concentrations of agricultural wealth was common to the Black Belt as well as to the Upcountry, and resulted from both the failure of land reform and the reorganization of labor during Reconstruction. Although the abolition of slavery struck the planting elite a telling blow, in a rural society control of land as much as control of labor defined the boundaries of social relations. Had the federal government embarked upon a policy of confiscating large plantations and dividing them among the ex-slaves—a policy anticipated by wartime military exigencies and supported by a handful of Radical Republicans—the postwar South would have been very different. The decision of President Andrew Johnson to

restore confiscated property to its former owners and the commitment of most Republicans to the sanctity of private property and the
revitalization of the cotton economy, however, combined to doom
the federal initiative.

The defeat of confiscation in the White House and Congress
did not lay the issue entirely to rest; it continued to influence
politics and race relations in the South. But the eclipse of land
reform as an element of national Reconstruction policy left intact
one of the vital foundations of the planter class. It is true that land
titles changed hands as the result of death, tribulation, and geographical mobility, though, significantly, at a rate no higher than
during the 1850s and certainly not in a manner that broke up large
holdings. Indeed, in some areas, planters not only persevered in
considerable numbers but actually enlarged their share of real
wealth. Whatever their trials, they were in a far better position to
withstand the economic woes of the immediate postwar years than
were their poorer neighbors. In the Upcountry, too, the richest
farmers and planters—as a group—had more success in weathering
the storm than did smallholders and often found themselves more
powerfully situated in 1870 than in 1860. If, for example, we
consider the distribution of real wealth among all white household
heads rather than simply among all white landowners, the top tenth
and top quarter in Carroll and Jackson counties claimed more than
55 percent and 80 percent respectively in 1870, sizable jumps over
the course of the decade. Once again, middling and lesser yeomen
stood as the relative losers.

If the failure of land reform along with economic dislocations
facilitated a greater concentration of agricultural wealth, the growing number of small farm units represented the outcome of the
planters' efforts to reestablish authority over the liberated black
labor force. Insisting that the freedmen were inherently lazy,
indolent, and unreliable and would not work unless compelled,
former slaveholders, while reluctantly accepting Emancipation,
hoped to maintain plantation organization and supervision. And for
the first year or two following the war they did just that. Blacks
continued to live in the old slave quarters, continued to receive
rations and clothing from the landowners, and continued to
cultivate the land in gangs, although now they were entitled to a
low wage or a small share of the crop as further remuneration. The

freedmen had other ideas, however. They wished to escape from the rigors of plantation life, farm their own land, and provide for themselves. Having meager resources and facing the fierce opposition of the landed elite, few attained the goal of independent proprietorship. But the ex-slaves did their best to force something of a labor market on planters who preferred "some species of serfdom or peonage, or . . . other form of compulsory labor," and thereby struck better bargains than white landowners had originally intended to offer. By resisting gang labor in a variety of ways, moreover, the freedmen helped bring about a major reorganization in the system of production. Gradual though the process was, as early as 1870 many plantations were being divided into small parcels farmed by black tenant and sharecropper families having a greater measure of personal autonomy. With few alternative employment opportunities, the freedmen remained tied to the land and subject to the exploitation of landlords and merchants, but the struggle for control of production and exchange was a persistent feature of economic and political life. . . .

By the late 1860s and early 1870s, sharecropping—which had the landowner furnish the laborer with a tract of land, farming implements, work animals, and seed, and pay him, perhaps, one-half of the crop—had become somewhat more common. The share might have been larger if the cropper owned livestock; in either case he had to purchase his own provisions. Renting farms to freedmen, on the other hand—when the landlord received a share of the crop as payment and allowed the tenant freedom from close supervision—was quite rare. But it appears that surprisingly few Upcountry blacks became even sharecroppers. In Jackson County, which boasted one of the region's largest black populations, almost nine of ten freedmen engaged in agriculture were reported as "farm laborers" in 1880. Only a handful cropped or rented; proportionately more, in fact, owned farms than worked on shares. In Carroll County, which had one of the region's smallest black populations, a larger percentage of sharecroppers could be found. Nonetheless, about half of the black agriculturists were farm laborers, a situation which seems to have prevailed elsewhere. While often living in scattered one-family houses, as did croppers, these blacks worked the land collectively. Tenancy and sharecropping in the Upcountry would be predominantly white institutions.

White landlessness, by no means inconsequential during the antebellum period, became more extensive after the Civil War. Though economic hardship affected both rich and poor, small farmers had a particularly difficult time of it. Generally in debt and left with depleted resources during the 1860s, they faced growing pressure from creditors who responded to the financial havoc and political uncertainties of Reconstruction by attempting to clear their balance sheets as quickly as possible. And they showed little reluctance to resort to the auction block if necessary. "I have now a large amount of executions in my hand for collection," the Franklin County sheriff told General John Pope, commander of the Third Military District, "which if done will cause a great sacrifice of property there being but little money in the country." Old political feuds also came into play. Complaining that the "Sheriff of this Co[unty] is a Strong Reb and all connected with the office is," a Jackson County Unionist advised federal officials that the "Secessionists have oppressed [my husband] ever since Georgia seceeded. They are as venomous now as they were then. . . . [H]e went Securrity for some of them during the war who have proved insolvent, now his little remaining Property is taken to pay other debts." She joined what had become a resounding chorus in asking that "the Sales of property [be stopped] until the people can make money to pay creditors with. . . ." Three-quarters of the state's citizens were debtors, W. L. Goodwin, an Upcountry delegate, apprised the Republican-dominated constitutional convention of 1868, and if judgments were pressed to the limit "the entire landed estates of Georgia will pass into the hands of a few extremely wealthy men." "This is a strife between the capital and labor; between the wealthy aristocrats and the great mass of the people," Goodwin proclaimed. "Let me appeal to you . . . stretch forth your helping hands, give the desired relief to the debt-ridden and over burthened people. . . ."

Responding to the pleas of men like Goodwin and hoping to court the favor of north Georgia yeomen, the convention effectively abolished debts contracted prior to June 1, 1865, and recommended substantial homestead exemptions on real and personal property, which the legislature promptly enacted into law. For many farmers, however, such relief measures came too late. Fewer Upcountry whites owned land in 1870 than in 1860, and the trend only worsened thereafter. An upswing in land values during the 1870s coupled with declining prices for agricultural commodities—especially cotton—placed real property increasingly beyond the reach of whites who began their adult lives in a condition of landlessness. As numerous participants in a survey conducted early in the twentieth century remarked, the "small white farmer did not find it easier to secure a farm after the war than before." . . .

More centrally, the growth of sharecropping reflected the expansion of staple agriculture, for a hallmark of contracts was a detailed delineation of the crop mix—a provision rarely found in antebellum agreements. Thus, when Lucius H. Featherston "allow[ed] . . . Moses Moreland to cultivate during the year 1870 fifty acres more or less, of his farm near Franklin [Heard county]," he supplied Moreland with "stock and farming tools necessary to cultivate said land in good farmer like stile," and directed Moreland to sow "30 acres in cotton and the balance in corn." "[A]fter all advances of money, forage, provision, and other things" were repaid, Moreland would have "one half of the crop." John H. Dent and Harvey Lemmings reached similar terms in Floyd County three years later. Dent was "to furnish a horse or mule, all implements and feed [for the animals]"; Lemmings was "to cultivate and harvest 15 acres of corn and . . . 5 acres of cotton," and "receive ½ corn and fodder and . . . ½ cotton" out of which he would pay for any provisions supplied by Dent.

Both Featherston and Dent plainly stipulated that "the title and possession of the entire crop is to remain in . . . [their hands] until said advances and debts are settled." As of 1872, such an inclusion was no longer necessary. In that year the Georgia Supreme Court issued a ruling that acknowledged the new aspects of the staple economy and bolstered the power of landlords by distinguishing the rights of sharecroppers and tenants. The tenant "has a possession of the premises, exclusive of the Landlord, [the cropper] has not," the court announced. "The one has a right for a fixed time, the other has a right only to go on the land to plant, work, and gather the crop. The possession of the land is with the owner against the cropper." In the eyes of the law, the cropper was no more than a wage laborer or, as men like Dent and Featherston would have it, a "hand." . . .

✳

"Hard times" was the cry in the Upcountry by 1890. Low cotton prices, short food crops, and indebtedness for supplies went into making of a vicious cycle that enveloped the lives of small farmers, white and black, owners and tenants, for during the 1880s staple agriculture fastened its grip on the region's economy. If the 1870s and early 1880s marked a transitional period, the direction of change was apparent, and as the last decade of the nineteenth century opened, the Upcountry stood fully transformed, wrenched from the margin into the mainstream of the cotton market. . . .

"Hard times," to be sure, proved ever present features of rural life in the Upcountry, and elsewhere, during the nineteenth century. The whims of nature and the fluctuations of the market placed farmers, especially family farmers, in a perpetually vulnerable position. There is no need to glorify the existences of yeomen, North or South, in early America, for whether or not they attained that fabled sturdy self-sufficiency, they labored long hours, had relatively few material comforts, and could never be certain that their efforts would be rewarded. Yet, the postwar years gave "hard times" a new and increasingly enduring aspect. Falling prices for agricultural produce on the international market, discriminatory freight rates, the erection of high protective tariffs, the demonetization of silver, and land policies that favored speculative engrossment combined to squeeze farmers throughout the United States as a national economy was consolidated under the auspices of industrial and financial capital. Supplying raw materials for Northern factories, the South in particular was relegated to junior partnership—if not colonial status—in a powerful industrializing society. Landlords, merchants, and petty cultivators alike groaned under the yoke of subordination fastened by "Wall Street" financiers.

All did not suffer like fates, however. For if the national and international market conquered and absorbed the Upcountry in the years after 1865, that conquest was not achieved by impersonal forces, by an "invisible hand," or by "Wall Street" financiers. It was accomplished, in large part, by landlords and, especially, by merchants who sought to make the best of postwar conditions, to extend the realm of staple agriculture, and to reap its profits. If they remained junior partners in an emerging, though unquestionably tense, sectional reconciliation, they tended to fare considerably better than the small producers whose economic surpluses they appropriated for their own. No wonder that yeoman farmers and tenants soon turned their wrath, not simply on Northern capitalists, but on local storekeepers and landlords as well.

James Turner

UNDERSTANDING THE POPULISTS

James Turner focused on Texas in his effort to understand why people became Populists. He discovered that the People's party had more strength in counties that were more rural, less affluent, and less developed than those in which the Democrats prevailed. These findings led him to suggest that we might understand Populism in the context of a broader pattern in American history that pitted those at the "centers of political and cultural influence" against those "living on the periphery of the dominant society." Professor Turner's other publications include *Reckoning with the Beast: Animals, Pain, and Humanity in the Victorian Mind* (1980) and *Without God, Without Creed: The Origins of Unbelief in America* (1985).

Pushing on toward a century after Populism burned its course across the American horizon, we have yet to puzzle out what impelled that brief meteor. This is not for lack of trying. Even the historian's infinite capacity for disagreement has barely accommodated the quarrels over the Populists. Were they racists? Were they anti-Semites? Were they victims of capitalism? Or of their own agrarian mythology? Radicals? Reactionaries? Conceivably liberals? Possibly Marxists without Marx? The reason for this confusion is simple. No one yet has plausibly explained why people voted Populist. But without understanding the motivation of ordinary Populists, it is impossible to get to the heart of their ideology or their politics. . . .

From "Understanding the Populists" by James Turner, *Journal of American History*, 67 (September 1980), pp. 354, 359, 362–364, 367–373. Reprinted by permission of the Organization of American Historians.

Texas offers a particularly good basis for informed speculation, not only because of its active role in the genesis of Populism, but because of its geographic location. Lying at the juncture of the two major Populist regions, the Great Plains and the South, Texas Populism combined characteristics of both the farmer's frontier and the sharecropping South. The experience of grass-roots Texas Populists in fact suggests a new understanding of the social basis of Populism that, taken in conjunction with writings on other periods of American history, may be of wider significance in comprehending the origins of American political dissent.

Well over two million people lived in Texas in the 1890s, most of them in a wide central belt running roughly north and south from the Red River to the Gulf of Mexico. Here black loam and (closer to the coast) rich alluvial soil provided fertile ground for the cotton that dominated the region's agriculture; here the cities and industries were found; here railroads proliferated. The business and commerce of Texas flourished within this middle region, but Populism did not.

It was in the peripheral, less populated regions of East and West Texas that Populism sank its deepest roots. Fifteen Texas counties voted for a Populist governor in at least three of the four elections between 1892 and 1898. Three or four of these hugged the less developed edges of the central belt; the rest lay well beyond it. Moreover, both within and without this Populist heartland, cities and towns gave the People's party a cool reception; the rural countryside accounted for its potency on the ballot. One suspects that, in Texas as elsewhere, Populism prospered outside of the social and economic mainstream. Other evidence heightens the impression. Not only were railroads thicker in the central portions of the state, but in every section Populist counties received service inferior to that in neighboring Democratic counties. This meant limited, even irregular commerce with the rest of the state. And the Populist regions were not fully integrated with the cotton economy. The leading cotton-producing counties shied away from Populism, while Populist counties tended toward agricultural self-sufficiency. This did not necessarily mean that Populists were poorer—in fact, throughout the state, Populist counties compared favorably with Democratic counties in farm income—but it did suggest that Populists live "on the outskirts" of Texas. . . .

Since a cursory view makes clear that Populism flourished especially in certain regions of Texas, what is needed is a closer examination of these general areas. They were not uniformly Populist; some counties stood by the Democracy as staunchly as any in the state. To try to determine what impelled some people into Populism, while others remained Democrats, the fifteen strongly Populist counties were paired with neighboring counties which consistently voted for the Democratic gubernatorial candidate. This permitted a comparison of farmers in roughly the same area, who engaged in pretty much the same types of farming, but who ended on different sides of the political fence. . . .

The comparison of Populist and Democratic strongholds immediately scotches any lingering notion that Populism attracted particularly those farmers who suffered most from the agricultural depression. Farm tenancy rates, often taken as evidence of economic conditions, fluctuated so peculiarly in Texas that one questions their usefulness. In any case, the difference between Populist and Democratic counties in both average tenancy rate and average increase in tenancy was marginal—only two percentage points—and hardly suggests unusual problems for Populists. Mortgages are even less helpful, for only a tiny fraction of farms in any of these counties were mortgaged, and the average difference between Populist and Democratic counties in both proportion of farms mortgaged and mortgage interest rates was miniscule. . . .

Probably the best indicator of relative prosperity, though hardly ideal, is the average value of products per farm: the closest approach in available statistics to the individual farmer's annual income. Here the Populist counties actually outperformed their Democratic neighbors. "Farm income" in Populist strongholds averaged $432, compared to $403 in the Democratic counties. Moreover, Populist counties showed a larger increase between 1880 and 1890: 111 percent to 78 percent. This does not prove, though it certainly suggests, that Populists were better off than Democrats in these counties. But the important point is that no reliable evidence indicates the reverse. Economic problems were a necessary condition for the Populist revolt. But they alone did not determine who became a Populist.

Other indices, however, do point to significant differences between Populist and Democratic areas. None of these counties had large towns, but the county seats in Populist counties averaged fewer than 1,000 people, while the Democratic seats averaged over 1,600. No county had major industry, but the Populist countries numbered fewer than a fifth the manufacturing workers of Democratic counties. Railroad lines less frequently crossed the Populist counties, and the Democratic counties had all but one of the six important railroad depots. Slightly less of the farmland in Populist areas had been improved. Formal church membership was somewhat less common in Populist counties, and fewer religious denominations were represented there. Populist counties also included fewer than a third as many inhabitants of foreign birth.

Individually, none of these circumstances amounted to much. But they linked together with remarkable persistence. . . . Taken together, they substantiate in some detail what recent writings on Populism have begun to hint at and what the general geography of Texas Populism suggests: that Populists lived in relative isolation from the larger society of their state and nation. . . .

Isolation meant, among other things, rather limited contact with other human beings. Populism appealed to farm families starved for social life—thus the camp-meeting political rallies, the picnics, the incessant fraternizing that characterized it. . . . The camaraderie it offered probably helps to explain how it mushroomed in a few short years. But its even more rapid collapse shows the limits of sociability, nor can the fraternal side of Populism account for its politics or world view. Isolation had a deeper impact. . . .

Isolation may also have shaped Populism in deeper, more personal, and more important strata. Here the historian treads on slippery ground, for ordinary Populists left little evidence of their interior selves. The shreds that survive consist mostly of scattered copies of county weeklies—important for not only the locally produced editorial content but especially the letters to the editor—and a rare letter or diary. These fragmentary remains often impart a sense of people bewildered by the complexities of the world around them. Populists struggling with practical political realities commonly wrote in real perplexity. One local "Investigator" could not fathom why the general economic discontent did not immediately produce a political remedy: "Why not change our statu[t]es so they will be in accordance with the will of the majority? It appears strange to me that the only obstacle that prevents it is a lack of agreement upon the best policy or methods by which it can be accomplished." . . .

Much of Populist rhetoric . . . suggests that third-party men felt themselves at sea in the society in which they lived. Bewilderment appears to have bred an incessant worry that more sophisticated men preyed on their naiveté. Populists saw themselves as cruelly hoodwinked for years, until the third party had opened their eyes. A greedy plutocracy controlled the government and economy of Texas and the nation, and the money kings remained secure in their high places through their success in duping the citizenry. "The brigand has his headquarters in legislative halls, and the pirate fees a lawyer and goes into business. Of course, the masses must be kept in ignorance and deceived, and nothing gives deception and error such power over men as to be clothed in the garb of law." "The trouble with us," one Populist sighed, "is that we have too many men who are too easily fooled." . . .

At the same time, this isolation may also have been the Populists' greatest strength. As strangers in their own land, Populist farmers would more easily have probed and questioned accepted political and economic verities. They could more comfortably desert the Democratic party, the party of the fathers, treason to which was betrayal of the South. They could even break the united front of white supremacy and breach the color line. Above all, they could support (though not necessarily generate or fully understand) the wildest, the most improbable—perhaps the most penetrating and hopeful—schemes for remodeling an industrializing America. Their relative isolation gave Populists enough independence from the dominant political culture to allow the growth of an original politics and ideology. Yet isolation was perhaps also the reason why Populism, so powerful, was so easily undercut, divided, and defeated. . . .

A puzzling question remains. If, as proposed here, social isolation is a key to understanding Populism, why did no farmers' revolt explode earlier? Tillers of the soil had lived in rural insularity before; they had suffered severe economic depression before. Yet never before had they responded with the intensity and power of the 1890s. Why was isolation especially galling at this particular moment of American history?

Between the end of the Civil War and the turn of the twentieth century, the United States underwent what time may demonstrate to have been the most fundamental transformation in its history: the change from a basically rural nation to an urban society. The cultural impact was radical. Especially with the advent of national chain stores, smaller towns grew more closely linked with the great metropolises. The huge mail-order houses brought home even to rural folk the new city-oriented civilization. The ideal of a single national pattern of life and set of values, reinforced by the proliferation of national circulation magazines, came much closer to realization. Even the county weeklies commonly read by Populists, though unconnected with the new wire services, usually filled half their space with nationally produced boiler plate. Ways of living in New York and Chicago were becoming the standard to which the rest of the nation wished to conform. The central culture was swallowing more and more of the diverse local cultures.

However, some citizens—very few in most of the country, but many in the recently settled Midwest and the war-retarded South— remained on the fringe of the metropolitan culture. Tantalizing tastes of the wider culture they certainly had; real participation they did not. Rural free delivery and decent roads, with the automobiles to travel them, still lay in the future. Although the offerings of Montgomery Ward tempted them along with other farmers, nevertheless, on the whole, these "backward" people remained the last outpost of the old America. . . .

This interpretation places Populism firmly in the broadest context of American historical development. The movement cannot be understood as simply a farmer's revolt against penury and oppression, a rebellion that could have flared up, given the right conditions, at any time in American history. Instead, Populism resulted specifically from the "ending of the frontier"—not in Turner's sense of the drying up of free land, but in a wider sense of the curtailment of social isolation.

Yet implicit in this view of Populism is a notion that applies, not only to a specific historical moment, but to much of American political history: that isolation breeds a political culture at odds with the mainstream of political habits and attitudes. It follows that the tensions thereby generated ought to have been a continuing feature of the politics of an expanding nation with a frontier that pulled many citizens into a relatively isolated life.

The limited evidence available points to precisely this conclusion. The most striking case is Jackson Turner Main's analysis of *Political Parties before the Constitution.* Main argues that a division between "Localists" and "Cosmopolitans" dominated politics in all the states during the 1770s and 1780s, foreshadowing the Anti-federalists and Federalists in the struggle over ratification of the Constitution. The well-populated, long-established economic and cultural centers were the strongholds of the Cosmopolitans. But away from the towns, away from the major rivers, in the inland villages and on the frontiers, where commercial agriculture gave way to subsistence farming, in regions "culturally backward" and cut off from "short, cheap access to markets," the Localists dominated. *Mutatis mutandis*, Main could almost have been describing the Populist heartlands. One cannot help wondering whether the politics of the Antifederalists—their suspicion of central government, their persistence in the "outmoded" whig radicalism of the early Revolution—owed much to the political culture of the relatively isolated areas in which many of them apparently dwelt.

Yet this was neither the first nor last conflict between established centers of political and cultural influence and people living on the periphery of the dominant society. Before the Revolution the Regulator movements of Carolina pitted up-country frontiersmen against low-country planters. Much of antebellum—and indeed postbellum—southern politics centered on tensions between Piedmont dirt farmers and lowland elites. The Great Awakening split New England along lines roughly corresponding to the division between established socioculture centers and culturally and commercially peripheral areas. The American Revolution itself was a conflict between the sociocultural center of the empire and a provincial region three thousand miles away.

To point to these examples is to raise questions rather than to suggest answers. Historians have seldom pursued the kinds of research that might reveal in these cases similarities to the Populist milieu such as Main's book indicates. But the possible inferences are intriguing. Do we need a richer, more complex interpretation of these persistent conflicts in American politics, an explanation in terms of clashing political cultures as well as inequalities of political and economic power? Does all of this hint at a much broader, more flexible, more subtle remodeling of the Turner thesis? Perhaps we should try to understand Populism, not only as a response to the economic modernization of America, but as a manifestation of one of the most central and venerable characteristics of the American political tradition.

II

Principles, Programs, and Party

Theodore R. Mitchell

THE ALLIANCE AND
THE PUBLIC SCHOOL

Like Lawrence Goodwyn (see Part I), Theodore R. Mitchell concluded that the primary significance of the Southern Farmers' Alliance stemmed from its having forged a mass democratic movement in an effort to offer an alternative to the concentration of power and wealth that had become so pronounced by the 1880s. Mitchell focused on the Alliance's efforts to improve public education so that ordinary people could think for themselves and thus challenge the prevailing social, economic, and political order more effectively. Theodore Mitchell is a professor of education at Dartmouth College.

"To arrange and display the needs of the South in their order as to importance, we believe the Alliance has well stated them: first we need education," wrote Congressman L. F. Livingston, President of the Georgia Farmers' Alliance in a contribution to Nelson Dunning's *Farmers' Alliance History*. In 1889, the same piece, "The Needs of the South," was run, with an approving introduction, in the *Annual Report of the United States Commissioner of Education*. For the Commissioner, N. H. R. Dawson, what Livingston was obviously talking about was schools. He was willing and eager to use Alliance sentiment in favor of education to spur efforts to improve the quality and quantity of public schooling in the South.

The Alliance leadership, too, seemed willing to be part of a movement to improve schooling. Livingston went on to argue that "we need, in the South, a thorough, practical, and economical system of common school education." [Charles W.] Macune, in the pages of the *National Economist*, wrote that "what we ought to do is build up our public school system, build it up by providing a more liberal school fund." Milton Park echoed the sentiments of the national leadership. "Increase the number of schoolhouses," he urged, and by so doing, the Alliance would "increase the power of the people by

From *Political Education in the Southern Farmers' Alliance, 1887–1900* by Theodore R. Mitchell, pp. 124–129, 133–140, Copyright 1987. Reprinted by permission of The University of Wisconsin Press.

educating them to independent thought." The People's party, when it emerged from the Alliance in 1892, supported public education. State and national Populist platforms carried planks demanding "an effective system of free public schools for six months in the year." For these national spokesmen, public schooling fit into their program of education and reform in several ways.

First, public schooling in the South lagged far behind schooling in other regions, in enrollment per capita, expenditures per capita, and length of school term. This educational underdevelopment contributed to high rates of illiteracy, which made the kind of active citizenship the Alliance advocated difficult, to say the least. In an age before the adoption of the Australian ballot system (in which a ballot contains the names of all candidates) men merely collected a party ticket from a campaign worker, signed it, and stuffed it into a ballot box. Under this system illiteracy was no impediment to casting ballots, but it was a sure deterrent to an understanding of whose names were on the ticket.

From the point of view of the Alliance leadership, illiteracy was a form of de facto disenfranchisement. Worse, it put the votes of a large number of citizens at the mercy of last-minute party maneuvering. In addition, literacy tests became, in the late 1880s and 1890s, a *de jure* means of denying voting rights to blacks and some poor whites in the South. "To take away a man's citizenship because he can not read and write," wrote one Louisiana man, "would be most unjust without first providing the means for such education." What the Alliance attempted, through its support of public schooling, was to erase the problem of illiteracy and of manipulated voters, seeking a fair count and honest elections through universal literacy.

Second, public schools were and are institutions of the state. As with other elements of the polity, Alliance leaders demanded that the public school be directed "to promote the welfare of the people, the great struggling, toiling masses." As in the larger political arena, the Alliance sought control over schools in part through the power of the ballot. To this end, every Alliance endorsement and every People's party ticket, even at the county level, targeted candidates for school boards and school superintendencies.

These direct electoral attempts to take control of the public schools were, however, halfhearted. The faith of the Alliance leadership in the ultimate importance of education could not compete for organizational resources with their immediate political aims in the direction of capturing legislative and executive control of government. Expenditures on these campaigns ran very low. Candidates for school posts languished in anonymity at the hands of reform editors. Park, a strong advocate of public schooling and a careful editor, misspelled the name of the People's party candidate for the Texas superintendency twice, before he finally gave the correct name. Even then, the retractions and corrections were the only bits of press E. P. Alsbury got from the *Mercury* in his losing campaign in 1894.

Even more important than the organizational imperatives, though, in explaining this neglect of local school politics, was the understanding among national Alliance leaders that the public school was only one component of what comprised education in the rural South. In the public school children learned the rudiments of literacy and numeracy; their minds were "hardened" in these mental "gymnasiums." In the family, children and young adults learned the values and ideas that focused their parents' understanding of the world. There children began to use the skills they learned in school in the context of their lives. Finally, the third piece of this configuration was the "enrollment" of whole families in the great school that was the Farmers' Alliance. They became members and learned that there were names and reasons for the miseries they shared, and they learned how to take action in their own interest. When they thought about education for their farmer members, the leaders of the movement thought about this configuration as an integrated and interdependent unit. The public school fit within the educational configuration as an important foundation through which future citizens could develop intellectual skills that would later be focused and directed within the educational program of the Alliance.

Thus the Alliance leadership supported public schooling on strategic, ideological, and pedagogical grounds, agreeing in general, if not in specifics, with the bullish school-building sentiment current in every region at the turn of the century. Over the period, public schooling was one topic upon which nearly every reform group could agree. Even in the South, where traditional opposition to public schooling continued into the 1890s, Alliance leaders could agree with industrialists and labor organizations that more schooling at state expense served the public interest. But this general consensus masked important particular conflicts over the nature and purpose of state supported schooling.

While national spokesmen and spokeswomen for the Alliance supported public education as an introduction to useful intellectual skills, they struggled politically and rhetorically against trends in educational governance that they believed would hinder the use of public schooling as a constructive element in their educational configuration. In fact, some feared that changes in schooling were fast making public schooling anathema to the reform cause.

These changes were of two kinds. First, the Alliance viewed with concern the growing power of private groups in the governance of education in the South. These groups, including the "school book trust" and various philanthropic organizations, were, through economic and bureaucratic means, wresting control of schools from the hands of elected or appointed school officials. Second, even worse was the fact that as they gained influence in the schools, these groups introduced a curriculum whose content contradicted the reform message of the Alliance educational program. Because of these changes, the use by the Alliance of public schooling as one leg of its educational triad became problematic. If the schools were teaching ideas antithetical to reform, then should the Alliance support public schools at all?

In some communities, the answer was no. According to the Choctaw, Alabama, *Advocate*, the county Alliance there established its own high school in 1891. In the same year, an Alliance cooperative school opened in Echo, Alabama, enrolling over one hundred students. The Echo Cooperative School employed two male teachers and held classes for seven months during 1891, nearly double the average length of school terms in the South. Unfortunately, we do not know the fate of either of these two schools, and examples of this kind of direct intervention into schooling were few. The creation of alternative schools for the children of members was not an Alliance priority. In addition to the philosophical and ideological impediments to devoting organizational resources to the education of children, the Alliance, particularly local groups, could ill afford, financially, to create a system of Alliance schools. Rather than create a parallel system of schools, the Alliance launched a rhetorical attack on the educational "trusts" and mounted a campaign to debunk and discredit the standard curriculum.

National spokespeople incorporated schooling issues as part of their campaign to illustrate how combinations of the wealthy and powerful always result in the immiserization of the poor. In other words, the Alliance leadership fashioned its role in school politics in the same mold used for shaping its role in politics writ large: the leadership took upon itself the task of illuminating the underlying structures of power and authority which determined the course of so many outwardly democratic institutions. In this way the leadership carved for itself a niche as educators about education.

In 1890, the National Alliance accused a group of publishers including Harper Brothers, D. Appleton and Company, and A. S. Barnes and Company, of conspiring to consolidate contracts, control competition, and raise prices in the schoolbook market through the creation of a holding company, the American Book Company. This combination not only raised prices to schools and to parents, but also propounded, in the pages of its texts, the virtues of American industrial progress, particularly the virtues of the American industrial giants, the very enemies of the Alliance. More, the Alliance found that the "trust" had ensured its insidious effect on the public schools through an intricate and secret system of kickbacks to local and state superintendents. "The farmer will find this class of educators in hearty sympathy with this combine, and to attack one is to fight both," wrote Macune. Unfortunately, the Alliance did not rally to Macune's cry for action, perhaps not yet convinced that schools were a legitimate target for their political efforts.

National opposition to the increasing influence of philanthropic organizations on southern education was even more lukewarm. Occasionally Alliance papers denigrated the directors of the Peabody or Slater Fund through statements such as "that old Fraud R. B. Hayes is a member." More often, though, they criticized philanthropy itself: "Charity," Macune argued, "covers up no sins when the gift has been stolen from the poor." Aside from these grumblings, the Alliance took no action against the philanthropic organizations which had begun to spread their money and influence throughout the South. One reason the leadership did not make more of the Peabody and Slater charity was that these organizations, officiated over by the ubiquitous Jabez Lamar Monroe Curry, ministered exclusively to black schools during the 1880s and until the late 1890s. While the Alliance leadership could and did disapprove of philanthropy and its effects, as long as the elite charities concerned themselves with black education they remained secondary targets, even within the realm of education. . . .

*

Professional educators and social elites believed that the classical curriculum wasted the time of children whose lot in life was to farm the fields of the South and West. Literacy and numeracy remained important within the school curriculum, dominating the common school. But in higher training, including both at the high school level and the land grant colleges, the skills and techniques of agriculture came to play a larger and larger role after 1880.

By 1880, the land grant colleges that Congress had authorized in 1865 had become well established, even if their purpose remained ill-defined. Their charge to instruct students in the mechanical and agricultural sciences had been interpreted loosely. In most of the southern states, the A & M colleges were ruled by the faculty of the classical departments, with a farm attached to the campus on which students worked during a good part of the day. In 1887, Congress appropriated funds for the establishment of agricultural experiment stations in the South; most were attached to these land grant institutions. At the stations, experiments were carried out with the goal of increasing per acre yield of various cash crops, including wheat, corn, and of course cotton.

The idea of agricultural education got a boost as well from the widely lauded industrial schools established for blacks. These schools, like Washington's Tuskegee and Armstrong's Hampton, became in the 1890s the paradigm for useful education for all members of the laboring classes. In industrial schools, blacks learned skills and habits commensurate with adult roles as hired labor or independent artisan. In other words, they were educated into, not out of, the lives assigned them through the rigid racial structuring of southern social life. Similarly, whites in agricultural programs within the public school learned modern methods of cultivation and fertilization. They learned how to make more from their lot (literally and figuratively). What Charles Dabney concluded about sentiment toward black education applied with similar force to whites by 1890. The question was not "whether he should be educated, but how he should be trained." The rise of vocationalism, of training, in southern education encouraged conservatives as well as liberal southerners to support the spread of universal public education.

The leaders of the Alliance saw the introduction of agricultural education in both the schools and the colleges as a good thing. At Clebourne, the Alliance approved a resolution demanding "for the masses a well-regulated system of industrial and agricultural education. Similarly, the constitution of the Agricultural Wheel stated that one object of the order was to work toward the "improvement of its members in the theory and practice of agriculture, and the dissemination of knowledge relating to rural and farming affairs." In its own educational campaign, the Alliance participated in the movement toward more thorough education in the science of agriculture. Most Alliance papers ran columns on farming and farming technique. The Dunning volume, *The Farmers' Alliance History and Agricultural Digest*, which was mailed free to every subscriber to the *Economist*, contained articles on "How to Plan a Barn," and "What is Under Draining." The *Digest* also included sections on fertilizers and soil chemistry. Suballiance meetings were arenas in which farming technique was discussed and new methods were disseminated.

In its support for better agricultural education the Alliance seems at, one level, to have been in sympathy with the school reformers and earlier agrarian groups, particularly the Grange. But the Alliance position regarding agricultural education differed from that of either the New South reformers or the Patrons of Husbandry. Alliance opposition to certain aspects of the agricultural education movement illustrates, again, the struggle underway over what, exactly, was useful knowledge.

The major complaint of Alliance spokesmen regarding agricultural education as practiced in the schools of the South was that it was technical in nature, to the exclusion of all other epistemological forms. Macune responded to the popularity of agricultural education with typical insight, arguing that

> the purely technical effort of improving our methods of farming, by which we may possibly increase the amount of products we make in return for a given amount of labor and expense, although it be praiseworthy, is not a force or remedy [to the conditions faced by farmers].

"The influences that tend to depress agriculture and render the pursuit of that occupation unprofitable," he continued, "have rapidly gained the ascendancy over and neutralized the beneficient effects that should have followed the introduction of wise methods and new machines." The old methods and the old logic—produce more to make more—had "proved ineffectual on every occasion," and the Alliance leadership found that political knowledge leading to political power held out hope where technical knowledge and technical prowess did not. The hope of the Alliance lay in changing the political economy in such a way that the laws and the courts worked in the farmers' favor, not in perfecting their techniques within a political economy structured against their interests.

L. L. Polk, speaking before an audience of the faithful in convention on a winter afternoon in Ocala, Florida, summarized the division he saw between technical and political means to achieve freedom from the grasp of poverty. "This investigation [into the causes of agricultural depression] has led to the general, if not universal conviction that it is due to discriminating and unjust national legislation. Were it due," he proclaimed, "to false or imperfect systems of farm economy, we would apply the remedy by improving systems of our own devising." For Polk, technical training and technical knowledge, when substituted for political training and political knowledge, masked the true nature of the farmers' plight and militated against the organization and mobilization of any kind of protest. Agricultural and industrial education were simply parts of the "miseducation" of southern farmers. Improved technical efficiency, by itself, promised to make farmers more productive slaves to the lien system, the usury, and the declining prices that marked southern agriculture during the period. Political knowledge, not technical knowledge, offered hope.

Some of the conspiratorially minded leaders of the movement saw an even more pernicious meaning in the rise of technical agricultural education. A second complaint about the increasing focus on technical/vocational education was that it would actually deprive farmers and workers of access to political knowledge and so limit their legitimacy in future discussions of politics. By limiting the education of the masses, black and white, to technical training, elites would preserve political knowledge, and so political power, for themselves. The introduction of agricultural training in the purely technical aspects of farming was, for these members of the Alliance leadership, a first step toward the creation of a hierarchy of kinds of knowledge and toward the segregation of access to different kinds of learning on the basis of social class.

Thus Milton Park noted in the *Mercury* that it was the organized politicians and the professional educators who "advise the farmers to raise more corn, cotton, and grain." "We [the Alliance] say, study political economy and the social conditions more, work less for the plutocrats and bosses, and you will come out ahead." The reform program of the Alliance depended on the movement's ability to appropriate the powerful language of politics for its own use. By limiting the curriculum for farmers' children more and more to technical, vocational areas, schools made it more difficult for the next generation of farmers to grasp political ideas, to form political opinions on their own, and to take independent political action—in short, to support any ideology different from that of the dominant classes.

If the farmers became technicians, and intellectually came to accept that the solutions to their problems rested with improved technique, then the battle for reform would be lost. The Alliance based its reform impulse on a critique of the American political economy. This critique relied on the farmers' ability to distill from their own particular experiences perspectives on the state of the nation. It required that farmers measure the state of the nation against a normative template fashioned of economic moralism and equality of opportunity. In short, reform depended upon the ability of the farmers to criticize the system of American politics and economics. Park, for example, worried that, as technicians, farmers would be trained to take that system for granted and to puzzle over how to maximize their returns, social as well as economic, within it. It was a prospect that animated Alliance opposition to exclusively technical training in the schools, colleges, and experiment stations in the South.

✳

When the Alliance leadership looked at the economy, they worried about and worked against the concentration of wealth in the hands of a few industrialists and financiers, and the corresponding concentration of political power in the same hands. When they looked at what was happening in education, a few, notably Macune and Park, saw that a similar process was at work: the "bosses" and the "plutocrats" intended to monopolize political language and political knowledge, setting themselves up as the experts in running the nation, and setting out for the farmers a limited and subordinate sphere for the development of their own agrarian expertise. As they had gained control over the mechanisms of economic production, the privileged classes were well on the way to controlling the means of the production and legitimation of knowledge, through the segregation of technical and political learning along class lines.

The leaders of the Alliance saw that exclusive concentration on agricultural techniques would limit their claim to political knowledge and their claim that their particular political ideology was legitimate. As a result, their efforts to retain access to political knowledge and to battle for the legitimacy of their ideology centered upon ways to continue to train farmers in the language of politics and in the ideals of democratic citizenship, in spite of changes in publicly funded educational programs. For the same reason, the leaders opposed technical education without compensatory political education, both in and out of the public school.

For this remedial political training the leadership relied on its own educational configuration: the rallies, the suballiance meetings, and the news organs. The Alliance supported the public schools, the agricultural experiment stations, and the agricultural and mechanical colleges, insofar as these other pieces of educational apparatus contributed to a well-balanced system of education, whose effect was "not only to teach our people to grow better crops," but also to "obtain control of products of the farm and prevent their passing into the hands of the great corporations."

To some extent the Alliance leadership depended upon the movement's ability to maintain an ongoing critique of "miseducation" that was powerful enough to overwhelm the antithetical elements of schooling. In this expectation they were disappointed. The educational movement that sought to redefine the family does not seem to have done so. The campaign that was to create a permanent system of suballiance discussion groups produced only temporary successes. In other words, the distance between Alliance educational thought and its formal articulation restricted the effectiveness of the educational campaign. At another level, the success of Alliance educational opposition was limited by the narrow distinctions national leaders made between acceptable and unacceptable public school curricula.

Unfortunately for the fate of the educational impulse of the Alliance, these distinctions were too fine in most cases to influence local Alliance groups in their day to day interaction with particular schools. Debates over the nature of history taught in school and over the legitimacy of political knowledge did not penetrate to the local level, with an ultimately negative impact on the general oppositional education campaign. At the local level, only the bare outlines of the leadership's position on schooling were visible, and these outlines suggested one main position, namely that public schooling was good for the children of the South. To local Alliancemen the difference between several types of knowledge, between divergent means of control over that knowledge, and even between the focus of Alliance and state education simply did not obtain. What did, however, were sets of local political, economic and social conditions that varied substantially between communities. As a result, local support for or opposition to schools depended more upon circumstance than principle.

It is important to remember that although poorly supported and most often poorly conducted, the public school was an integral part of southern communities. In the South and in other rural areas, schools were much more than buildings in which children learned to read and write. The school was often a focus of public life, serving as an auditorium for community meetings and debates; as a courtroom in which the justice of the peace and the circuit judge presided; and as a hall in which community groups, including the Alliance, might find a temporary home. In the black half of town, the public school often doubled as a church, or the church as a school—at times it was hard to tell. But for both blacks and whites, in addition to its educative function, the public school served as no less than a community center in the postbellum South. As a community center, the school was symbolically and logistically important for local Alliance groups, and this importance favorably disposed local officials in their handling of public school matters.

The first meeting of the Arkansas Agricultural Wheel—one of the several organizations Macune brought together in Shreveport to create the National Alliance—took place in W. T. McBee's schoolhouse, eight miles southwest of Des Arc, Arkansas, in Prairie County, in February 1882. From that early moment in the history of the movement, local chapters of the Wheel and the Alliance met in schoolhouses throughout the South. The connection was auspicious, promising reform-minded farmers a firm link with the communities in which they lived and worked. For, from the first, the Alliance fought the stigma of a foreign element in the community body politic. Members of the Wheel and the Alliance did not fit into traditional political categories; their allegiance to the agrarian cause was something new. Naturally the movement came under suspicion. By tying their organization to one of the pillars of the community (the school), local leaders gained some measure of legitimacy. This linking with the school meant more than simply using the building for Alliance events. In most communities it also meant supporting the public school in every way possible.

Ideological and rhetorical support for the schools came naturally to local Alliance groups. From the national leadership they had learned the value of education, which they translated into support for the schools. Wrote the editor of the Tarboro, North Carolina, *Southerner*, "our public schools are the mainstay of our republic." The *Farmers' Advocate* of Tarboro echoed this sentiment, urging the members of the Edgecombe County Alliance to "send the boys and girls to school while they are young . . . educate your children by all means." The schools could "make them not dumb-driven cattle, but help them to be heroes in the strife." . . .

Michael Schwartz

THE SOUTHERN FARMERS' ALLIANCE: GROWTH AND MERGER

Michael Schwartz, one of the first scholars to address the issue of class divisions within the Southern Farmers' Alliance, argued that although the organization initially consisted largely of yeomen and tenant farmers, it eventually expanded its appeal. When planters, who came to dominate the organization's leadership, took the Alliance into politics in 1890

From *Radical Protest and Social Structure: The Southern Farmers' Alliance and Cotton Tenancy, 1880–1890* by Michael Schwartz, pp. 91–104; copyright © 1976 by Academic Press, Inc. Reprinted by permission of the publisher.

without a mandate from the rank-and-file members, Schwartz concluded, they undermined its support among the small farmer class and reduced it to an empty shell. A member of the Sociology Department at the State University of New York at Stony Brook, Michael Schwartz is the author of *The Power Structure of American Business* (1985).

The Southern Farmers' Alliance flowed through the 1880s like a river on its way to the ocean. The tributaries began as small farmers' clubs in the early part of the decade, and each small stream grew as it gathered strength from the misery which the tenancy system created. As the clubs grew, they flowed into each other and contributed to the growth of the movement. As the decade progressed, clubs that had merged then recombined into larger and larger organizations; each one of these large groups was the summation of its many tributaries. Finally, in 1892, the Alliance, one million members strong, lost itself in the Populist party, as a river into the sea.

But unlike a river, the Alliance absorbed two different kinds of streams as it proceeded. The main tributaries were large organizations of small yeomen and tenants who sought to use boycotts, form cooperatives, and engage in other locally based mass activities to reverse the process of tenantization and overcome the immiseration brought about by the crop lien system. The other tributaries were small organizations of large owners, which gathered together the leading farmers in a county or state to work out suitable solutions for the entire farming population and then attempted to use the power and prestige of the individual members to carry out the prescribed changes. The process of merger and absorption that occurred as the stream of Southern farmer protest grew is a good beginning focus for an analysis of its activities.

✳

Historians of the Southern Farmers' Alliance trace its beginnings to Texas in the middle 1870s, but the original group, which remained small and collapsed several times in its early years, bore almost no important relation to the later group which reached maturity in the 1880s. Only in early 1882, with a substantial organization in Parker County, Texas, and a few members in neighboring areas, did the Alliance undertake its first attack on the tenancy system: a selective buying project aimed at reducing merchants' prices. That fall, a state organization was formed and membership rose to 5000; 1883 saw it decline to 2000. . . .

The Alliance survived these early tribulations and it entered the middle 1880s as a healthy and growing organization of some 40,000 members, almost all of them in Texas. It was joined by the Louisiana Farmers' Union, the Agricultural Wheel, and the Brothers of Freedom, all of which had sprung up in much the same way and had developed into remarkably similar organizations. All four were membership groups which had local clubs as their basic building blocks. They directed their initial recruiting efforts at yeoman farmers, and their activities centered around reforming or reconstructing supply and sales systems of Southern cotton farming.

Since activities were generally centered around a county seat, where the farmers of a community bought supplies and sold crops, expansion within county limits was a natural outgrowth of any activity. But further growth was unwieldly and "unnatural," and at first cross-county expansion was haphazard at best, depending on the more or less problematical communication of the activities of small local clubs. Rapid statewide and interstate growth began only when the farmers' groups deliberately pursued it through the establishment of a statewide organizing apparatus capable of entering new areas and mobilizing potential members. In the case of the Alliance, this took place in 1882 and resulted in the expansion from 2000 to 38,000 members. The 1000-member Arkansas Agricultural Wheel formed a statewide organizing committee in 1883 and increased its membership to 25,000 in 2½ years. The Louisiana Farmers' Union and the Brothers of Freedom experienced similar growth for similar reasons, entering the middle of the decade with 10,000 and 15,000 members, respectively.

As these groups expanded, they began to run into each other. The Wheel and the Brothers of Freedom were the first to make contact, and their merger—voted in October 1885 and consummated in July 1886—was the first important merger among the groups that ultimately formed the Farmers' Alliance. The second such merger united the Texas Alliance and the Louisiana Farmers' Union. Like the Wheel–Brothers juncture, it was managed with little difficulty, though unlike its predecessor, the prelude was tumultuous.

The Texas Alliance convened at Clebourne August 3, 1886, with membership at an all-time high of 110,000. Nevertheless, the organization was in deep trouble. It was becoming clear that the initially successful county-level activities were failing, and the group needed new programs which could successfully ameliorate the oppressive conditions created by the cotton tenancy system. The convention decided to pressure the state legislature for "such legislation as shall secure our people freedom from the onerous abuses that the industrial classes are now suffering at the hands of arrogant capitalist and powerful corporations." The list of demands included the opening of new farmlands through confiscation of large holdings and legislative attacks against railroads and other large enterprises affecting agriculture. The new program was accompanied by the structural alteration necessary to convert a locally based economic pressure group into a statewide electoral action group. The Texas Alliance Constitution was altered to give greater strength and initiative to the state leadership, and a legislative lobbying committee was set up and began its work by monitoring the Democratic convention which was being held in Clebourne at the same time.

However, less than a week after the close of the convention, a group bolted the Alliance, called a rump convention, and elected new officers. This group claimed that the previous convention was void because it violated the constitutional stricture against partisan politics. Since this insurgent group contained local leaders who exerted great influence in the theretofore locally oriented Alliance, their protest threatened the very existence of the organization. As a consequence, C. W. Macune, the chairman of the executive committee, nullified the program of the August meeting and scheduled a unity convention in October. However, when Macune's efforts to negotiate a merger with the very large Western Farmers' Alliance foundered, he postponed the convention until he could offer a substantial program to the membership.

Such a program was ready by January, and the unity convention at Waco was greeted with three major proposals. The first was a new economic strategy built around an ambitious Farmers' Alliance Exchange. This exchange was intended to replace the retail and wholesale merchants by acting as supplier to the Alliance farmer during the crop growing season and as sales agent during harvest. . . . The second was the institution of an ambitious organizing drive which involved a strengthened *national* organization with paid agitators in every Southern state. The third was the easily accomplished merger with the Louisiana Farmers' Union.

The logic behind Macune's program was twofold. On the one hand, the exchange strategy headed off the move into electoral politics by offering plausible economic action for the immediate alleviation of the farmers' situation. At the same time, the expansion to a national organization held the promise of a vast pressure group; a huge farmers' organization to impress the government with the gravity of the farmers' plight and alter national policy. Thus, specific electoral action was replaced by a less particular strategy—the arousal of national public opinion.

Macune united the Waco convention with his proposals. The result was a new vibrancy in the organization and the beginning of the Farmers' Alliance as a major force for reform. By the next year, it had spread to five states and doubled its membership to over 250,000.

The Clebourne crisis in 1886, like the organizational crisis of 1882, is a window into the internal dynamics of farmers' protest. The failure of local activities created the pressure for change which found expression in two tendencies. The conflict between these tendencies was unresolvable through debate: Though the politically oriented group won the vote, the economically oriented group wielded the structural strength to emerge victorious. Finally, the key element in restoring the health of the organization was the institution of a program that offered the promise of successful reform, in this case locally oriented economic action together with the creation of a national organization potentially capable of affecting national politics.

*

During 1886 and 1887, the Farmers' Alliance and the Agricultural Wheel expanded rapidly on a course which carried them closer and closer together. As they grew toward each other, they absorbed smaller and larger groups which had sprung up in their paths. Among the groups they absorbed were the farmers' Associations, which based themselves among large planters. These groups, which sought to redress the grievances of the many landlords who felt the pressure of the Southern agricultural system, were destined to provide both the Alliance and the Populists with a substantial proportion of their leadership.

A good example of such a group is the North Carolina Farmers' Association, led by L. L. Polk, who later became the president of the national Alliance. Polk, a descendant of President Polk and formerly North Carolina commissioner of agriculture, founded what was to become the most important agrarian reform newspaper of the period, the *Raleigh Progressive Farmer*, in February 1886. Soon afterward, he began organizing farmers' clubs to advance his reform programs: an expanded agricultural college, the reorganization of the North Carolina Department of Agriculture, and immigration to increase the supply of farm labor. The club movement met with some success, especially among the most prosperous farmers, who would have benefited from these programs.

After nearly a year of existence, the club movement held its first statewide convention in January 1887. The call was so moderate that it won the endorsement of the governor. Despite some discontent among club members, this endorsement led to cosponsorship by the North Carolina Board of Agriculture and a list of prominent speakers, including a former governor and the president of the University of North Carolina. The attenders were primarily wealthy planters and the resolutions reflected their interests: a call for a national department of agriculture oriented toward research, and a host of legislative acts aimed at protecting large landlords. These programs did not look at all like the calls for cooperatives, the protests against landlords and merchants, and the challenges against the whole government which the Alliance and Wheel regularly approved at their conventions.

The convention formalized the club movement into the North Carolina Farmers' Association, which functioned until spring 1888, when it was absorbed by the Alliance. The Farmers' Association concentrated on organizing large rallies whose purpose was to educate farmers about modern techniques. This emphasis appealed to large farmers, who had the freedom to experiment and the resources to expand, but it had little relevance to the indebted small farmer, who needed to reduce supply costs or increase returns within the context of crop lien. Consequently, the organization did not prosper, and even the rallies owed their success in part of the publicity given them by the hardworking

Farmers' Alliance, which had entered the state in January 1887, just after the Waco convention.

In August 1887, Polk first met C. W. Macune; they both addressed the Interstate Convention of Farmers in Atlanta. . . . Upon his return to Raleigh, Polk fully endorsed the burgeoning Alliance, printed its organizational chart weekly in his paper, and began reporting its news on a regular basis.

The dissolution of the North Carolina Farmers' Association into the North Carolina Farmers' Alliance during the ensuing 6 months created an influx of a large group of relatively prosperous tenantholding farmers who had decidedly different interests from those of the earlier Alliance members. "Where at first the leading and most influential men stood aloof," wrote one Allianceman, "they are now the most enthusiastic members." The Long Branch Alliance in Paw Creek was made up of individuals who were "not only good citizens who mean to do well, they are well-to-do."

These new members—large landholders and local politicians—were immediate candidates for leadership positions. They were accustomed to prominence; many were expert public speakers; they had access to the press; they had the time and money to devote to organizational work. Polk became the new state Alliance secretary. S. B. Alexander, the new state president, was a college graduate, a high military officer in the Confederacy, a three-time state senator, and a candidate for governor, as well as "one of the leading farmers" in Mecklenburg County. . . .

This marriage of planter groups with yeoman and tenant groups produced latent or overt conflicts and contradictions. These conflicts had many facets, including a racial ambivalence which was introduced by the uncomfortable coalition of planters and yeomen inside the Farmers' Alliance. Consider, for example, the fact that the inclusion of landlords made it difficult for the organization to appeal to the tenants who rented from the planters. Since many of these tenants were Black, the Alliance was tempted to organize only white yeomen and . . . landlords, and to develop a program that advanced the interest of these two groups. Unfortunately, this was extremely difficult for three reasons, none of which involved race. First, all successful landlords were also merchants; therefore, any antimerchant programs the group approved would at least in principle attack the landlords. Second, there were many white *tenants* inside and outside the Alliance; this meant that the exclusion of Blacks could not prevent tenant-landlord tensions from splitting Alliance membership. Third, the yeoman-tenant distinction was by no means clear. . . .

At first, the problem was minor. The Alliance began in "yeoman" areas, and it recruited planters from the Black Belt. The yeoman membership mounted struggles against local merchant-landlords in one part of the state, while the planter leadership in another part of the state excluded its black (and white) tenants from membership and focused energy on railroads and other purely mercantile interests. Racial exclusion was not obtrusive, and at the local level, Black yeomen might easily join in Alliance actions with or without being members. Thus, in North Carolina, L. L. Polk could call for the exclusion of Blacks from Southern agriculture yet not arouse visible opposition from the yeoman base of the Alliance.

However, as soon as Alliance programs required support above the local level, real problems arose. In 1888, when North Carolina was still attending to local action and L. L. Polk was denouncing Blacks, the older state groups in Texas, Arkansas, and Louisiana had already begun organizing Black farmers to support various statewide projects. The Texas Alliance supported the establishment of the Colored Alliance and gave resources and public endorsement to its efforts to establish a national organization parallel to the white Alliance. When organizers for this group appeared in North Carolina, they caused grave problems for the planter leadership, who not only feared that the group would select them as a target, but that the association of the two groups would antagonize their planter constituency. Thus, when North Carolina Alliance President Alexander was asked about the Black Alliance's relationship to the white Alliance, he replied with a genuine lack of candor, "It is a separate and distinct group with which we have nothing to do."

But this distance was hard to maintain, especially when the Alliance's national convention, held 2 weeks after President Alexander's statement, began to work toward the merger of the two groups. Moreover, so powerful were the antiracist forces that the convention passed what may have been the most encompassing and economically radical resolution ever promulgated by a Southern white organization:

> Resolved, that it is detrimental to both white and colored to allow conditions to exist that force our colored farmers to sell their products for less, and pay more for supplies than the markets justify.

Since it was these very conditions which allowed planters to grow cotton at a profit, action around the resolution would have seriously threatened the newly installed planter leadership of the North Carolina Alliance. However, the entire matter was delivered to the states for their action, and this guaranteed that the racial stance of the North Carolina Alliance would remain ambivalent.

Even the removal of the ban on Black membership the following year did little to alter the North Carolina situation. In some areas, the Colored Alliance made good progress, participated in parallel and joint protests with the white Alliance, and even coalesced with it. However, this unity was balanced by the activities in the eastern half of the state, where the Alliance became an instrument of planter attacks upon Black tenants, a lobby for labor control legislation, and an object of Black tenant protest.

In some states, there was little planter presence inside the Alliance: The interests of the large landlords found adequate expression through less problematical channels. South Carolina planters, for example, rallied behind the banner of Pitchfork Ben Tillman:

> Captain Tillman married young and settled on a plantation of four hundred acres. He was successful until 1881, then enlarged his operation, and went into debt. He ran thirty plows—which means that he had thirty one-horse farms in his plantation and with all conditions favorable might have made two hundred and fifty to three hundred bales of cotton. Then set in a decline of prices and a succession of poor crops—in other words, after the manner of planters (and other people) he had speculated and suffered losses. He looked about for explanations and a remedy and saw, or thought he saw, them in state government and agricultural education.

Tillman formed a farmers' club and soon after, at the invitation of the state agricultural society, delivered a widely publicized and very abusive attack against the state government. This led to a column in the Charleston *News and Courier*, one of the principal daily newspapers in the state, through which he organized a statewide Farmers' Association. The founding convention in 1886 was attended by 12 state legislators, 2 lawyers, 12 doctors, 3 or 4 editors, and a good many merchants; the rest were prominent planters.

The program called for an agricultural college and other reforms similar to those demanded in North Carolina. But unlike the North Carolina group, the South Carolina Farmers' Association met with tremendous success. Tillman was publicized extensively by many newspapers, and he soon became a force in the South Carolina Democratic party. In less than a year, he was a leading candidate for governor. Lavishly financed in his campaign by many prominent farmers, and extensively supported by planter-oriented newspapers, he had a growing base among the less prosperous farmers. Tillman's ability to mount a serious challenge for state office in a short period of time gave credibility to his argument that meaningful reforms could be obtained through elections.

During this period, the Alliance arrived in South Carolina and began to eat away at the poor farmer support of Tillman. Tillman, unlike Polk and despite his early friendship with the group, was unwilling to adopt a more directly yeoman and tenant oriented program, and this earned him the opposition of the Alliance. As the Alliance began to take root, Tillman turned against it, and when he became governor, he did all he could to destroy this source of opposition to his rule. This attack in part explains the limited—50,000 members—size that the Alliance attained in the state.

Here we see the strength of the planter class in South Carolina. Because an exclusively planter-oriented group could gain great strength and mobilize those segments of the press which allied with planters, and because planters had much greater strength in South Carolina than in less cottonized states like North Carolina, a planters' movement could sustain itself without significant accommodation to the less prosperous agricultural groups. Then, when the conflict among these groups arose, it did not arise as a battle *within* the Alliance, but rather as an *external* battle of two markedly opposite movements. In this situation, the tendencies within the movements were less ambiguous than in a combined group like the North Carolina Alliance. Thus, Tillman led South Carolina to disfranchisement of Blacks and Jim Crow legislation in 1896, many years before other, less planter dominated, states. The only state that enacted these laws earlier was Mississippi in 1890, another state where the conflict between the Alliance and the planter class was open and bitter, and the only state in which agriculture was as cottonized as in South Carolina.

The middle 1880s saw the absorption—or nonabsorption—of elite Farmers' Associations into the growing Alliance. Thereafter the activities and program reflected this tension, and the history of the Alliance reflects the organizational ambivalence such tension created.

*

By 1888, the Agricultural Wheel, centered in Arkansas, had expanded into several neighboring states. Its membership of more than 100,000 made it the second largest agricultural organization in the South after the Alliance. Merger seemed inevitable, especially in light of the almost identical programs and structures of the two groups, but there was little impetus for such a unity. As late as October 1887, a leadership conference in Shreveport produced no conflict and no progress.

Along with the influx of elite leadership into both organizations came forces that sought to utilize the national strength of a united group to develop an articulated farmers' voice. Moreover, leaders with political ambitions realized that a single large group would better be able to publicize and promote them, bringing them to the broader public's notice.

While the merger was therefore highly likely, the developing class antagonisms created an uneasiness not present in previous amalgamations. As the December 1888 conventions drew near, the differences crystallized around the racial issue. The Wheel, even more so than the Alliance, had resisted the forces of racial exclusion. Whereas the Alliance had excluded Blacks while maintaining fraternal relations with the all-Black Colored Alliance, the Wheel accepted Black members—though in many areas, it maintained segregated locals clubs. Correctly anticipating the merger proposal, the Mississippi Wheel attempted to prevent exclusionary policies from prevailing by passing an antimerger resolution at the state convention in fall 1888. . . . However, this opposition was in vain. The two organizations met simultaneously in Meridian, Mississippi, in December and, despite considerable opposition, succumbed to the exclusionists. The newly merged organization was designated for whites only, with the understanding that close fraternal ties would be built with the Colored Alliance. After ratification by the states, the merger was completed the following October.

Much is made of the racism of Southern white farmers and of the Farmers' Alliance, but even the policy of fraternal relations with a separate Colored Alliance stands in stark contrast to the policies of the Democratic party, the richer farmers' organizations, and the federal government, all of which advocated explicitly discriminatory policies. The Alliance and the Wheel undertook to create unity between Black and white farmers and to build a mutually beneficial relationship.

✳

The 1888 merger created a new organization, formally entitled the National Farmers' Alliance and Laborers' Union, of about 300,000 members. By early 1890, membership was nearly 1 million. The organization, together with the Colored Alliance, could validly claim to speak for the mass of Southern farmers. The leadership's vision of a national farmers' voice was within reach, and this led to simultaneous national conventions of the four major farmers' groups in Ocala, Florida, in December 1890. In addition to the Southern Alliance and the Colored Alliance, the National Alliance, centered in the Great Plains, and the Farmers' Mutual Benefit Association, centered in the Midwest, gathered to join forces. A merger was not consummated, but a set of joint demands was passed. These demands lent credence to the claims of the leadership that they represented the united voice of American farmers.

From this pinnacle, the organization disintegrated with startling rapidity. The 1891 national convention was canceled, and subsequent conventions were not even scheduled. By late 1891, the Alliance's enemies were writing obituaries, and by 1892, its leadership began to desert it.

This puzzling collapse is partly understood in the history of the Populist party. Alliance leaders and members created the Populist party in 1892 and built it with such energy and enthusiasm that it immediately became the largest and most threatening third party movement in the post–Civil War period. However, this is only part of the answer. People do not abandon large and vibrant organizations without cause. There was a push as well as a pull to this exodus, a push that was the culmination of Alliance activities in the 1880s. The discussion of this collapse is therefore properly placed with the discussion of these activities.

✳

The organizational history just reviewed can be threaded together into a causal pattern that reveals close connections among seemingly independent events. . . . [The] early period culminated in the crisis at Clebourne, brought on by the failure of local activities. This crisis was marked by an ideological debate, one side of which was defeated by the structural blocks inside the organization. The victory of the Macune plan committed the organization's resources to rapid expansion at the same time that it erected state bureaucracy. And from this flowed two important structural consequences. First, the Alliance entered a period of very rapid growth as it quickly reached an extremely receptive population. Second, the state organizations became important, visible centers of power and prominence, and this made them potentially independent of membership control.

These two outcomes were the enabling legislation for the influx of elite elements into Alliance leadership. In highly cottonized states like South Carolina and Mississippi, most large farmers and the politicians associated with them had little incentive to seek yeoman and tenant support. But in states like North Carolina, Texas, and Arkansas, where large farmers were not strong enough to enforce their own political programs, the large and enthusiastic Alliance membership was a powerful incentive for elite participation.

Landlords and other elite individuals sought Alliance office, and the tenant and yeoman membership, recognizing the superior resources and skills which qualified the elites for leadership, endorsed this process, even if some policy disagreements had already begun to appear. Much of the later story remains to be told, but we can briefly sketch it here. The ultimate outcome of the failure of local actions was a sizable state apparatus controlled largely by elite elements whose class interests were different from those of the rank and file. As this division crystallized, the leadership pressed for independence from the membership, an independence which would free it to pursue policies that advanced its own distinct needs.

The collapse of the Alliance makes sense when viewed through the lens provided by this structural analysis. In the first instance, it was difficult for it to settle upon economic programs that could help the small farmer rank and file which did not attack the increasingly powerful planter-oriented leadership. For this reason, membership enthusiasm diminished even before large members began to leave. This created the "push" away from the Alliance. In the second instance, the elite leadership sought to affect state and national politics for precisely the same reasons that the Farmers' Associations had done so. They energetically built the new Populist party and successfully rallied the Alliance rank and file to its banner. This plausible electoral strategy was the "pull" that reduced the Alliance structure to an empty shell by 1892.

It was the history and development of the Alliance which made it possible for the Populist party to become the largest third party movement in the history of the United States. And it was the creation of the Populist party which ensured a rapid and unambivalent death for the moribund Alliance.

Peter H. Argersinger

POPULISM AND POLITICS

Just as Michael Schwartz (see the previous selection) found that the Southern Farmers' Alliance failed to maintain unity among its members, so too have students who addressed the difficulty that Populists confronted in trying to establish a new political party in a traditional two-party system. Peter H. Argersinger discovered that the Kansas Populists, who won a majority in the state legislature in 1890, represented an uneasy coalition of people united by common problems and the resolve to exercise political power. As the forces within the new party calling for free silver and fusion with the Democratic party became strong, the coalition unraveled, and the Populists lost control of state government. Like many other third parties in American history, the Kansas Populists had failed to maintain their separate identity as a party. Many of

Reprinted from Peter H. Argersinger, *Populism and Politics: William Alfred Peffer and the People's Party*, pp. 302–310, copyright © 1974 by the University Press of Kentucky. Reproduced by permission of the publishers.

Argersinger's important articles on Gilded Age politics and populism are available in *Structure, Process, and Party: Essays in American Political History* (1992).

Whatever their views on the merits of Populism, scholars have frequently agreed that it was ultimately successful if originally rejected. To list the Populist demands, declared one historian, "is to cite the chief political innovations made in the United States during recent times." Many Populists in the first decade of the new century leaped eagerly and hopefully to the same conclusion. William Peffer expressed great pleasure that the principles which he had championed as a Populist and which were, he said, "laughed to death at the time are now considered respectable," and that in 1907 "the country now hotly demands legislation it abused me for advocating." He maintained that "today I do religiously believe in all the fundamental principles of the People's Party and have at no time cast them from me," and he continued to advocate reform in the social, political, and economic structure of the nation. But he accepted the hegemony of the GOP and eventually became an admitted Republican ("I'm an insurgent, though," he insisted). He had great praise for Theodore Roosevelt, believing that the president was "applying the principles of Populism."

But Peffer must have known that this was a fiction. Roosevelt had regarded Peffer as an "anarchistic crank" in the 1890s and at one time urged that the Kansan be summarily executed. As president, Roosevelt's words remained more radical than his actions, and the transformation of American society promised in original Populism never occurred, despite the minor, palliative reforms of the twentieth century. The vaporings of Roosevelt became the triumph of Populist principles only through the cataracts of an old man's eyes and the mists of history.

*

Death of Populism

Populism died because it failed to transcend the American political system. It was killed by those very factors of politics that its founders had intended to kill: prejudice, elite manipulation, corruption. Populists decried the divisive sectionalism still rampant in the 1890s and attempted to overcome it by promoting a union of sections based on generally shared interests; Populists arraigned partisan prejudices as destructive of the general good and urged the formation of a new grand union to surmount the obstacles provided by traditional and emotional party loyalties. Instead, the South rejected the Western yearnings in 1892 for the intertwined sectional and partisan appeals and stood as the Solid South for the Democratic party. Faced with this sectional and partisan rebuff of their good intentions, aggravated by the consequent election of a conservative Democratic administration, many Western Populists surrendered again to the intolerance and prejudices that had previously guided their political lives, reacting bitterly to the South and to Democrats. Thus, early, Populism underwent a significant change, with many former Republicans returning to the GOP, never to leave again, even in 1896. The People's party itself, too, became a sectional party, perhaps more so than either of its opponents, and yet it was unable to use effectively the possible advantages of sectionalism, which continued to be directed against it. In the West and in the South, the dominant party induced great instability in the Populist coalition by appealing to traditional loyalties and threatening the pending triumph of the despised minority party through the People's party. Ignatius Donnelly argued that popular prejudice against Democrats disrupted the People's party and destroyed the possibility of its success. "The Republican speakers claim[ed] that the People's Party men have all turned Democrats," he wrote, "and then they raked over the Democracy during the War, and drove our Republican friends back to their 'first love.'" In the South, Republicans, especially black Republicans, served as the bête noire to keep party lines firm against Populism. Racial bigotry joined sectional provincialism and partisan prejudice in the triumphant assault on a Populism which, despite its rhetorical hyperbole, preached a realistic politics.

The struggle between partisans of different political traditions continued within the People's party. A Minnesota lawyer warned William Jennings Bryan against "the tyranny of political partisanship," which "is fundamental, all pervasive and permissive of all other political evils. As long as men regard the political instrumentality through which a principle is to be obtained as of more moment than the principle itself, just so long will we have corrupt politics." That statement cogently explained the predicament of the third party, but Bryan already understood the problem and he knew that too often Populists themselves, despite their intentions, remained slaves to the same tyranny. In his own 1894 attempt to elect a fusionist legislature to send him to the Senate, he learned that "the Republican members of the Populist party voted almost to a man for the Republican candidate for their legislature." And, the Nebraska Democratic state chairman told him, "so it would be on every occasion when the issue is between a Democrat and a Republican." Indeed, at least part of the fight over fusion involved simple distrust of Democrats, and Peffer's course during the 1890s typified that of the Populist who tried valiantly to overcome the partisan prejudice of his personal heritage and ultimately failed. The *Topeka Capital* had commented shortly after his senatorial election in 1891 that it was a "moral and physical impossibility for a man of Senator Peffer's antecedents and acquaintance with the differences between the Republican and Democratic parties to turn himself politically inside out at this late day." The issue was unsettled for nearly a decade, but perhaps never in doubt. Peffer was not the only major Populist who campaigned for McKinley in 1900; Mary Lease supported the GOP because "as I take it the issue has resolved itself into the old issue of copperheadism versus Republicanism, and as the daughter of an old Union soldier I feel that my place is with the Republican party." Thomas F. Byron, the anti-fusion editor whom Weaver forced from the *Des Moines Farmers' Tribune*, did not even wait till 1900. In 1896 he organized McKinley clubs in Iowa and supported the GOP rather than accept a national fusion with the Democrats. The Populists had hoped to transform politics but had fallen under its dead weight; as the products of years of elite manipulation of passions and prejudices, they ultimately failed to escape from their past. But they had tried, something most Americans never considered doing.

Not just the trappings of the American political system, but the very nature of American politics also destroyed Populism. There were formal aspects to this: the biopolarizing effects of single-member legislative districts and other statutory features of the structure of American politics militated against third-party action. But the informal, though no less certain and decisive, features of politics proved eventually more destructive. The impulse of American politics was not toward a realistic appraisal of societal needs and a sincere attempt to solve the nation's basic problems. Rather, political parties were concerned with winning elections and more interested in votes than principles. Thus, the tariff, the bloody shirt, the Lost Cause, and white supremacy dominated political discussion before Populism: issues essentially irrelevant to the massive problems the nation confronted in industrialization, urbanization, expansion, and immigration; but issues which would, because of their emotional content, mobilize electorates in state, section, and nation to maintain the dominance of self-seeking groups and parties. More than that, such sham issues often intensified national problems which continued to fester, unsolved, and diverted attention from real problems. Dependent upon traditional loyalties or ethnic-cultural cleavages for electoral support, old parties could not or would not formulate relevant policies for pressing economic, social, racial, and political difficulties. The two-party system did not meet the need to articulate constituent demands directly into the political framework.

What was significant about original Populism, after all, was that it developed outside the political system—and precisely because the system had proved incapable of responding to real needs. Yet in the transformation of Populism from a mass movement into the People's party, much of its democratic and directly responsive nature was lost. Populism became incorporated within the same system and the People's party became subject to the same influences that guided the other parties. The history of the People's party became one of a continuing struggle against the subversive tendencies of politics, undermining the original goals of Populism and substituting those of the old parties. The People's party, if originally for different reasons, became concerned with winning office and gradually accepted institutional objectives. Under the direction of professional politicians such as Taubeneck, Breidenthal, and Butler, Populist politics too became more of a struggle for office and power than for reform. The party became increasingly oligarchic and more easily dominated by its officials, and it became more and more difficult for the rank and file to influence policy. In Kansas, for example, as early as 1892 the party leadership rigged conventions, lied to its rank-and-file members, and overturned duly nominated candidates in the search for office.

In 1897 Davis Waite looked back at the Populist failure already evident and blamed the party organization. There had been no means to hold the party to principle, he lamented. It had adopted the same caucus system and the same party committees, used the "rotten delegates" and the "bossism" of the old parties. An "inside ring" had usurped the rights and circumvented the action of the rank and file, Waite asserted. "A few leading officials of the People's Party by as bald trickery in the way of bossism, bogus proxies, and paper delegates as ever distinguished 'Tammany Hall,' assumed supreme control of the party and exercised that control without consulting the popular will and without appeal." Henry Lloyd also complained about the increasing oligarchic control of his party. "When I see the selfishness, and stupidity, (synonymous terms) which appear in organizations, seeking to usurp the common sacrifice for personal advantage," he confessed to a friend, "I find it hard to keep my footing as a believer." Peffer similarly declared that local, independent action by autonomous popular groups would never interfere with the goals of Populism but that "the danger to Populism lies in the tendency of the party to go backward instead of forward."

Annie Diggs recalled in 1901 that the true strength of Populism "never did lie in its party organization" and that in fact one of the roots of the movement was "a protest against the dangers and tyranny of permanent party organization." More important as a cause of Populism than economic distress, she argued, "was the discovery that the national machinery of both the Republican and the Democratic parties was set to the service of privileged classes and of commercial combinations." The people became furious when they understood "the humbuggery of the protective tariff. . . . the hypocrisy of the national party policies, the sham battle between Democracy and Republicanism over free-trade and protection." That vast mass movement of "the memorable revolt of 1890," she declared, was above narrowly "partisan politics." But "later, when success and official reward entered the minds of the people who came as recruits, the dominant spirit of the People's Party became less fraternal and unselfish."

Percy Daniels saw the tragedy of the People's party. "It came. It saw," he wrote. "It has been conquered." Populism had repudiated "the methods of the old party machines" and denied "the celebrated theory of Mr. Ingalls that intrigue and corruption are essential to political success." But the party leaders set aside the original purpose of the movement, disobeyed the wishes of the rank and file, and adopted as legitimate tactics and appropriate goals what had been condemned. By 1898, Daniels denied that any party was controlled or directed in the interest of justice and declared that henceforth he would work outside the party system. "Parties as they exist today are bellowing imposters and organized frauds," he wrote, "sowing little but deception and garnering little but spoils and corruption. . . . They are either reliable machines of plutocracy and the corporations," he concluded, "or they are the handy tools of hypocrites and harlequins, and are as much responsible, through the deceptions they have practiced and the corruption they have defended, for the servitude of the masses to plutocratic usurpers, as are the lawless exactions of organized capital for their plundering."

Those in control of the party machinery justified their manipulations in the name of "practical politics." Such machinations, however antithetical to the original professions of the movement, were necessary, argued Taubeneck, Weaver, Breidenthal, Butler, and Latimer, if the party were to secure election. Those who disagreed with such a policy were "impractical visionaries" and hopelessly utopian. It was not practical politics that the country needed, however; it had that in the Democratic and Republican parties. America needed realistic politics, a policy of ignoring facile prejudices, investigating the realities of problems, and formulating relevant programs without resorting to traditional and outmoded dogma. There were those who demanded just such a necessary radical reappraisal of American society, but they were precisely those damned as impractical visionaries. Gradually the Populist politicians succumbed to the same temptations affecting the old party leaders; too often converts to an elitist ideology, they proved as cynical as any of their opponents and certainly no more open and honest. But ultimately with less experience in dissembling, they lost to past masters. As much as the irrelevant tariff had served the old parties, the practical Populists used the issue of free silver as a political panacea. Essentially a minor reform, clearly of limited effectiveness, free silver nevertheless promised an electorate to the People's party because as a panacea it was attractive to those who shrank from the requirements of realistic politics. Populist party leaders seized upon the issue to the exclusion of a consideration of vital problems and realistic reform proposals that the People's party had been created to advance. Silver and fusion, the tangible death instruments of Populism, did not domi-

Death of the party

nate the People's party until its leaders subordinated the early demands of the movement in a practical grasp for power. Henry Lloyd wrote bitingly in 1896 of this Populist abdication of responsibility:

> The men in the management of the P.P. who are specially and bitterly traitorously opposed to the real issues now before the public are the ones who have fanned this free silver back fire. All the rail-road, telegraph, telephone, trust, bank, and other monopolists could ask nothing better than that the dangerous—to them—sentiment among the people be beguiled into believing that *the* principal cause of their woes was that the privilege of the silver owners to compel the people to accept their product as legal tender had been taken away. . . . [Demonetization, however, occurred long after the basis for the nation's social and industrial problems had been laid. But now] the poor people are throwing up their hats in the air for those who promise "to lead them out of the wilderness" by the currency route. It is awful. The people are to be kept wandering forty years in the currency labyrinth as they have for the last forty years . . . over the tariff bill.

But the practical Populists suppressed the realistic Populists, and with the use of a prime old party technique. They condemned as "socialism" every suggestion that free silver coinage was not the primary and essential reform. Thus discredited in the eyes of those voters educated to the acceptance of panaceas, superficial solutions to nonexistent problems, and the avoidance of questioning the accepted myths which formed the bulwark of those in power, the radical Populists were pushed aside. Those such as John Willits who refused to acquiesce in the slightest to the demands of the party leadership were pursued with ever greater villification. A pariah in 1897, Willits explained his treatment as a mid-roader in 1896: "Because I refused to bolt our national convention, abandon the only Populist on the national ticket, and yell for the Democratic nominee and the Plutocratic Sewall, I was denounced as a 'Hannacrat' by the whole gang of Democratic hirelings and cowardly, truckling, would-be Populists. You know too well the results," he continued. "Kansas went Democratic, the People's Party lost its identity, and the hands of time are turned back."

Just as important as silver to the practical Populists was fusion, the policy of making concessions to other groups in hopes of finding a shortcut to political power. Fusion was a practical political maneuver in a political system that rewarded only one winner, but too often it required the betrayal of the promises of Populism (Peffer marveled at "how filthy the corruption of 'practical politics' among Reformers" became), and it gradually changed the composition, ideals, and objectives of the People's party. Too, fusion was addictive and once taken it made the new party dependent and circumscribed its options.

Fusion and its requisite attendants of compromise, coercion, and constraint became the touchstone of Populism. Those who opposed fusion were interested in thorough, racial changes, focused on political reform which would provide a method to right any future abuses through establishing a responsive, realistic, and genuinely democratic political system. Fusionists were never as interested in political, or general, reform as in limited measures of economic reform. Lacking the great overall reformatory zeal, they were willing to refuse implementation of Populism where it was immediately possible—within the People's party—in futile hopes of achieving their own perverted program of personal power and a truncated economic Populism. . . .

Mari Jo Buhle

WOMEN IN AGRARIAN REFORM

The role of women in agrarian reform movements of the late nineteenth century has received relatively little attention. In the following selection, Mari Jo Buhle addresses this subject by briefly discussing how gender manifested itself in the Grange, Alliance, and Populist movements. Perhaps the least-studied aspect of Populism, gender warrants far more attention than it has received to date. A faculty member in history and American civilization at Brown University, Professor Buhle has edited *Women and the American Left: A Guide to Sources* (1983) and *Encyclopedia of the American Left* (1990).

From *Women and American Socialism, 1879–1920*, by Mari Jo Buhle, pp. 82–90. Footnotes omitted. Copyright 1983, reprinted by permission of The University of Illinois Press.

Women's position in Populism had been prepared by decades of participation in agrarian movements, particularly the Patrons of Husbandry. Organized in the late 1860s as a secret society devoted to cooperation, the Grange invested womanhood with a mystical significance rooted in ancient lore. The founders described the Eleusinian mysteries wherein male and female cult members worshipped the goddess of agriculture, Ceres. Modern-day Grangers continued to revere women. "Like a bright star in the dark pathway of life," as a Minnesota Worthy Master said to a Grange convention in 1879, women guided human existence, her "purity, tenderness and delicacy" an inspiration for the Patrons of Husbandry. Support for her cause "more than all else," he added, was destined to "make our Order live forever."

On a more mundane level, Grangers considered women a necessary element in rural association. Because the Grange emphasized the unity of the family, women served jointly with their husbands. A local assembly, for example, could acquire a charter only by demonstrating that at least four women as well as nine men were ready to enroll. Women possessed full voting rights, had access to any office, and enjoyed special posts created for women's affairs. In a majority of assemblies the lecturer who directed its programs was female, as were the leading officials of several state organizations. At picnics, processions, banquets, concerts, and other social events, women took the more familiar role of preparing refreshments and caring for children. Often relegated to positions of nominal equality, especially in southern assemblies, women gained at the minimum a sense of participation comparable to that of German-American women in the Socialist fraternal network. But in many midwestern Grange chapters women shaped the social character of local institutions along more egalitarian lines and won support for both temperance and women suffrage campaigns.

In its first years the Grange served to strengthen the western woman's movement. By the mid-1870s, when the organization had grown to nearly 25,000 chapters and three-quarters of a million members, its geographical center was the Ohio River Valley and adjoining states where the WCTU [Women's Christian Temperance Union] gained its first ground. The temperance crusade profited directly as the Patrons of Husbandry placed itself squarely on the side of the WCTU. The Grange required a vow of abstinence for admission and included temperance instruction in its ritual. In Ohio, home of the women's crusade, the first links between the Grange and the WCTU were established. While the state Grange met in Xenia, women's crusaders struck at a local tavern and forced the owner of the "Shades of Death" to empty his kegs. The Grange voted unanimously to join the ceremony, the State Master delivering a temperance speech atop the empty whiskey barrel. The sentiment spread rapidly among Grangers, pushed to such an extreme that the Illinois order officially condemned the use of tobacco as well as spirits. WCTU activists could find among their Grange friends across the Midwest and Plains states ready listeners and collaborators in their sacred vigil.

The Grange also became a force for woman suffrage. As early as 1876 one Granger predicted that their assemblies would "prove a more powerful organization for the inauguration of Woman Suffrage than even the Woman Suffrage organizations themselves." In western Kansas some of the ablest lecturers routinely presented woman suffrage arguments; one claimed that the "nation's safety lies in the political advancement of Woman." The southern sector obstructed any uniform position until 1885, when at a national convention the Patrons of Husbandry finally passed a resolution recognizing the equality of the sexes as one of the order's cardinal principles. Grangers avowed they were "therefore prepared to hail with delight, any advancement of the legal status of woman, which may give to her the full rights of the ballot box, and an equal condition of citizenship." Grangers subsequently reaffirmed this policy, blessed the WCTU for its salvational roles, and established a special committee to accelerate programs on women's behalf. Admittedly the southern delegates continued to harbor more conservative opinions, and committee work often relegated women to traditional pastimes, such as kitchen duty. Despite these limitations, many women used their Grange experiences to prepare for wider political roles. Some rank-and-file women actually became locally notorious in the 1880s when they initiated the first discussions of the forbidden political issues. During the severe rural recession of 1887–88, when the political taboo became impossible to enforce, women in states ranging from Texas to Michigan, Minnesota, and Nebraska to Colorado and California rallied to the banner of Populism.

Although the most militant sector of the Populist movement at large originated among farmers in the South and Southwest, it was not surprising that women organized as a distinct force where they had struck the deepest roots. True to its woman's rights heritage stretching back to the bloody strife of the 1850s, the historic woman suffrage campaign of 1867, and the early temperance victories, Kansas became the organizational epicenter for Populist women. Residents of the state's growing commercial centers, urban women likewise found an opportunity to participate in a far-flung movement not merely agrarian—contrary to belief common at the time and since—but profoundly radical.

The most prominent Populist women—Fanny Randolph Vickery, Marion Todd, Sarah Emery, Mary E. Lease, and Annie Diggs—had gained their spurs in a variety of antimonopolist movements foreshadowing Populism. Significantly, none had been a lifelong resident of a farm. Mary E. Lease, for example, before calling upon farmers to raise less corn and more hell, lived as a housewife in Wichita, where she cared for her family, handled the usual household chores, and took in laundry to supplement the family budget; her first political act upon moving to Wichita had been the organization of a women's discussion club. Women like Lease displayed an acute awareness of the plight of the urban working class, particularly its female component. They typically had helped organize institutions for workingwomen and often joined the Knights of Labor in recognition of its pledge to equal wages for equal work. Observing the intensification of urban woes most especially among women fresh off the farm, these experienced activists felt a strong kinship with their rural sisters and served as their voice within the movement's leadership.

Populist women in cities or on farms shared a common aspiration. Transcending all differences was foremost a universal commitment to women's enfranchisement that found its ideological and organizational base for women of varying backgrounds within the WCTU. Annie Diggs, for example, had begun her career in Lawrence, Kansas, as a pollwatcher in a prohibitionist campaign, later to become vice-president of the state suffrage organization. Sarah Emery, known as the "Elizabeth Cady Stanton of the Michigan Home Crusade," served as national superintendent of the

WCTU's department on temperance and labor. Mary E. Lease claimed a half-million "white-ribboners" in the Populist ranks, and WCTU officials reciprocated, blessing the Farmers' Alliance as a major temperance ally in the struggle to abolish the liquor traffic and unearned wealth. This sense of shared perceptions created an

Mary Elizabeth Lease. Born in Pennsylvania in 1853, she moved to Kansas in 1873. There she married, bore four children, practiced law, and became one of Populism's most famous orators. *(Kansas State Historical Society)*

ideological continuity, from the WCTU to Populism, almost precisely parallel to that between the urban-based woman's movement and Nationalism. Women had moved in their own ways from self-interested causes to broader radical concerns.

Populist ideology reflected vividly the sentiments put forth by the WCTU, especially as thousands of alliance women helped revive the struggle for temperance and woman suffrage in the late 1880s. But even more as symbols, temperance and woman suffrage conveyed the special significance the WCTU had invested in the concept of womanhood. The rhetoric of Populism alone was testimony to this fact. Womanhood embodied, as Grangers had likewise insisted, the moral imperative against evil.

If Nationalist women found their desires expressed in *Looking Backward*, Populist women located their own literary idol in master politician Ignatius Donnelly, whose sequel to the famous *Caesar's Column* (1890) tells the story of the reconstruction of a new order along feminine lines. *The Golden Bottle* (1892) incorporated the popular faith in the power of womanhood to purify the civilization and to guide the entire process of reconstruction. The great struggle is led in unison by two characters, Ephraim Benezet and his wife, Sophie. Ephraim, a Plains state lad who discovers a liquid that turns base metals into gold, uses his rapidly accumulating fortune to secure a place for himself as reform demagogue, finally to become president of the Untied States. From his position Ephraim directs a worldwide revolution. In weaving this tale, Donnelly suggests only a faint blueprint of the future political order but provides massive details on how the revolutionary struggle is to be waged. He exalts the concept of womanhood as symbol of morality and political wisdom.

In many respects it is not Ephraim but Sophie who emerges as the major protagonist. After a close call with the ultimate degradation brought about by a forced move to the city, Sophie is awakened at a tender age to the reality of women's powerlessness and sagely turns to political action. She first organizes the women of Omaha into a grand sisterhood. She speaks to the middle-class women and explains the horrible plight of farm families, the desperation which allowed farm parents to send their daughters off to the cities in search of work. The family, Sophie explains, was being destroyed, "crushed under the rolling rock, the Sisyphine weight of interests, of taxes, of monopolized markets, of cruel trusts, of every form of human selfishness and cunning." The poor country girl is thus driven into the "great wicked city" to find work or to perish. But even if she does find work, it is usually of some unhealthy type paying only starvation wages. This girl, Sophie explains further, "becomes a merciless hunter of men, armed with the poison darts of disease and death" as she turns to the only good-paying occupation available. Having moved her audience to tears, Sophie pleads with these women to recognize their duty to their sisters and to aid them in some substantial way.

The women of Omaha form the Woman's Cooperative Association, a self-help society gathering both middle- and working-class women and spreading to every ward of the city. The association erects a splendid building to house workingwomen, to provide fine reading and music rooms as well as large halls for dancing and lectures. These establishments were, Sophie remarks, "little paradises on earth." The project succeeds so well that the workingwomen are uplifted from their abject misery and the entire city is transformed into a pure and moral place.

Sophie then builds upon her initial success and forms a national society, the Woman's League of America, which pledges to buy no goods made by women except from women themselves. Then the "race rose with the elevation of the *matrix* of the race; for the river of humanity cannot ascend above the level of its fountain—woman. . . . The earth became beautiful, peaceful, happy, hopeful; full of all kindness and goodness." Rich women were released from enforced idleness and dissipation and walked hand in hand with their "sisters of one blood." The solution was "Not charity, but justice. Not stealing from the poor and giving them back part of it, with many airs and flourishes and ostentation; but stopping the stealing, and *permitting industry to keep the fruits of its own toil.*"

As the quintessential Populist novel of social reconstruction, *The Golden Bottle* focuses clearly on woman's role in transforming the industrial order into the Cooperative Commonwealth. There is, notably, no nostalgia for the preindustrial past, no backward glance at domesticity. Rather, the inequities and degradation of modern life are met head on, their eradication premised upon a collective solution to economic problems with women taking a major part in the effort. At the conclusion of the novel, a grand finale indeed, the readers follow Sophie's triumph as, mounted on a white horse, she gallops across the Russian steppes leading the masses out from under czarist oppression and darkness, completing the last chapter in the revolutionary purification of the world.

Behind the gripping action of Donnelly's tale, his depiction of womanhood has a ring of familiarity. Like Bellamy, he drew on the sentiments of his milieu and rendered them a literary device of far-reaching significance. As in the case of *Looking Backward, The Golden Bottle* owed much of its popularity to the seedwork of the woman's movement in creating a female audience eager to accept its political message. At rank-and-file levels the positive images of womanhood which women leaders put forward and Donnelly converted into a literary metaphor became Populist icons.

This praise of women's role could prove deceptive in certain respects, for women did not share leadership or gain a consistent leverage region by region. The Farmers' Alliance and its electoral arm, the People's party, did not provide women with as much organizational space as did the Grange. Whereas the Grange viewed itself as a cooperative and fraternal order, Populism spread like wildfire as a protest movement. Cooperative marketing, widespread agitation, and electoral activity directed against the railroads and other monopolies launched the agrarian movement almost overnight as a major regional political force. By 1890 the alliance appeared to many observers to lack only urban allies in its campaign to take control of American society. But a price had been paid, better understood by women than by their brother comrades. The family-based and socially oriented activities familiar to the Grange had given way to an apparatus more like that of a traditional political movement. Populists abandoned the dual representation of men and women in its internal offices, jettisoned much of the elaborate ceremony that ensured women's centrality, and relegated voteless women to an ancillary role.

Yet women re-emerged near the movement's center by virtue of their energy and self-organization, the authority they wielded as wives and mothers, and the ideological position they gained in the Populist articles of faith. At the local level especially, individual women participated as chapter secretaries, stump speakers, newspaper writers, and editors. As groups they inevitably took in hand the social services that kept the movement alive and thriving. Like the German-American Socialists' summer outings but larger and more dramatic, massive tent meetings reached across the southern and western states in the late 1880s, adapted both from the educational Chautauqua meetings and from the revivalist gatherings common to the region. Through their own initiatives in the national organization and with the hope of forging a far-reaching political alliance, Populist women pushed the movement to its limits.

Especially in states where women were well organized, Populist agitators could turn their demands for the ballot and equal wages into a wider program. Writers in the local and regional press thus hammered away at the fact that woman's sphere was not, properly speaking, the home. The movement's female base was, of course, the "farmer's wife," and the primary description of the home still reigned as the "sacred refuge of our life." But essayists frequently addressed the largest fact of rural domestic existence: drudgery. They commonly implored women to resist the temptation of excessive cleanliness and order, to let their household chores slip by the wayside if necessary, and to make more time for themselves and their loved ones. Ordinary Populist women developed their own strategy along lines paralleling the cooperative politics of the Grange and the Farmers' Alliance: the cooperative household. With home care shared systematically by all family members, they argued, women would be freed from their bonds and capable of doing anything they chose. As one woman wrote, "Some people think it is acutely funny if a woman anywhere is not devotedly attached to making biscuits and darning socks. And yet men have been known who preferred other occupations to plowing and cleaning sewers, and no one seemed to think they were monstrosities."

Years of devotion in the WCTU had, necessarily, instilled in Populist women a great respect for women's traditional roles, but they affirmed the goodness of woman innate to herself rather than to her current drudgery. The fate of civilization rested in the hands of those who had gained moral sensibility as guardians of the family, they believed. But to exercise that power, women had to be more than dutiful housewives. Thus Bettie Gay gave a Populist gloss to the sentiment the WCTU had done so much to make popular:

> What we need, above all things else, is a better womanhood, a womanhood with the courage of conviction, armed with intelligence

and the greatest virtues of her sex, acknowledging no master and accepting no compromise. When her enemies shall have laid down their arms, and her proper position in society is recognized, she will be prepared to take upon herself the responsibilities of life, and civilization will be advanced to that point where intellect instead of brute force will rule the world. When this work is accomplished, avarice, greed, and passion will cease to control the minds of the people, and we can proclaim, "Peace on earth, good will toward men."

Much like their sisters in other sectors of the woman's movement, Populist women named men's political hegemony as a major cause of civilization's decline. Only as women assumed their rights would the republic return to its proper course.

So well entrenched in the philosophy of the woman's movement and committed to women's prerogatives, Populist women sought alliances with other women reformers. They dispatched delegates to suffrage conventions, to WCTU meetings, and to the National and International Councils of Women. In 1890 a group of Topeka, Kansas, women took a portentous step further. They established a newspaper with the expressed purpose of fostering a new, national women's reform coalition. The monthly *Farmer's Wife*, emblazoned with the time-tested motto "Equal Rights to All, Special Privileges to None," urged women to communicate with one another and to promote the "natural unity" of temperance, suffrage, labor, and agrarian radicalism.

In September, 1891, Populist women founded the National Woman's Alliance with presiding officers Fannie McCormick, a Kansas "foreman" in the Knights of Labor, and Emma D. Pack, *Farmer's Wife* editor and honored women's club leader in Topeka. Women in twenty-six states served as vice-presidents, and the adopted charter carried the signatures of Annie Diggs, Mary E. Lease, Sarah Emery, Marion Todd, and other leading Populist women. The "Declaration of Purposes," a representative document of Gilded Age woman's reform, read:

In view of the great social, industrial, and financial revolution now dawning upon the civilized world, and the universal demand of all classes of our American citizens for equal rights and privileges in every vocation of human life, we, the industrial women of America, declare our purposes in the formation of this organization as follows, viz.:

1st. To study all questions relating to the structure of human society, in the full light of modern invention, discovery and thought.

2d. To carry out into practical life the precepts of the golden rule.

3d. To recognize the full political equality of the sexes.

4th. To aid in carrying out the principle of co-operation in every department of human life to its fullest extent.

5th. To secure the utmost harmony and unity of action among the Sisterhood, in all sections of our country.

6th. To teach the principles of international arbitration, and if possible, to prevent war.

7th. To discourage in every way possible the use of all alcoholic liquors as a beverage, or the habitual use of tobacco or other narcotics injurious to the human system.

The thirst for enlightenment, the demand for equal political rights, and the faith in women's regenerative power rendered the Woman's Alliance the logical successor to the WCTU and women's clubs. Far from the rural paranoia often attributed to Populists, the *Farmer's Wife*, as official organ of the National Woman's Alliance, carried column upon column of news and encouragement from countryside and urban areas alike. The federated plan of organization accommodated various possible models, from the Illinois Woman's Alliance that the paper publicized, to the Woman's Christian Alliance of Lufkin, Texas, which was launched after an alliance organizer toured the area.

The success of the National Woman's Alliance would depend upon a favorable response from allies in the urban woman's movement and from the Populist leadership itself. Organizers therefore asked Populist politicians to lend their official endorsement to woman suffrage and to women's rights as laborers. They asked, too, for statements of encouragement. Pungent epigrams in the *Farmer's Wife* expressed better than any theoretical treatise the weight Populist women placed upon a positive response:

Give our women encouragement and victory is yours.
Be as true to the women as they are to you.
Don't give us taffy; we are too old for that.
Give the women a suffrage plank: you may have the rest.
Rule the women out and the reform movement is a dead letter.
Put 1000 women lecturers in the field and revolution is here.

This buoyant sentiment fed expectations of cataclysmic change, no less for women than for men. The Populist political momentum, gaining steadily since the late 1880s, seemed to need only an urban counterpart to become the major force in the nation. That necessity required in turn the kind of alliance women prided themselves in having pioneered and which could evidently become whole only through their participation.

∗

The women who rose to prominence in the major radical movements of the late 1880s and early 1890s—in the "Americanized" sections of the Socialist Labor party, Bellamy Nationalism, and the Farmers' Alliance—carried with them certain articles of faith from earlier involvements. They clung to a romantic notion of womanhood expansive enough to encompass a vision of women organized as the ultimate force against corruption. As principal organizers, renowned orators, or activists of regional standing, women began to seek alliances with various elements of the nascent protest movement, and they endowed this new endeavor with distinctive qualities transferred from their own organizations. Decades of preparation in the independent woman's movement had firmed their faith. As Mary E. Lease announced at the peak of the People's party campaign in 1892: "Thank God we women are blameless for this political muddle you men have dragged us into. . . . Ours is a grand and holy mission, a mission as high and holy as ever inspired the heart, fired the brain, or nerved the sinew . . . ours the mission to drive from our land and forever abolish the triune monopoly of land, monopoly, and transportation. Ours is the mission to place the mothers of this nation on an equality with the fathers. . . ." Women's accession to political and economic power was, in this perspective, not merely a desirable goal but the prerequisite for the establishment of the Cooperative Commonwealth. . . .

Robert W. Larson

POPULISM IN THE MOUNTAIN WEST: A MAINSTREAM MOVEMENT

For a long time, students have attributed the success of Populism in the Rocky Mountains solely to that section's support for free silver. Robert W. Larson takes issue with that view. Silver was important, he says, but mountain Populism embraced other issues, one of the most important being antimonopoly. In addition, mountain Populism won more support from industrial laborers than did Populism in the South and West. A professor of history at the University of Northern Colorado, Larson is the author of *New Mexico Populism: A Study of Radical Protest in a Western Territory* (1974) and *Populism in the Mountain West* (1986).

Twenty-seven years after Appomattox the American electorate was presented with a presidential ticket designed to please both North and South. A new political organization, the People's party, was offering voters during the 1892 election an ex-Union general for president and an ex-Confederate general for his running mate. The former was James B. Weaver of Iowa and the latter James G. Field of Virginia. But the primary objective of the new party was not to reconcile the Union, although the bitterness caused by the Civil War still lingered. Rather its major purpose was to begin the long-delayed process of solving the myriad of ignored social and economic problems that had accumulated during the nation's unprecedented industrial growth following the Civil War. Moreover, the political movement that had launched the new party had started in Kansas, Nebraska, and the Dakotas, which were located along the fringe of the wilderness when Union and Confederate armies first clashed at Bull Run. In these Middle Border states dissident and independent third parties first made their challenge in the 1890 elections; their successes in these midterm contests gave impetus to Populism as a national movement and led to the nomination of the Weaver and Field ticket in July of 1892.

In the autumn campaign that followed, zealous Populists, or Pops as their detractors liked to call them, took their crusade for reform to as many citizens as possible. Even such remote areas of the far-flung republic as Montana were visited. Indeed, Weaver was the first presidential candidate to campaign there. But the results on election day were to bring them profound disappointment. The new party's standard-bearers won less than 9 percent of the national popular vote. Although Weaver and Field were able to poll more than 15 percent of the votes in six cotton-producing states of the South, they could not count one electoral vote from that region. In the wheat-raising Midwest the results were more encouraging: the Weaver-Field ticket polled almost half the votes cast in Kansas and North Dakota, making a clean sweep of all state offices in the Jayhawker State and capturing five of that state's eight seats in Congress.

The mineral-rich Mountain West was another area of success. Half of the electoral votes won by Weaver and Field were from this region and their percentage of the popular vote was as high as 54.66 percent in Idaho, thanks largely to Democratic support, and 66.76 percent in Nevada. In Colorado, where their popular vote was 57.07 percent, the local ticket captured the governor's office, won the state's two seats in the House of Representatives, and almost gained control of the state senate—success made possible in this state and elsewhere in the West and Midwest by fusion with the Democrats.

Because Populism has been regarded by many historians as the beginning of major reform in the United States, the professional time and talent devoted to its study is impressive. Most attention has been concentrated on those areas where the movement had its widest appeal—the West and the South. But, curiously, the focus on the West has not included until recently the Mountain West. Rather, the scholarly emphasis on western Populism has been directed almost exclusively toward the wheat-raising Great Plains. The reasons for this striking imbalance have been baffling to some. There are, however, possible explanations; the remoteness of the Mountain West, for instance, may be a factor. How could a sparsely populated area just emerging from the rawest of frontier conditions have any real impact on national politics? But a more likely cause for neglect is the belief held by a number of Populist scholars that the movement's success in the mountain country was due almost exclusively to that section's strong support for free coinage.

John Hicks is perhaps most responsible for the Mountain West's one-dimensional silver image. In his comprehensive *The Populist Revolt: A History of the Farmers' Alliance and the People's Party*, published in 1931, Hicks, while admitting that the Weaver-Field ticket gathered half of its electoral votes in the silver states of the West, concluded that there was a "fly in the ointment." Support for the third party among westerners was not due to an interest in Populism, but rather to a preoccupation with silver. "They were interested in *silver*, and they supported the Populist ticket solely because of this one item in the Populist creed. Had the Populist program not included free coinage it could hardly have appealed seriously to any of the mountain states."

Hicks's view of the Mountain West was endorsed a quarter of a century later by Richard Hofstadter in his Pulitzer Prize-winning book, *The Age of Reform: From Bryan to F.D.R.* Although Hofstadter's essentially revisionist view of Populism clearly put him at odds with Hicks in his interpretation of the movement, he could agree with the dean of Populist historians on one point: the Mountain West was a one-issue region. "The free-silver Populism of the mountain-states variety was not agrarian Populism at all, but simply silverism." Thus two giants of the profession had effectively written mountain Populism out of the mainstream of the movement.

Nevertheless, a number of monographs, articles, and theses written since the publication of Hofstadter's book in 1955 have challenged the one-issue thesis. In 1968, David B. Griffiths published an article in the *Annals of Wyoming* on the Populist movement in the cattlemen's commonwealth. Basing a part of his findings on two carefully researched master's theses that reached the same conclusion, he determined that a celebrated cattle war, the Johnson County War, had more to do with the growth of Populism than the silver issue. In 1970 Thomas E. Clinch published his monograph, *Urban Populism and Free Silver in Montana*, in which he concluded that Populism in the Treasure State was much more complex than a case of "simply silverism." In 1974 James Edward Wright published a study, much of it based on quantitative evidence, entitled *The Politics of Populism: Dissent in Colorado*. Wright also perceived the complexities of Populism in the mountain state he chose as his case study, an especially significant subject for this kind of project because Colorado produced three-fifths of the national silver product in 1890. During the same year this writer published his *New Mexico Populism: A Study of Radical Protest in a Western Territory*. Again the one-issue concept simply did not stand up to the facts.

Despite the patterns suggested by these individual state studies, Lawrence Goodwyn in his *Democratic Promise: The Populist Movement in America* chose not to treat mountain Populism as part of the movement's mainstream. Published in 1976, Goodwyn's study was to be the first general history of the movement since Hicks's monumental work. It was the hope of western historians interested in Populism that Goodwyn would make a more serious effort than Hicks did to integrate mountain Populism into the national movement. Unfortunately, although Goodwyn acknowledged many of the individual state studies already alluded to, the patterns they suggested did not impress him enough to give them more than scant attention. Thus, while he recognized that the Johnson County War in Wyoming had great relevance to Populism and that the movement in Montana had an intriguing urban quality about it, he too dismissed the Rocky Mountains as a one-issue region: . . .

. . . [U]ntil someone pulls together [the] individual studies of western Populism, . . . Populism in the Mountain West will continue to be ignored or misconstrued. The purpose of this study, then, is to integrate the more recent and updated histories of Populism in this region into one suggestive article that will provide a start for a much-needed reinterpretation of Populism as a national movement.

As such an effort could involve eight states or territories . . . four have been selected for purposes of manageability: Montana, Wyoming, Colorado, and New Mexico. These are called the Front Range states today by people who live in the area. . . .

Colorado is the logical state to start with in this synthesis of Populism along the Front Range. If Hicks and Goodwyn are right that the movement in the Mountain West was a single-issue one, then Colorado, as the leading silver-producing state in the nation, should be their prime example. It should certainly be easier to prove [the] case in this state than elsewhere. But any systematic analysis of Populism in Colorado must begin with one very striking fact. It was the discovery of gold, not silver, that led to the settlement of the Centennial State. The rush of the fifty-niners to the Rockies of Colorado was in search of the yellow metal, not the white one. And the result was almost overnight growth. Population for the New California soared to 34,277 in 1860, while gold production amounted to an impressive $3,400,000 per year in 1862 and 1863. It was not until 1874 that the output of silver surpassed that of gold.

Regardless of which precious mineral was mined, however, it soon became evident that overcoming the obstacles of mining required more capital than the ordinary prospector could provide. The terrain of the central Rockies was rugged, and there were also rather distinct metallurgical combinations found locked beneath Colorado's steep mountainsides. Eastern and European capital was by necessity courted, and soon an influx of outside money flooded the young territory.

This development turned out to be a mixed blessing, though, as much of Colorado's economy fell under the control of absentee bankers and entrepreneurs. And if laws in harmony with laissez-faire economics are any indication, these absentee investors had an immense influence on the legislators of the mining commonwealth. For example, when Colorado achieved statehood in 1876, it had the dubious distinction of being one of the twelve states in the Union without legal restrictions on usury. Although a one-man railroad commission was established, the state legislature rather characteristically appropriated no money for it. Moreover, railroad interests, also largely controlled by outside capital, minimized what little authority that commission had.

By the 1880s, certainly, Colorado had become what modern historians and social scientists call a colonial economy. Leon W. Fuller, a historian writing during the Great Depression, came up with an even harsher characterization, regarding the state as "little more than a pocket borough of the corporate oligarchy."

But most citizens of the new state seemed willing to tolerate this outside control until the late eighties, when the glowing promise of much of Colorado's booming economy began to fade. Fuller insists that a downward trend in the business cycle was

Baring
crisis
1890

perceptible as early as 1889. It was undoubtedly aggravated by the Baring crisis of the following year, when Baring Brothers and Company, the leading financial firm of England, was imperiled by an Argentine revolution. This development, which threatened the supply of foreign capital, caused panic among many eastern creditors, who began to liquidate their capital holdings in the West. Thus, the Baring crisis acted as a catalyst for the accelerated economic deterioration that occurred in Colorado during the nineties.

The disillusionment that accompanied this slowdown, however, is more germane to this study than its causes. One result that considerably lessened the exuberance of the Colorado miner was the transfer of mine ownership from the hands of the individual prospector to the corporate entrepreneur. By 1900, for instance, although there were 822 mines in Colorado, 64 of them controlled 80 percent of the state's mining production. Indeed, countless miners were becoming wage earners instead of mine owners, and their awareness of this new and diminished status is evident from the fact that the state in 1892 had a greater percentage of its citizens unionized than any other.

One labor organization that played such a crucial part in this unionization was the group so prominent in the formation of Populism nationally, the Knights of Labor. First organized in the coal fields north of Denver, this union became prominent in 1884 when it won a major regional rail strike against the Union Pacific. The leader most responsible for that success was a radical Denver editor, Joseph R. Buchanan, who became known as the "Rip-roarer of the Rockies" and was later appointed to the prestigious three-man executive board of the national organization.

Perhaps even more disillusioned with their future in the new state than the miners and the workingmen were the farmers. They originally came to Colorado to feed the miners; their small irrigated plots around Denver were feeding hopeful fifty-niners in practically no time at all. And these Coloradans would soon develop an irrigation system along the rivers of the east slope that would eventually become the model for much of the semiarid West. But disenchantment also developed among them, particularly among those farmers who were irrigating the South Platte and Arkansas river valleys. Their distress was largely the result of the practices of privately owned water companies, enterprises which often promised more water than they could deliver and charged royalties above the standard water rates. One water company that was particularly resented was the "English Company," which had built immense reservoirs and canals adjacent to the Front Range. It bore a double stigma: it was allegedly guilty of the abuses commonly attributed to the water companies and it was alien owned.

But nonirrigation farmers had their grievances, too, compounded by the severe droughts of 1888 and 1889 in Colorado. Their faith in the future of the so-called "rain belt" in Colorado was so diminished that the population of Baca County in the southeastern corner of the state dropped from three thousand in 1888 to one thousand in 1890. Like other farmers of the Great Plains, though, they were not inclined to blame all their woes on the weather. The railroads became for them what the water companies were for the irrigation farmers. The rate structure of the railroads servicing eastern Colorado was regarded as inequitable, placing Colorado farmers at a disadvantage in competing with wheat farmers and cattlemen outside the state.

Farm organizations like the Grange and Northern Alliance tried to represent the interests of these disenchanted Colorado farmers, the Grange for the irrigation farmers and the Northern Alliance for the nonirrigation farmers. But it was the Southern Alliance that would become the dominant organization, because it seemed more willing to take a tougher stand on the issues confronting both groups. As a matter of fact, Southern Alliancemen took the lead in organizing the Independent party, which would launch the Populist movement in Colorado.

With delegates representing the Knights of Labor and even Edward Bellamy's Nationalists, this new Independent or Alliance party gathered in Denver during the summer of 1890 to nominate candidates for state and national office. Much of the new party's platform predated the Omaha platform of the national Populists by two years. It called for national ownership of railroads to satisfy the "rain-belt" farmers and state ownership and management of the ditches and reservoirs of Colorado to appease the irrigation farmers. Also, in a plank aimed at the English Company, there was a call to prohibit alien landownership. Keeping in mind, no doubt, the importance of support from miners and urban workingmen, there were also calls for an eight-hour day and an employer's liability act. As for the free coinage of silver, it was only of secondary importance at this time.

Although the Independent party garnered only 6.23 percent of the total vote, its existence helped to promote a reform coalition known as the Citizens' ticket. This alliance was organized by reform-minded men of both major parties in response to a notoriously corrupt Republican-dominated legislature known as the "Robber Seventh," also one of the targets of the new third party. Undoubtedly this Citizens' alliance blunted the thrust of the reformist Independent movement; Wright, as a matter of fact, believes that the Citizens' coalition may have neutralized the strength of the Independents among the irrigation farmers, who seemed genuinely ready to sever old political ties.

The new third party, however, finally found a man who could win in 1892. He was Davis H. Waite, an editor from the silver-mining camp of Aspen. But to call this controversial editor from the silver-producing Western Slope a silverite is to misgauge the man badly. He was a multi-issue-oriented reformer who, if he had one passion, it would be his unequivocal opposition to monopoly. Waite once characterized monopoly as a Frankenstein monster, who was "sucking the lifeblood of the prosperity and liberty of the nation." As a matter of fact, silverites at the Populist nominating convention of 1892 would have preferred as their gubernatorial candidate an ex-Republican and silver mine owner from Dolores County by the name of Julius Thompson. Thompson had the support of the powerful state Silver League organized that year, which had sent observers three weeks earlier to the Populist national convention in Omaha. Waite's selection over Thompson, then, represented a triumph for those agrarian leaders of 1890 who were most responsible for Populism. In truth, the candidates chosen along with Waite were identified with a number of agrarian doctrines of which silver was only one. Nevertheless, the Silver League endorsed the Waite ticket, which, with substantial Democratic support, won a surprisingly decisive victory for a new third party.

It is undeniable that from 1892 on silver would dominate Colorado politics; the fact that the new Populist party did not have a record to defend on such controversial pieces of silver legislation as the Bland-Allison, Sherman, and other disappointing half measures undoubtedly helped Waite in his victory. Colorado would now move into what Goodwyn calls Populism's *shadow movement*. But so would much of the third-party movement in the South and

True reason - not only
silver - monopolies
Populism in the Mountain West: A Mainstream Movement **109**

the Midwest. O. Gene Clanton noted in his study on Kansas Populism that it was "the issue of free silver that relegated other Populist reforms in Kansas to a secondary position." Hicks, himself, admitted that the free coinage issue invariably received a more enthusiastic response among the farmers who voted Populist in 1892 than any of the other issues.

The important thing to remember is that protest and Populism in Colorado grew out of a variety of issues of which antimonopolism was the prime one. Helplessness among little people to cope with the monopolistic power of the railroads, water companies, and absentee investors and owners during a time of economic downturn gave Populism its birth. Silverism came later, just as it did in other parts of the country where Populism enjoyed its greatest success.

The free coinage issue did not dominate Populism in the state north of Colorado either. Indeed, as mentioned before, it was the Johnson County War of 1892 that gave Wyoming Populists what power and influence they enjoyed during the troubled nineties. But even before the famous range war, Wyoming Populism was a multi-issue movement, supported by both rural and urban workingmen.

In 1890 a rural group, the first local Farmers' Alliance, was organized in Crook County in the northeastern corner of Wyoming. By January of 1891 there were other Alliance locals operating in the newly admitted state. But agriculture was a relatively small industry in Wyoming at this time. There were only 4,584 acres of wheat raised in 1890 and 14,607 of oats. Hay was the most important crop, with nine times more acreage devoted to it than wheat and oats combined. Such acreage figures are unimportant, however, when compared to the millions of acres devoted to the grazing of cattle. Stock raising was Wyoming's future in the view of most of the state's early settlers. And yet that future was imperiled by the Wyoming Stock Growers' Association, which enjoyed a virtual monopoly of the state's grazing land. Many recruits to Populism would come from small stock grazers challenging this local monopoly, some of whom joined the Northern Wyoming Farmers and Stock Growers' Association, which precipitated the Johnson County War.

There was one urban group responsible for the birth of Wyoming Populism too, the familiar Knights of Labor. The two leading Knights were Henry Breitenstein and Shakespeare E. Sealy, both of whom worked for the Union Pacific Railroad and became Populist organizers. Breitenstein, the ideological leader of Wyoming Populism, was as suspicious of capital and wealth as Waite, believing that bankers and bondholders "were ticks that fattened on the body of the laboring honey bee." He was one of those responsible for the state's first Populist platform framed in Laramie, the planks of which were largely drawn from the statements of principle enunciated in St. Louis in 1889 by a resolute gathering of Alliancemen and Knights of labor.

But this platform, oriented as it was toward national issues, attracted little support for the new party. It was not until some of the members of the Wyoming Stock Grower's Association hired twenty-five Texas gunmen and fifteen cattlemen in 1892 to eliminate alleged rustlers in Johnson County that the Populists found their opportunity. Believing that the true purpose of this effort was to oust small stock grazers, the Populists, along with the Democrats, condemned the action. In their national Omaha platform Populists characterized it as an "invasion of the Territory of Wyoming by the hired assassins of plutocracy, assisted by federal officials." The reference to federal officials was a politically strategic one: there is strong circumstantial evidence that both Republican United States senators were involved and that the Republican governor did not intervene until the association's hired mercenaries were trapped by an enraged posse organized by the sheriff of Johnson County.

About three months after the Johnson County War local Populists gathered for their first state convention on June 29. Their platform, unlike the earlier one formulated in Laramie, focused on local issues, many of its planks being critical of Republican involvement in the Johnson County War. Interestingly enough, the issue of free silver was ignored. At their nominating convention in September, the Populists agreed to fuse with the Democrats: Democrats would support the Weaver-Field ticket and Populists would vote for the Democratic gubernatorial candidate. Other candidates were agreed upon for mutual support too. The main issue for these Populist and Democratic fusionists was the Johnson County War. But during the campaign they would also attack United States Republican Senator Frances E. Warren's Arid Land Bill to give the states control over irrigation and land development.

This measure, it was argued, would allow big corporations to steal the land; no doubt the fusionists feared a monopoly of land grabbers to match the one enjoyed by Wyoming's cattle barons.

In the Wyoming election of 1892 the Weaver electors lost to the electors pledged to Republican Benjamin Harrison. The Democratic gubernatorial candidate John Osborne, however, won the fusionist support. But the disappointed Populists received no more than 13 percent of the total vote, electing only five of their candidates to the lower house of the state legislature compared to the sixteen Democrats and twelve Republicans who were elected. The even balance between Republicans and Democrats did make Populist support crucial in organizing the House. Consequently, to get the necessary Populist votes, Democrats agreed to the election of Sheridan Populist Lewis Cass Tidball as speaker. With the Republicans in control of the Senate, however, there was little the fusionists could do. Tidball introduced a bill to create a board of railroad commissioners that could fix freight and passenger rates, a measure that could not help but antagonize the powerful Union Pacific, the great rail monopoly in Wyoming. He also offered an amendment to the state constitution to legalize the initiative and referendum. But neither effort succeeded. Another Populist in the House introduced a bill to protect the small settler from absentee corporations, but his measure failed also.

As it turned out, the year 1892 was the peak one for Populists in Wyoming. In 1894 they refused to fuse with the Democrats and elected only one member to the state legislature. Although the party fielded candidates as late as 1908, after 1896 the party hardly made a ripple in the state's political waters. Silver did become an obsessive issue in 1896, as it did in Colorado, but Breitenstein, who believed in fiat money, thought that free coinage was just one way of inflating money. Strongly antimonopoly and expedient, Wyoming Populism provides an even poorer example of "simply silverism." . . .

. . . [T]he evidence gathered for . . . states in this region is most suggestive. Antimonopolism was evident almost everywhere. Railroads were at issue in a particularly conspicuous way in . . . Colorado. . . . Irrigation monopolies [also] gained notoriety [there] . . . . Big cattlemen triggered agrarian radicalism in Wyoming . . . , which ultimately benefited Populism. . . . Workingmen's issues

were important to the growth of Populism in those states where mining and railroad laborers were numerous. . . . Such classical Populist
positions as the prohibition of alien landownership were also found
in the Mountain West, with . . . Colorado being most important in
this regard. Certainly there is sufficient diversity here to question seriously the one-issue interpretation of Mountain Populism. Indeed, it
seems a most arguable proposition that Populism in the Mountain
West was so varied in its concerns that it belongs in a very real sense
to the mainstream of the national movement.

Gene Clanton

CONGRESSIONAL POPULISM

**Gene Clanton supports his contention that Populism represented a
genuine democratic reform movement, distinct from twentieth-century
liberalism, by examining the handful of Populist congressmen who
served between 1891 and 1895. After demonstrating that the Populists
supported a wide range of fundamental reforms, he concludes that
perhaps "Populism was . . . America's aborted attempt at the creation of
a truly radical and democratic working class movement. The party was
certainly mass-based, redistributionist in tone, and outspoken in
suggesting major economic adjustments that assumed the value and
necessity of helping small-scale operatives survive in a modern-industrial
world." A long-time student of Populism, Professor Clanton's publications include *Kansas Populism: Ideas and Men* (1969) and *Populism: The
Humane Preference in America, 1890–1900* (1991).**

Eleven Populists were elected to the Fifty-second Congress. Six of
the eleven were Kansans—William Baker, Benjamin Hutchinson
Clover, John Davis, John Grant Otis, and Jerry Simpson to the
House; William Alfred Peffer began his term in the Senate. Peffer

was joined there by James Henderson Kyle from South Dakota. The Populist contingent in the House also included Omer Madison Kem and William Arthur McKeighan from Nebraska, Kittel Halvorson from Minnesota and Thomas Edward Watson from Georgia. Watson was the choice of his colleagues for speaker. Seven of the eleven were farmers.

Thirteen Populists participated in the Fifty-third Congress. Nebraska elected William Vincent Allen to the Senate; the House delegation again included Baker, Davis, and Simpson, while Thomas Jefferson Hudson and William Alexander Harris replaced Otis and Clover from Kansas. Kem and McKeighan returned to represent Nebraska; Haldor Erickson Boen replaced Halvorson from Minnesota; and John Bell and Lafayette Pence from Colorado and Marion Cannon from California completed the delegation. Simpson replaced Watson as caucus leader in the Fifty-third Congress.

Pure agriculturalists were slightly less prominent among the Populists of the Fifty-third Congress than the Fifty-second, since the replacements and new members were all lawyers, except for Boen and Cannon. The change in composition was beneficial, however, because Halvorson and Clover were inactive, and Otis, while active, was quite ineffectual. Their replacements were all more active and effective spokesmen. Watson's failure to return to the Fifty-third Congress was a significant loss, but overall the Populist delegation to the Fifty-third Congress was stronger, obviously more experienced, and more capable than that of the Fifty-second.

Little space needs to be consumed in exploding the 1890s Neanderthal, "Uncle Hayseed" stereotype of the Populists. . . . Suffice it to say, the stereotype is no more valid, probably less so, than most stereotypes. Historically, it is important, however, as a barometer of how serious a threat these leaders of radical agrarianism posed to the powerful, procorporation spokesmen of the urban-industrial complex, whether those spokesmen resided in the manufacturing East or elsewhere in the nation. . . .

The strength of the stereotype, especially its longevity, owes much to a powerful assumption, well established by 1890 and growing thereafter, that nothing "progressive" could possibly emanate from the ranks of the working classes—particularly those who populated the rural hinterlands. "Everything" was truly "up to date in Kansas City," or should one say New York City. Conversely, backwardness must reign elsewhere. The fact was, of course, that no village, farm, city, or region had a monopoly on greed or altruism, but the rural-urban dichotomy that had been exacerbated by post–Civil War economic development certainly encouraged contemporaries to believe that they or their opponents had cornered the market on one or the other. Images were grossly distorted. Populist congressmen, on the average, were every bit as capable and qualified as were their old-party opponents—if one injects the "soul supremacy" ingredient, as one Populist suggested, even better qualified. They hailed from *undercapitalized, underindustrialized, underurbanized, underprivileged*, and therefore *undercoopted* areas of the nation (not necessarily *undercivilized* areas, as some of their congressional opponents were fond of suggesting); nonetheless, or perhaps because of it, they were, if anything, less inclined to seek scapegoats and more inclined to engage in fundamental analysis than were most of their congressional opponents. . . .

. . . They were "nineteenth century men in their values and assumptions, not precursors of the fiscal liberalism, the welfare philosophy and the statist orientation of twentieth-century liberal reformers. . . . They believed in an older order, a world of self-regulating, not selfishly manipulated, mechanisms and processes." Obviously, they were men of the nineteenth century, but were their values, assumptions, and policies consistent with what one ordinarily thinks of as reactionary or conservative? . . .

. . . [P]opulism represented a missed opportunity of significant magnitude and . . . Populists called for fundamental changes that have not yet been achieved. To back up that judgment, while at the same time responding to the issue of reactionary conservatism, what follows is a partial list of the changes that would have taken place had the Populists been able to work their will on the national government. At the top of the list, because it was basic in congressional Populist thought and all other reforms were clearly secondary, would be a system of public banking—one that completely divorced the banking and financial community from control over the nation's monetary system. Money would be no more than a medium of exchange, would be increased or decreased by the national government to adjust for deflation or inflation, and introduced directly into the stream of commerce, without the intervention of banks, at a minimal (cost of administration) rate of interest, to meet the changing needs of a growing industrial society. The subtreasury system of populism . . . was only one, albeit the first and most important, of several devices proposed by Populists to implement their idea of a truly just monetary system. Railroads, at least those engaged in interstate commerce, would be owned and operated by the public. All institutions involved in the transmission of intelligence—in their day the telephone and telegraph businesses—would likewise be owned and operated by the public, just as the postal service was then operated. In the Fifty-third Congress Senator Peffer even called for government ownership and operation of the coal industry in order to make that critical resource available at cost and also to improve the lot of mine workers. . . . All government revenue would be derived, without exemption, except for what was considered necessary for a bare standard of living, by means of a graduated income and/or land tax on the great wealth of the society. The president and vice-president would be elected by a direct vote of the people. Subsidies to corporations, but not necessarily to individuals, would be strictly prohibited. Bonded indebtedness as a way of supporting public functions, particularly on terms favorable to monied interests, would be out and congressmen would be required to divest themselves of corporate stock.

. . . When the worst depression the country had experienced hit the urban centers beginning in 1893 . . . and more than 4 million men and women were unemployed by early in 1894, in a still predominantly rural nation of about 63 million people, the Populists were the only ones to sponsor, advocate, and defend legislation to put the unemployed to work. In fact, throughout the Fifty-third Congress they introduced and pleaded for quite a variety of emergency measures for that purpose. . . . Perhaps of most interest would be John Davis's proposal for the creation of a 500,000-man industrial army of the unemployed "to be put to work on authorized public improvements." Davis defended his measure by arguing it was wiser "to furnish work for starving men in order to prevent the necessity of increasing 'the standing Army' to shoot them down."

Almost all the Populists, at one time or another, proposed action to assist starving and destitute people in the *urban* centers. Senator Peffer at one point endorsed a system of old-age assistance.

In the Senate on June 1, 1894, Peffer stated, "I would have every poor man have a home. And I would do more than that. Every old man and old woman who have passed through a lifetime of toil and have not saved anything for their old age I would pension the same as I would pension a soldier who had risked his life for the safety of the Republic. I would send the old people down to the grave in comfort instead of sending them to the almshouses and to the poorhouses." That certainly has a New Deal ring to it. Herbert Hoover, to say nothing of his "leave-it-alone liquidationist" advisors, might well turn over in the grave to hear such proposals described as conservatism! But let us not be misled. One is correct in divorcing Populists from "twentieth-century liberal reformers," but let us *not* do it for the wrong reasons. New Dealers were a bit too paradoxical in their goal of accommodating some of the security features of socialism while at the same time saving capitalism. Without populism's basic, structural national reforms, you have only the ghost, or pseudo-populism. To this list one could add a number of other measures, among them mortgage relief, woman suffrage, the advance payment of pensions due Civil War veterans in one lump sum, . . . direct election of senators, rural-free delivery, postal savings banks, and the Australian ballot. . . .

In view of the programs they supported, were the Populists proponents of socialism? . . . Their congressional opponents, on a number of occasions, accused them of being socialists; they denied that they were. And if they were, they were advocates of a peculiar brand of socialism—the socialism of agrarianism or . . . "grass-roots socialism." Public ownership, in their scheme, was to serve the interests of millions of small-scale, land-owning farmers, businessmen, and wage-earning laborers. Their basic, structural reforms in finance, land, and transportation, they sincerely, perhaps naively, believed would render unnecessary a wholesale change in the existing arrangements regarding private property and private production. . . .

The well-being and viability of small-scale agriculture was, not surprisingly, also an important aspect of their outlook on the world. No question about it, they could not conceive of a future America composed of tenant farmers and large corporate farms, with a population massed in urban centers and conspicuous for its great pockets of destitute and dependent workers, as compatible with democracy and human freedom. . . . They were indeed convinced that agriculture was one of the basic (if not the basic) industries, and much of their struggle was aimed at making changes that would enhance the viability of the family farm, reversing the trend toward tenancy. It was a goal that many, from their day until the present, have seen as unprogressive, inefficient, and not worth the price—easily dismissed as a product of rural "fundamentalism" or "provincialism." That may be, but who can say that the ultimate price of the massive exodus of rural blacks and whites to urban centers and the gigantic farm programs since the 1930s have not been even more costly? . . .

To return in this essay to the more specific question of congressional performance, two generalizations concerning Populist behavior must be confronted. It has been confidently asserted that "legislative activity with a humane or 'liberal' rationale—child labor reform, the eight-hour day, woman suffrage—was exceedingly uncommon in Populist congressional circles." . . . As regards Populists in the Fifty-second and Fifty-third Congresses, nonetheless, these undocumented generalizations are simply examples of "Alice in Wonderland" history. Child labor, to this researcher's knowledge, did not emerge as an issue. Populists supported the eight-hour day at every opportunity (Peffer would reduce it to six) and they were the only congressmen to speak in favor of woman suffrage and to introduce bills to accomplish that long-overdue reform. Their support of woman suffrage, as a matter of fact, was one of the reasons given by a Connecticut Democrat in the Fifty-third Congress for why the nation should ostracize Populists. . . .

Regarding the plight of black Americans, that disgraceful situation was not prominently at issue except during the debate over the repeal of the federal election laws in the Fifty-third Congress. No Populist employed racist language, as did a number of southern and border-state Democrats. . . . Watson, in the Fifty-second Congress, as part of his eulogy for a fellow southern congressman, courageously appealed for justice for the 8 million oppressed blacks. In the Senate during the Fifty-second Congress, Peffer also presented a petition on behalf of the "colored people of Riley County, Kansas," who were protesting "mob or lynch law" throughout the nation. Peffer called the petition "very timely." He stated, "It is time for the American Congress to take prompt action in such cases." . . .

For certain, Populist economic measures were designed to aid poor blacks and whites. From 1891 to 1895, moreover, racial and ethnic arguments simply were not involved in the Populist call for immigration restriction—and this was in a Congress that was not reluctant to make them openly. Populist reasons were wholly economic and the concern was directed at controlling the supply of "cheap labor" that was used all too frequently to keep down wages and to frustrate the organizational drive among laborers. Simpson, a Canadian immigrant himself, called the Chinese exclusion measure a "disgrace to any civilized nation," and when asked why he planned to vote for a measure he considered a "disgrace" he explained that he had no choice, until greater economic wrongs were righted, in order to protect the wages of labor. Populists were prominent in opposing an anarchist exclusion provision, on the other hand, favored by conservatives fearful of radicalism, because of the measure's vagueness and potential for political abuse. Even after they had been told that many dangerous anarchists were on the way and the bill had been rewritten to provide a definition of anarchism to include only those who advocated violent overthrow of the government, one of them invoked parliamentary procedure to scrap it. . . .

It has also been stated that "Populist congressmen had little time, and apparently little inclination, for promoting the specific causes of agrarian or labor interest groups" and that "almost without exception the Populist approach to public spending was that of the meat-axe." A more accurate generalization would be to say that they continually endeavored to cut appropriations in areas they regarded as wasteful or primarily beneficial to corporate interests. They were consistent foes of military spending, which they regarded as uncalled for in a time of "profound peace" with so many millions of unemployed and underemployed people in need of assistance. They were warm friends of appropriations for education and for the destitute. Although they often called for cuts in appropriations, they constantly attempted to increase them for particular measures they saw as beneficial to the disadvantaged— and not just rural Americans. In August 1894 one congressional opponent calculated, with much exaggeration made possible by double counting their programs, that if all their measures were enacted the cost would amount to over 35 billion dollars.

As regards labor, Populists were strong defenders of labor's right to organize. Among other things, they repeatedly insisted that labor be granted as much protection by the government as was management; they led a successful move to condemn the use of Pinkerton detectives in labor disputes, fought energetically to require automatic safety couplers on railroads, called for investigations into several labor-management disputes and industrial disasters, and, what was news to this historian, they initiated the successful effort that led to the establishment of a national holiday for labor. They also called for and obtained an investigation, at the behest of the Knights of Labor, into the "slums of cities of more than 200,000 population," which was viewed by them as a preliminary to doing something about improving the living conditions of all kinds of urban workers—unemployed, child, sweating, tenement house, etc. In fact, on more than one occasion, Senator Peffer earnestly tried to commit the Congress to a thorough investigation of the whole range of relationships between management and labor. They were lonely defenders of the right of Coxey's unemployed "armies" to petition Congress for relief and employment in person at the nation's capitol. . . .

. . . Congressional Populists were not, as has been said, "admitted and unabashed inflationists." Actually, they were staunch foes of deflation and determined to create a monetary system that was relatively stable and, above all, removed from private control. Because the dollar had been appreciating for a number of years, they advocated reflation to arrive at that point of stability. They frankly conceded the injustice of an inflationary or deflationary monetary system. . . .

. . . [T]hey were not oblivious to the harmful consequences of injecting an unlimited quantity of money into the economy. Apparently, it was because many of them came to view the subtreasury system as likely to create just that kind of money expansion, coupled with the fact that the land and commodity loan plan was so immediately and so one-sidedly an agrarian relief proposal, the congressional Populists gradually backed away from it. And of course they were never fooled by the silver issue. It was for them only one of the milder reforms conducive to money expansion to counter the contraction (deflation) and to frustrate the intense drive then under way to "irrevocably" commit the nation to the gold standard. They opposed the Cleveland administration's bond and debt policies for that reason also. In their eyes the use of bonds and the creation of a national debt thereby was merely a means of maintaining and extending a financial system that enriched the few, impoverished the masses, and needlessly burdened future generations of taxpayers with a huge unearned increment due bill.

In conclusion, without having demonstrated the point as completely as can be done, the writer will submit that the Populists require no apology. Congressional populism, the first phase at least, was indeed a democratic phenomenon. Obviously, congressional Populists won only a limited number of victories . . . but they tried, and the record of that effort turns out to be most revealing. What they had to say is, of course, somewhat circumscribed for Americans almost a century later. They represented a large underclass that was in certain ways historically unique and that is by now virtually extinct.

To paraphrase Shakespeare, in the course of democracy, as "in the affairs of men," there would appear to be a tide, "which, taken at the flood, leads on to fortune; omitted, all the voyage of their life is bound in shallows and in miseries." Perhaps populism was, in the final analysis, America's aborted attempt at the creation of a truly radical and democratic working-class movement. The party was certainly mass-based, redistributionist in tone, and outspoken in suggesting major economic adjustments that assumed the value and necessity of helping small-scale operatives survive in the modern urban-industrial world. . . . Anti-Populists and most academic interpreters since the 1890s did not share the assumption that democracy required the kind of survival program Populists advocated; in fact, the opposite more nearly represented their position.

According to a recent constitutional study, one of the "transcendent values" expressed in American culture has been the idea that "a primary purpose of the law should be the furtherance of *economic progress and social mobility*, and that the maintenance of such progress and mobility is the best means for implementing democratic theory." Another, more powerful, "transcendent" value of the late nineteenth century held "that the law ought to construct and maintain a large area for the functioning of *private enterprise* relatively immune from the incursions of public power." Populists

and anti-Populists could both draw inspiration from these proposi-
tions, but the Populists were more clearly champions of the first
and therefore prime targets of the proponents of the second. The
movement was, however, by no means a monolith, and the elements it sought to unite were even more disparate. The fact that it
was aborted certainly owed something to this diversity. It owed
much more to the kind of society the nation had become and was
becoming by the 1890s. . . .

III

Populism and Race

Carl N. Degler

BEYOND RHETORIC

In the 1950s, C. Vann Woodward argued that in place of the paternalism of white conservatives and the blatant racism of whites who espoused segregation and disfranchisement, the Populists urged blacks to join their party in an effort to solve common economic grievances. During the 1890s, Woodward concluded, those blacks and whites who became active in the Populist movement "achieved a greater comity of mind and harmony of political purpose than ever before or since in the South."* Two decades later, Carl Degler responded to criticisms that were elicited by Woodward's work. Although he did not present the Populists' attitude toward race as idealistically as had Woodward, Degler nevertheless believed they had offered an important alternative. Additionally, by challenging the dominant Democratic party, the Populists provided blacks with the hope for a better day. The Margaret Byrne Professor of American History at Stanford University, Carl N. Degler is a prolific author, whose works include *Neither Black Nor White: Slavery and Race Relations in Brazil and the United States* (1971), *At Odds: Women and the Family in America from the Revolution to the Present* (1980), and *In Search of Human Nature: The Decline and Revival of Darwinism in American Social Thought* (1991).

Behind the fear and hatred of the Republican party was the fact that the party depended upon and supported Negro suffrage and office-holding. Not only had the Republicans introduced the idea of political equality for blacks, they had become in the deep South a largely black party. And in South Carolina, Louisiana, and Mississippi, where blacks constituted a majority of the population, political equality meant a black electoral majority. It was largely because of this fear that there were virtually no Populists in South Carolina at all and that in Mississippi the Populists were always weak.

Text excerpted from *The Other South: Southern Dissenters in the Nineteenth Century* by Carl N. Degler, pp. 337–343, 345–347, 349–354, 357; copyright 1974, Harper & Row Harper Collins, Publishers, Inc. Reprinted by permission of the author.

*C. Vann Woodward, *The Strange Career of Jim Crow* (New York: Oxford University Press, 1957), 46.

White Populists were all too well aware of the damage association with blacks might do to their cause. Yet, as they surveyed a political scene in which the Democrats were unwilling to adopt a legislative program helpful to the farmer, they saw no alternative. A similar conclusion had been reached by the Readjusters a decade earlier in regard to another economic issue. The Populists, in short, were no more ideologically committed to equality for blacks—even political equality—than most other Southern white men. Moreover, unlike the Scalawags, the Populists had no political experience with, or commitment to, Negroes. The white Republicans of the South not only had a historical and ideological obligation to blacks, they also had a dependence upon black votes for election. Most Populists, on the other hand, were former Democrats. In time they might have reached the same conclusion that the Republicans and many Readjusters did after they had worked with blacks. They might have come to recognize that the South's best future lay in political cooperation between black and white rather than suppression of one by the other. But at the opening of the nineties, as Populists looked to Republicans and blacks for support and votes, they still had not reached that point. They simply were willing to ignore some old prejudices in exchange for a chance to defeat the Bourbons.

Once it is recognized that Populists began with little or no ideological commitment to black political equality, then the lengthy debate among historians as to the degree of sincerity of Populist appeals to blacks can be put into a realistic and historical context. The historians' debate has been able to last so long because the evidence has been so ambiguous and even contradictory. Populists supported and denied blacks at the same time. We shall look at some of the evidence. . . . But here it is simply worth noting that such conflicting statements and behavior are to be expected when a deeply accepted social ideology like white supremacy is being undermined, but not being confronted directly by a clearly articulated counter ideology. The Populists were not philosophical egalitarians; they were simply Southern farmers who wanted to defeat the Bourbons, and they needed black votes to do it. And as we shall see, too, when the Populists sought to develop an ideological conception of race relations by drawing a distinction between political and social equality, their practical approach to the question of the Negro resulted only in confusion and inadequacy.

Sharecroppers in Virginia. In the 1890s African Americans constituted a large portion of the South's population. White politicians—Populists and Democrats alike—tried to win the support of black voters. (*The Granger Collection, New York*)

The significance of the Populist movement in the South, however, lay not in the consistency of its behavior, the clarity of its ideology, or the purity of its motives, but in the fact of its challenge to the existing racial-political order from whatever motive. In the 1890's, for the third time since Appomattox, white Southerners out of the necessities of their history and society challenged the political rigidities of the one-party system, which white supremacy had demanded and constructed. The challenge was admittedly not intended to change race relations, but by its very nature it could not fail to do so. For if the new party was to succeed, blacks would have to be induced to vote Populist, and to do that they would have to be worked with, appealed to, and recognized. In the context of the late nineteenth-century South that fact alone was a threat to the racial status quo. And if that racial order were disrupted, even a little, who could say what more far-reaching changes might follow?

✳

The novelty of the Populist appeal for Negro votes is reflected in the fact that the farmer organizations from which the Populists derived had shown little or no interest in Negroes. There was a Colored Farmers' Union in the South, to be sure, but it had no formal organizational connection with the white farmers' groups. Furthermore, in Louisiana in 1890, most of the legislators who had been elected by the Farmers' Union voted without complaint for a bill making segregation compulsory on trains in the state. Similarly, the Alliancemen who sat in the Georgia legislature in 1891 voted for Jim Crow legislation and primary election restrictions against blacks. In both Louisiana and North Carolina, it is worth noting, too, the official newspapers of the farmers' organizations were entitled *The Caucasian!*

Once the farmers moved into politics, however, their interest in Negroes noticeably quickened. The most obvious form this new interest took was to assert the black man's right to vote his political conscience. For some Populists that was a major concession in itself. William H. Kitchin, for example, had been a Negrophobic Democrat before he became a Populist in 1894. He had often spoken publicly against black civil and suffrage rights. Yet as a Populist he said, "We must lay prejudice aside and come together, regardless of party or color, and make one common fight for our common interest." . . .

No Populist became better known for his appeal to blacks than Thomas Watson of Georgia. Elected to Congress in 1890 as a farmers' candidate, Watson went on to become one of the leaders of the People's party in the South and in the nation. In 1896 he was the national party's candidate for the vice-presidency. Because he is so well known, he has been subjected to much analysis by historians, particularly since 1938, when C. Vann Woodward published a biography of him in which he emphasized the strong class appeals made by Watson and the Populists in general. As one examines Watson's words and record it is evident that he was hardly a friend of what today is called integration, but it is also clear that he was quite willing to encourage Negro political equality in an effort to defeat the Democrats. . . .

Perhaps the best-known example of Watson's appeal to class as a counter to race appears in his article published in 1892 in the national magazine *Arena*. Watson advanced the same argument in the South, but his *Arena* article brought to national attention the Populist effort to win blacks and whites on grounds of a common class interest. "Now the People's Party says to these two men [black and white], 'You are kept apart that you may be separately fleeced of your earnings. You are made to hate each other because upon that hatred is rested the keystone of the arch of financial depotism which enslaves you both. You are deceived and blinded that you may not see how this race antagonism perpetuates a monetary system which beggars both.'" This is the closest, incidentally, that Watson or any other Populist came to saying that racial prejudice and hostility were deliberately created to gain advantage for the dominant economic interests.

✳

Words, one might say, are cheap. And that has often been the response of some skeptical historians to Populist statements in behalf of Negro rights. There are two responses that need to be made to that skepticism. One is that even to make the remarks in the context of the late nineteenth-century South is at once an act of audacity and a shift in ideology that ought not to be ignored. Words, as well as deeds, may change men's minds and even their behavior. The second point is that the words were not alone. Populists did act to put them into practice. One such act was an incident connected with Watson himself in 1892. H. S. Doyle, a black preacher who had been speaking in behalf of the Populists, came to Watson pursued by angry white Democrats. Watson offered Doyle a place to stay and sent word into the countryside that he needed armed support. Ultimately two thousand white men came to Watson's plantation, prepared to defend a black man's right to speak against other white men. As C. Vann Woodward wrote in describing the incident, "the spectacle of white farmers riding all night to save a Negro from lynchers was rather rare in Georgia." At the conclusion of the incident Watson said, "We are determined in this free country that the humblest white or black man that wants to talk our doctrine shall do it, and the man doesn't live who shall touch a hair of his head, without fighting every man in the People's Party." . . .

As during the Reconstruction, the rise of a rival party to the Democrats produced a new intimacy and mingling among the races at barbecues, picnics, suppers, and speakings. When the national Populist candidate for President, James B. Weaver, came to Raleigh, North Carolina, in 1892, he was escorted to the park in which he was to speak by 300 white men and 50 black men mounted on horseback. Reuben Kolb, the Populist candidate for governor of Alabama, spoke in Opelika in 1892 to a crowd of eight thousand, of whom a quarter were blacks.

One immediate consequence of the mingling with and the speaking to blacks in public was that all white men, Democrats as well as Populists, at least up to a point, had to moderate the expression of their hostility toward blacks. As occurred during Reconstruction, Democrats made appeals to blacks, too, inviting them to barbecues and picnics and making them promises. Occasionally the Democrats showed more interest in black voters than the Populists did, a development that was one of those unintended, but potentially significant, consequences that sometimes follows a break in an established racial-political order. Carried on long enough, it even might have worked a permanent change in outlook and social behavior. Whites might have begun to become familiar with and therefore accepting of black participation in politics.

A more concrete measure of the impact of Populist appeals to Negroes was the violent reaction from Democrats. When the Populists in Arkansas, for example, condemned lynching of blacks, the party came in for sustained and severe attacks from the Democratic newspapers. One of them made quite clear that it took seriously the Populist appeals to blacks. In fact the paper contended that it was their very concern for blacks that would ensure their defeat. "This is a white man's country, and white men are going to rule it," asserted the *Arkadelphia Siftings* in 1892, "and when the third party opened its arms to the Negro at its State Convention, it invited its certain death at the polls next fall." . . .

A revealing vignette of the way in which whites and blacks responded to the novel and fluid political relationship occurred at the Texas Populist Convention of 1891. A white man tried to deny blacks representation on party committees, even though Negroes were members of the convention. At that point a black delegate rose. "The negro vote will be the balancing vote in Texas," he pointed out. "If you are going to win, you will have to take the negro with you. . . . You must appoint us by convention and make us feel that we are men." The white president of the convention expressed his agreement by saying, "I am in favor of giving the colored man full representation. He is a citizen just as much as we are, and the party that acts on that fact will gain the colored vote of the South." The convention then elected two blacks to the state executive committee of the party. Negroes remained on the committee until 1900. . . .

When it is recalled that Southern Populists were largely small farmers, usually from the more remote and unsophisticated areas of the South, the mixing between black and white at these political gatherings is even more remarkable. Ordinarily it was the small farmer, the man without much education, but with many problems, who least understood or felt a connection with blacks. Often these small farmers were not even familiar with blacks in their everyday lives, since most of them did not live among Negroes as the whites of the Black Belt did. Thus when the Populist convention of Louisiana met in 1892 with 24 of the 127 delegates being black, it was a new sight and experience for many of the white Populists from the hill country, where almost no blacks lived. At that convention two blacks were placed in nomination for the state ticket, but then some more cautious black delegates questioned whether such a ticket might not be too stiff a dose of biracial politics for white Louisianans to take. They asked that the black nominees withdraw. The whites said nothing, leaving the delicate matter to the blacks to decide. Both blacks withdrew. Both of them, however, were then made members of the state executive committee of the party. . . .

An even more dramatic example of the persistence of white Populist support for black suffrage occurred in Grimes County, Texas. All through the 1890's black and white Populists in this east Texas county worked together politically, including the election of a Populist white sheriff, who appointed black deputies. The unity of black and white lasted until white Democratic terrorists killed one black leader and seriously wounded and drove out the white sheriff, Garrett Scott, and his family. As late as 1970 a descendant of Scott's defended that cooperation between blacks and whites. "They said that Uncle Garrett was a nigger-lover," his niece remembered. "He wasn't a nigger-lover, or a white-lover, he just believed in being fair to all, in justice."

*

To concentrate on examples of Populists' defenses of black participation is to present a distorted and therefore misleading picture of what was going on in the South of the 1890's. The evolution of a working relationship between blacks and whites in the same political organization was much more uneven and fluid than a catalog of such examples suggests. Individuals as well as groups of Populists shifted on the question during the decade. Indeed, it is this shifting on the race question that has allowed historians to maintain contrary positions on Populists' attitudes and behavior toward blacks. The fact is that, for reasons already suggested, Populists were ambiguous on the subject, often inconsistent, and sometimes hypocritical. . . .

Probably the most common form that the ambivalence of white Populists assumed toward black suffrage was to deny that there was any danger of Negro domination. Tom Watson spelled out the groundlessness of the fears in such a way that his own sense of white superiority was obvious. " 'Dominate' what? 'Dominate' how? 'Dominate' who?" he asked. "It takes Intellect to dominate: haven't we got it? It takes Majorities to dominate: haven't we got them? It takes Wealth to dominate: haven't we got it?" As Watson made clear, there could be no doubt that, given their advantages, the whites would always rule in the South. Trying to shame those who uttered the cry of Negro domination, he fell back upon an appeal to white supremacy: "What words can paint the cowardice of the Anglo-Saxon who would deny 'equal and exact justice' to the ignorant, helpless, poverty-cursed Negro in whose ears the clank of chains have scarcely ceased to sound." Then came the near-racist clincher: "No power on this earth will ever reverse the decree of God."

That Watson's appeal was at least paternalistic and perhaps tinged with racism was clear from the remarks he once directed to a predominantly black audience. You ought to be ashamed to allow white men to buy your vote, he told his listeners. "You are doing nobly in the way of educating your children; your daughters are *beginning* to dress nicely and behave themselves decently, and be respected, and now will you throw all this away in a campaign that your false leaders have been bribed to delude you?"

When Watson addressed a national audience he emphasized . . . the economic and social importance of blacks in the South. "They are a part of our system and they are here to stay," Watson wrote in *Arena* magazine in 1892. To believe, as some white Southerners do, that blacks are a dying race is false, he asserted. Nor were mulattoes increasing in number. "Miscegenation is further off (Thank God) than ever. Neither the blacks nor the whites have any relish for it," he assured his Northern readers, who believed the same thing. Once again he denied any danger of "Negro supremacy." As things now stand in "this country there is no earthly chance for Negro domination unless we are ready to admit that the colored man is our superior in will power, courage, and intellect." Obviously, Watson, for one, was not ready to admit it. . . .

The heart of the Populist argument in behalf of political participation by blacks was that it would not threaten white supremacy. It was, said one Alabama Populist, simply "making a practical application" of Booker T. Washington's famous metaphor of the fingers of the hand, which Washington had set forth in his Atlanta Exposition speech in 1895. Washington's views, the Populist noted, had received high praise from traditional white Southerners for being practical and helpful to both races. In cooperating with the Republicans "for the purpose of restoring the purity of the ballot, of having once more honest elections and majority rule," the Populists said that they were doing no more than following Washington's advice. . . .

For some sophisticated Populists the justification for black suffrage derived from what George Frederickson has called romantic racialism—that is, the idea that in some ways Negroes were superior to whites, though those ways were not necessarily ones the white man would want to emulate. Usually they consisted of "soft" or "feminine" traits like faithfulness, or patience. Joseph Manning, a radical Populist from Alabama, justified Negro suffrage on these grounds in a speech in 1903. During the Civil War, Manning said, the Negro was not and "he is not now, and had never been, turbulent or anarchistic as a race. No people on earth would have deported themselves during the Civil War as did the Negro, and no other race would have" remained faithful to a society "then ruled by a passionate belief, sustained by an unyielding prejudice, that the Negro should never himself either be a free man or the owner of a free man's home." . . .

No one, however, put more forcefully or clearly the assumption that underlay the relationship between blacks and whites in the Populist party than Tom Watson. At his best, Watson was without sentiment or illusion. (By 1895, however, his best was behind him, for after that year he was having increasing doubts about working with blacks.) He did not expect to convert whites to appreciation of or even sympathy with blacks, nor did he expect blacks to support Populists out of gratitude. After all, he pointed out, "gratitude may fail, so may sympathy and friendship and generosity and patriotism; but in the long run, self-interest *always* controls. Let it once appear plain that it is in the interest of a colored man to vote with the white man, and he will do it. Let it plainly appear that it is to the interest of the white man that the vote of the Negro supplement his own, and the question of having that ballot freely cast and fairly counted, becomes vital to the *white man*. He will see that it is done." On this ground Watson confidently predicted that "the People's Party will settle the race question."

Watson was right when he said self-interest would be controlling. What he forgot, however, is that not all interests are equally powerful. When he talked of self-interest he meant concrete economic concerns, that is, class interests that white and black farmers had in common. But there was another interest that white men had, and it was even stronger than class. Watson and the Populists knew that, too, and they feared its power. As a result they sought to erect additional defenses against it.

✳

That powerful interest was the belief in the superiority of the white race. Like the Scalawags and Readjusters before them, the Populists sought to allay white fears of compromising that belief by drawing a line between political equality, which they defended, and social equality, which they scoffed at as not worth discussing, much less fearing. "The man who alludes to Social Equality" when talking about Negro suffrage "insults the intelligence of those to whom he talks," declared the *People's Party Paper* in 1892. "Social equality is a question which every citizen settles for himself. The law never did, and never can, interfere with it." ("Social equality does not exist now among the whites." Republican Thomas Settle had asserted in 1867, "and no law has ever attempted to regulate that matter. . . . Every man chooses his own company. The virtuous form one association and the vicious another. This matter regulates itself, law cannot do it.") Tom Watson himself phrased the argument this way: "No statute ever yet drew the latch of the humblest home—or ever will. Each citizen regulates his own visiting list—and always will." . . .

. . . [W]hen we understand why most white Southerners found it difficult to abandon their ideas of racial superiority we also understand why the Scalawags, Readjusters, and Populists did not advance more sophisticated—or modern—arguments against racism. For they were a part of the same world. What is more remarkable is that those white Southern dissenters were able to go as far as they did in the direction of acceptance of Negroes. It is not given for many men and women to transcend their history; most are lucky if they can make even a few changes in their vast and varied inheritance from the past. The Populists and Republicans of the South were among those exceptions.

These three unsuccessful efforts by white Southerners to counter race allegiance by class appeals should remind us of another fact. Class and race are certainly among the elemental allegiances, but in the American South of the nineteenth century, class appeals when placed in opposition to race allegiance have been like a summer breeze against a juggernaut. . . .

Barton C. Shaw

THE POPULISTS AFTER DARK

In his work on the People's party in Georgia, Barton C. Shaw demonstrated how tenuous the relations were between Populists and African Americans. Although the Populists appealed for black votes and even made concessions to get them, they remained ardent white supremists. Like the Democrats, they were not above using terror and bribery to control black voters. Shaw concluded that it was highly unlikely that the majority of blacks voted for Populist candidates. Professor Shaw teaches history at Cedar Crest College.

Reprinted by permission of Louisiana State University Press from *The Wool-Hat Boys: Georgia's Populist Party* by Barton C. Shaw, pp. 78–90. Copyright © 1984 by Louisiana State University Press.

The notion that the black man had somehow betrayed Populism would constantly haunt the Georgia People's party. From the very beginning Populists had realized the political importance of blacks. Of the state's forty thousand Republican voters, a considerable majority were former bondsmen. If the white vote were to split, they might decide the outcome of any state election. But therein lay a predicament. How were the Populists to court the black vote without losing the white? How were they to keep whites from thinking of them as the "nigger party," the party willing to truckle to the former slaves? Clearly, however, an attempt had to be made to win over blacks. It was a dangerous scheme, but it contained a degree of precedent in state politics. In the 1870s and 1880s, Democrats and independents had sometimes used the same device when the white vote split. In those days many whites were willing to allow the black man the ballot, especially when it could be sometimes bought for as little as a dime or a mouthful of whiskey.

But to lure the Republican vote the Populists refused either to give up leadership of their party or to advocate the social equality of the races. The first was a question of power, the second of prejudice. On the issue of social equality, William L. Peek declared: "Us white men will not tolerate it, and the negroes don't want it." Time and again, Populists stressed this point. "Miscegenation," wrote Tom Watson, "is further off (thank God) than ever."

On other issues the Populists were willing to compromise. Their demand for an end to convict lease was enthusiastically supported by blacks. After the Civil War, Georgia had little money to spend on prisons, and so it leased its convicts to mining companies owned by Joseph E. Brown, John B. Gordon, and others. Deep beneath the earth, the prisoners lived in a world of dimly lit shafts, savage guards, and crushing toil. Cave-ins and gas took their toll, and many convicts never lived to see freedom. The shabbiest corruption preyed upon this form of legalized slavery. To maintain their labor supply, mine owners encouraged judges to pump as many men as possible into the system. . . .

Besides their position on convict lease, the Populists were willing to make other concessions to blacks. They demanded the secret ballot and honest elections that were free from intimidation and said this could be done by instituting the secret ballot. They reminded blacks that the predicament of farmers was the same regardless of race; therefore, Populist reforms would help them all. Finally, the third party added one more spice to the brew it offered the black man—representation in Populist councils. Out of about 150 delegates at the 1892 state convention, 2 were black. In the First District, the Populist nominating convention likewise included a black delegate, who was later appointed to the campaign committee. Although hardly monumental concessions, these acts gave credence to the notion that the Populists were interested in the problems and opinions of former slaves.

On the local level, some Populists also offered enticements. Occasionally ·black orators were invited to speak from the same platform with whites. One district convention unanimously passed a resolution condemning lynch law. In a few places third-party members promised that if victorious they would put blacks on juries, an alluring prospect because of the salary of two dollars a day. Some third-party men seemed especially sensitive to the feelings of blacks. "The *Chronicle* said I shook hands with negro men, women, and children at Sparta," Tom Watson declared. "I say yes I did it, and have no apologies to make.". . .

Yet some blacks remained unimpressed with third party promises. They remembered that many Populists were poor whites, their traditional enemy since slavery. They were likewise suspicious of the People's party support of the honest ballot. A resolution attached to the Populist national platform condemned federal supervision of elections, one of the few devices that had given the black man political power in the South. Instead, third-party members called for the secret ballot. But most Georgia blacks were illiterate and thus could not read the ballot, let alone fill it out. When Populists answered that they would pass laws allowing officials at the polls to help illiterates vote, blacks became even more wary. Georgia election officials were notoriously corrupt, were largely white, and were the last people they wanted help from when voting. Nevertheless, the majority of Republican leaders, white and black, favored some form of assistance to the Populists. It came on August 11, 1892, when their state convention decided not to nominate a state ticket. Instead, the convention advised party members to vote for the Republican presidential candidate, Benjamin Harrison, and to follow their consciences in the gubernatorial contest. With one exception the Republican congressional nominating conventions did the same. Later Alfred Buck, the most influential white Republican in the state, endorsed William L. Peek [the Populist gubernatorial candidate].

Democrats constantly asserted that a formal union existed between the Republicans and the Populists. They made the far-fetched charge that the national Republican party was sending the People's party vast sums of money to defeat the Democrats in one of their strongholds. The Populist campaign was such a threadbare effort—donations were usually in small change—that it was unlikely to have obtained much Republican aid. In October, however, a schoolgirl in Thomson noticed Tom Watson tear up a letter and throw it into the street. She retrieved the scraps, pieced them together, and showed the results to her father, who was a Democrat. When published, the letter caused a sensation. The sender was D. N. Sanders, the secretary of the *People's Party Paper*. Sanders reported to Watson that the newspaper had been short of funds and that he had paid a freight bill with cash borrowed from Alfred Buck. Although the letter made it clear that Watson knew nothing about the deal, the damage had been done. Gleefully, the Democratic press proclaimed that Republican money was indeed helping the Populists. This letter, however, was the only evidence of aid they ever produced.

The Democrats also realized the importance of the former slaves and were quietly at work trying to entice them to their party. They, not the third-party men, first employed black speakers in Tom Watson's district. But the Democrats found other ways to show their regard for blacks. During his first administration, William J. Northen used his influence to increase appropriations for black schools. More important, he seemed to have an honest hatred of lynchings, doing everything he could to prevent them (a risky policy in Georgia, which in 1892 had more lynchings than any other state in the nation). On one occasion he used his personal funds to have a black man, who was accused of rape, rushed out of the hands of a mob to the relative safety of Atlanta. In May, 1892, a triple lynching in Clarksville again brought forth his wrath. "The outrage committed upon the lives of these defenseless men is absolutely without excuse or palliation," he said publicly, and he offered a $200 reward for the arrest of the culprits. . . . Although there were limits to his tolerance (as governor, he had favored a bill making it illegal to chain a white convict to a black convict), many Georgia Republicans planned to reward him with their votes. Among them was Bishop Henry M. Turner, the most respected black clergyman in the state.

Blacks had other reasons for objecting to the third party. William L. Peek seemed to possess little friendship for them, and few could forget his slave bill. James Barrett, the People's candidate for commissioner of agriculture, had earlier declared that the more education the former slaves received, the more dangerous they became. Barrett had advised that, if it was necessary to instruct them, the teachers should be white "in order to protect white society." Tom Watson's record also left unanswered questions. While a member of the legislature he had worked to reduce funds for black schools, and on a technicality he had opposed a black man's obtaining a contested seat, even though the black had received more votes than his white opponent. Finally, in 1883, Watson voted for the Tutt bill, an early version of the Peek slave bill. But blacks feared not only Populist leaders. Many had a visceral dread of poor whites—the people whom they believed were most responsible for lynchings in the South. W. A. Pledger, a prominent black Republican, stoutly objected to a union between his people and the Populists: "The men who have lynched the colored people in the past; the men who have shot and robbed the colored people; the men who precipitated the 'Camilla riot' years ago and who marshalled the red shirter and night riders are now the followers and shouters of Peek and his crowd." Pledger pleaded with blacks to vote for Northen, the man who had "done all in his official power to keep these Third partyites from lynching my people."

On the local level blacks were also suspicious. The white citizens of Tom Watson's McDuffie Country had always been hostile to the former slaves. Intimidation was so great that blacks could never hold a political meeting or cast a ballot for any local candidate who was not a Democrat. The Ku Klux Klan was active as late as 1884. When the Populists came to power, all this changed. Abruptly, the former slaves were allowed to vote, a demonstration, the wool-hat boys* argued, of their respect for the black man and his rights. They

---

*By the 1890s in Georgia the term "wool-hat boys" referred to the honest, hard-working yeomen farmers who became Populists.

neglected to point out that some of the men who disfranchised McDuffie blacks in the 1870s and 1880s became Populists in the 1890s. It was unlikely that these public officials suddenly became more tolerant of black voters. Instead, they were faced with the classic Populist dilemma: because the third party would split the white vote, they were forced to appeal to blacks.

White Populists insisted that the blacks' fears were groundless, that they bore them no malice. As election day approached, however, the cheerful grin of the wool-hat boy occasionally changed, and a darker, sometimes even ghastly, visage appeared. What were blacks to make of one Populist's stand against lynch mobs that appeared in the Carnesville *Enterprise*: "Now as to lynching I am opposed to it except in extreme cases. I never was in but one. . . ."?

Many blacks believed the Populists exposed their true racial feelings on October 23, 1892. Late that evening 150 riders, all wearing masks, galloped into Dalton, Georgia. Quietly they turned out the street lamps as they passed through the darkened streets. After finding the marshal, they put a gun to his head and ordered him to take them to the home of a black man named Tom Harlan. There, by the light of flaring torches, they dragged Harlan and his wife from bed and ferociously beat them until they were nearly dead. Then the men rode to the house of Jack Wilson, another black. When they broke down his door, Wilson resisted and was shot through the head and heart. He died instantly. More homes of black people were visited, but their inhabitants heard the riders coming and fled. Having finished their work, the masked men galloped into the night, firing their pistols and waving torches.

No one ever discovered who the riders were or the reason for their crimes. But Dalton Democrats believed they knew and raised a $1,000 reward. Both Wilson and Harlan had voted Democratic in the October election.

No one was able to prove unequivocally that Populists had murdered Jack Wilson and beaten Tom Harlan and his wife. But there were circumstantial reasons to think that they had. In other parts of the state Populists had employed similar methods. The sworn testimony of William Oxford of Jefferson County at the contested election hearings between Watson and Black in 1896 shed light on the matter.

Q. What is your politics?

A. I am nothing.

Q. Did you not formerly belong to the People's Party?

A. Yes sir.

Q. How long did you belong to the People's Party?

A. Since it started in 1892.

Q. For whom did you vote for Congress in 1892, 1894, and 1895?

A. I voted for Watson.

Q. What time did you quit the People's Party?

A. Last fall [1895].

Q. State what incidents of attempted and actual intimidation by the Populists you know of that occurred in any of the elections, both State and Federal, in 1892, and what since then up to the present time.

A. From that time up to now I have been in a good many meetings with the Populists, and the most they did was to try to keep negroes from coming to Louisville [Jefferson County] to vote. They tried to do this by threatening to whip them and do a heap of things to them if they didn't vote for Watson.

Q. Do you know anything about Calvin Joiner [a black man who had supported the Democrats] being whipped by the Populists to keep him away from the polls unless he would go and vote their way?

A. Yes, sir.

Q. Who whipped Calvin Joiner?

A. I did.

Q. Do you know of any other acts of violence the Populists did to scare the negroes and keep them away from the polls?

A. They organized and rode everywhere in the county at night in order to scare them and keep them away.

Q. How did they arrange these squads to ride over the county?

A. There were men appointed in each district to select a squad of men to ride around at night and to scare the negroes either into voting for Watson or staying away from the polls altogether.

Q. These riders who went around among the negroes—didn't they threaten the negroes with what they might do unless they voted for Watson or did not vote at all?

A. They would go to the head or leading Democratic negroes in the districts and threaten to kill them if they didn't vote for Watson or stay away from the polls, and they threatened to whip all the negroes if they didn't vote for Watson or stay away from the polls. That was the rule of the club that I was a member of, and I suppose the other clubs did the same.

Q. Did you ever whip any negro before you did Calvin?
A. Yes, sir; I have whipped a heap of them. I whipped them before
    I became a Populist and since, too.
Q. Did you ever kill a negro?
A. Yes, sir; about twenty years ago. It was in self-defense.
Q. Haven't you killed more than one negro?
A. I decline to answer.

Oxford explained not only the methods but also the motive of Populist terrorism. In many places Populists wanted blacks to vote only if they intended to support the third party. Yet Oxford's testimony did not describe how far Populists would go to intimidate the black man. M. G. Gamble, a Democrat from Jefferson County, swore under oath that when he rode to the polls on election day, the Populists there were carrying sticks and wearing red caps—the symbol of the old Ku Klux Klan of Reconstruction. Another Democrat from the same county said that the night before the October contest, third-party men had ridden about the countryside dressed in "red shirts and red caps." Stopping at one plantation, they fired pistols and threatened black tenants with murder if they voted against Watson. The previous night, a black man from the same plantation was supposedly shot at by Populists wearing red caps. Pleasant Stovall, the Democratic editor of the Savannah *Press*, toured the Tenth District shortly before the congressional election and reported that in places third-party threats were forcing blacks to vote for the Populist party. Stovall asked Judge William Gibson of Warrenton what was afoot. The judge declared that it was a "union between the blacks and the kuklux; and that the lawless element is holding the negro in line at the muzzle of a gun."

Similar coercion broke out in Screven County. A black man who had helped in the Democratic campaign received a letter from the "Unknown Club," cautioning him not to take bribes from "lawyers or merchants with Wall Street money." The letter warned that if he ever again aided the Democrats, he would have his "God-damned brains shot out." In Briar Creek, C. N. Robinson, a black teacher who had given speeches endorsing Governor Northen, bitterly wrote that Populist threats had compelled him to leave his position and flee for his life.

There can be no doubt that Georgia Populists used terror and intimidation to influence state elections. The cry for an honest ballot was sincere up to a point—as long as the black man voted for the third party, white Populists demanded that his ballot be counted. Otherwise, they did not, and in many places they tried to keep him from the polls—sometimes by means of the Ku Klux Klan. This was especially true in the "terrible" Tenth. There black people realized the consequences of voting or even speaking against the Populists. During the Watson-Black contested election hearing, one black refused to answer a question about a third-party man. When asked the reason, he said that he feared the Populists "after dark."

It was not altogether surprising that some Populists resorted to the regalia and methods of the Ku Klux Klan. The old Klan of Reconstruction had been strong in northwestern Georgia and the area that later became the Tenth Congressional District. The crimes in the latter region were especially heinous. Among other horrors, the Invisible Empire was guilty of murder, rape, bludgeoning, ear cropping, and castration. . . .

Finally, what of that famous day in Thomson, when Tom Watson protected the black minister, Seb Doyle, and hundreds of poor whites galloped to the rescue? How can that response be reconciled with the Populists who, in the same locale, rode the countryside at night terrorizing black people? The answer is fairly simple. The farmers rushed to Thomson to save Watson, not Doyle. The word that went out into the country was that Watson had been murdered, or at least was in danger. It is certain that some farmers did not know of Doyle's involvement until after they reached Thomson. The Democratic editor of the Lincolnton *News*, when describing the moment word reached his town, said only that Watson was supposedly in danger and made no mention of Doyle. Only when the Lincolnton Populists returned did the press mention the black minister. But the clearest reason for the incident came during the contested election hearings. "The rumor was that they went to Thomson . . . to protect the negro Doyle, was it not?" Watson's lawyer asked a witness from Lincolnton. "No sir; the rumor was that the [Democratic] mob was trying to mob Mr. Watson." And Watson's answers during the same hearings show that other towns besides Lincolnton had received this report. "They came over to Thomson . . . greatly excited," Watson testified, "because news had reached Lincolnton that I had been killed. Numbers of men came in from Columbia, Warren, and perhaps other counties on account of the same rumor."

White Populists did indeed feel sympathy for Doyle. For weeks he had campaigned for the third party at considerable personal risk. Once the farmers were in Thomson, they were willing to protect him as well as Watson. It is doubtful, however, that they would have ridden to save only the black minister. About a week before the Thomson incident, a white man nearly killed Doyle in Sparta. And on that day, no one rode to the rescue.

Whatever the case, the Thomson affair demonstrated that in the Populist mind there were two kinds of blacks: those who supported the third party and those who did not. But only the former—the "good" blacks—deserved protection and free and unintimidated access to the ballot. Besides an end to the convict-lease system and token representation at a few Populist meetings, this was the only concession the Georgia People's party offered the former slaves in 1892. For the black man at least, this was the meaning of the third-party motto, "Equal rights for all, special privileges for none."

Thus William L. Peek's charge that blacks did not fully support the Populist Party was true. Peek assumed that most of the forty-eight thousand Republicans who voted for Harrison in the presidential election should have favored him in the gubernatorial contest. He lost the support of twenty-three thousand of these voters. Because Northen gained only six or seven thousand, roughly fifteen thousand blacks refused to vote for either candidate—an extraordinary demonstration of their distrust of both parties.

Peek believed that at most twenty-five thousand blacks (or roughly 50 percent of those who voted) supported him. In reality the figure was probably lower—perhaps as little as ten thousand. One historian has recently estimated that Peek received only about 20 percent. Those blacks who favored the Populists did so for a number of reasons. Government ownership of the railroads, the subtreasury plan, and inflation were issues that were color-blind. The Populists, moreover, advocated an end to the convict-lease system and had permitted two blacks to attend their state convention—both unheard-of in Georgia except within the Republican party. Still, most blacks must have supported Populism with trepidation, realizing that they were engaging in a risky union. Just a few months earlier, many of those with whom they were allying had been their mortal enemies—the men who had made Georgia the lynching capital of the nation. It was a strange alliance, and it would bear strange fruit.

Gregg Cantrell and D. Scott Barton

TEXAS POPULISTS AND THE FAILURE OF BIRACIAL POLITICS

Based on a careful state-level study, Gregg Cantrell and D. Scott Barton
concluded that race was a major weakness in Populism because most
whites in that movement remained highly susceptible to racist appeals. In
the elections of 1894, when the Texas Populists had their greatest success
with African-American voters, they won a scant 17 percent of the black
vote. Two years later, Populist leaders tried to promote fusion with the
Republicans but failed because the rank-and-file Populists refused to
support a scheme that might weaken white supremacy. Later, in 1902,
when Texas restricted black voting by enacting a poll tax, about half of
the former Populists did not vote. Of the half who did, almost three times
as many supported the poll tax as opposed it. Professor Cantrell teaches
American history at Sam Houston State University, and Professor Barton
teaches American history at New Mexico State University.

Scholars have found the racial aspects of southern Populism exceedingly difficult to study. The urban daily newspapers and well-known
manuscript collections that are often relied upon by political historians rarely allow one to proceed beyond generalizations about the
Populists' racial approaches. The present study overcomes these
obstacles in two ways. First, by limiting the scope of inquiry to one
state, it is possible to survey a wide range of traditional primary
sources that explore Populism at the local level. These sources
include major daily newspapers, the Populist press, numerous small-
town weeklies, and one important manuscript collection that never
before had been utilized in the study of Populism. Second, ecological
regressions have been employed to analyze actual county voting
returns, making possible the measurement of racial voting patterns as
well as crossover voting from one election to another. Among other
things, this methodology enables us to estimate the success of fusion.

"Texas Populists and the Failure of Biracial Politics" by Gregg Cantrell and D. Scott
Barton, *Journal of Southern History*, 55 (November 1989), pp. 661–665, 667,
672–679, 685–687, 689–692. Copyright 1989 by the Southern Historical
Association. Reprinted by permission of the Managing Editor.

The People's party was officially organized in Texas in 1891. Meeting in Dallas one day before the state Farmers' Alliance convention, the small group of Populists debated how their new party would approach blacks. . . .

By the time of [the 1892] state convention a few black Populists in south Texas were reporting . . . that "the colored people are coming into the new party in squads and companies." But the commitment of white Populist leaders and the enthusiasm of a handful of blacks did not translate into significant black support for Populism at the polls. The 1892 Populist state ticket finished a poor third. Estimates of voting behavior reveal the distance Populists had yet to travel if they were to form a biracial coalition: virtually no blacks voted for Thomas L. Nugent, the Populist gubernatorial candidate, and over one-third of the blacks cast no ballots at all. Populists must have been terribly frustrated at this turn of events. Black Republicans had faced three choices: they could vote for James Stephen Hogg, a reform (or progressive) Democrat; George Clark, a conservative (or Bourbon) Democrat; or the Populist Nugent. The state Republican party, traditionally the political home for blacks, had "fused" with the Bourbon Democrats. Blacks who could stomach neither Hogg nor Clark had simply sat out the election rather than support the third party. Populist appeals to blacks had fallen on deaf ears. . . .

The Populist had to find a way to make both blacks and whites in the regions where the black population was significant place reform ahead of racial anxieties. Populists had to show white Democrats that the desperate financial plight of farmers would never improve under Democratic rule and that whites and blacks could honorably cooperate for the common good without inviting "social equality" for blacks. Populists also had to convince blacks that the new party was sincere in offering them meaningful political participation. There were good reasons to be optimistic about the chances of recruiting more white Populists as the agricultural depression deepened. Many whites were already familiar with Populist demands via the Farmers' Alliance and the reform press. But black "Pop clubs" could not organize themselves, and few blacks could read (or afford) newspapers that would instill in them the vital "education" of Populism. The party needed to find more blacks with leadership ability, courage, dedication, and the wherewithal to travel and work tirelessly as organizers and educators.

The Populists found one such man in John B. Rayner, a fair-skinned mulatto preacher, teacher, and politician from Robertson County. Born a slave in North Carolina, he was the son of U.S. Congressman Kenneth Rayner. John B. Rayner came to the People's party with an impressive classical education acquired in two North Carolina colleges and years of experience in the labyrinthine world of black southern politics. His work in the 1887 Texas prohibition campaign had led even a white Democratic opponent to concede that "Rayner is a shrewd politician and understands to a dot how to organize a political campaign. . . ." By 1894 the state press was reporting that Rayner was traveling throughout the state speaking at picnics, political meetings, county conventions, and Populist encampments. In his announcements for speaking engagements, Rayner invited "all who favor justice, liberty, a higher price for labor, and a better price for products. . . ." Billed as the "silver tongued orator of the colored race," Rayner crisscrossed the eastern half of the state in April, May, and June 1894, leaving in his wake a sprinkling of black Populist clubs.

Of course, thunderous oratory alone would not win statewide campaigns. Rayner and his white and black comrades in the movement knew that the pitfalls inherent in interracial cooperation called for a well-thought-out strategy, especially in the racially volatile areas with large black populations. In the 1894 campaign, therefore, the strategy of Populists of both races was to seek local alliances between Populists and Republicans. Indeed, the importance of such arrangements and their frequency in the 1894 and 1896 campaigns can scarcely be overemphasized. In areas with significant black populations, potential fusion deals were almost always explored at the precinct and county levels. Sometimes committees appointed by the Republican and Populist county conventions would confer with each other, divide the county offices between the two parties, and report back to their respective conventions. The parties then could accept or reject the agreement. When the arrangements were rejected by one or both parties—which happened frequently—on election day, that county would have Democratic, Republican, and Populist tickets in the field. Another approach was for one party's county convention to agree unilaterally to seek fusion and then send a representative to the other party's convention to seek approval for the plan. At other times, the local Republican organization simply declined to field a county ticket and instead endorsed the Populist ticket. The Populists preferred to "convert" black Republicans to Populism, but loyalty to the party of Lincoln ran high among ex-slaves. Before Populists could hope to achieve anything, they had to defeat the Democrats. And fusion was a necessary expedient. . . .

By the time of the 1894 Populist state convention, both blacks and whites felt that real progress was being made in attracting blacks to the reform party. At that meeting the "colored brother" did not stay in the background, and the white Populists did not attempt to keep him there. Throughout the convention black speakers mounted the podium to proclaim the new gospel of Populism. Their message always revolved around a common theme: the dire economic hardships being endured by poor blacks and poor whites and the mistreatment of both at the hands of the old parties. Rayner was named to the committee on platforms and resolutions, which framed a number of planks addressing the needs of blacks, including reforming the brutal convict lease system and placing control of black schools in the hands of black trustees.

The convention's high point came on the second day, when the Populists nominated their state ticket. In a dramatic moment Judge Thomas L. Nugent was nominated for governor. Then, at the peak of the convention's euphoria, Rayner took the floor to second the nomination. The "colored delegate from Robertson" made an eloquent plea for interracial cooperation. Rayner said that "he came from a race which had endured 4000 years of savagery and 245 years of slavery, only to find that the white man of the south is the negro's first, best and firmest friend. 'Nominate Nugent and the negro will be as faithful to your flag as he was to your wives and children when you were fighting the battles of your country'." Rayner's brief speech masterfully appealed to Confederate sensibilities without downplaying the fact that slavery was an evil that blacks had "endured." Obviously, each race was seeking to accommodate the other. Rayner's speech was met with "loud applause" by the enthusiastic delegates, who nominated Nugent by acclamation. . . .

The 1894 state elections did not bring victory to the Populist state ticket, but in many respects Populists had cause to feel encouraged. With the Democrats reunited behind a single gubernatorial candidate and a Republican ticket again in the field, the election provided the best opportunity yet to gauge Populist strength. Thomas L. Nugent, once more the Populist gubernatorial candidate, finished second to Democrat Charles A. Culberson by a vote of 207,171 to 151,595. The Republicans and Prohibitionists polled a combined vote of 62,875. Nugent's vote had increased by over 40,000 since 1892, and the Democratic party was now a minority party. Populism was growing in Texas.

A closer examination of the 1894 election reveals the sources of the Populist gains as well as their continuing weaknesses. Eighty-two percent of Nugent's 1892 voters again cast their ballots for him. Blacks, who in 1892 had evenly split their votes between the two Democratic candidates, now found that they had more palatable options. One-third of the adult black males voted the Republican ticket, casting their ballots for William K. Makemson, and 29 percent of the adult black males voted Democratic, probably as a result of fraud and intimidation. In 1892 the Populist Nugent had received no measurable black support at the polls, but in 1894, 17 percent of the state's adult black males voted for him. Overall black participation increased from 62 to 79 percent.

Populists had finally made significant gains in their quest for black support, but the gains were far less than party leaders had hoped for. As in 1892 the Democratic governor of Texas had received a minority of all votes cast. The Populists naturally hoped that they could continue to recruit white Democrats and black Republicans. After all, 20 percent of Nugent's 1894 voters had been Democrats two years before. But the potential for the Populists was obvious from the returns: If all the votes against the Democrats could be combined under the Populist banner, the hated Democrats could be ousted.

As the 1894 congressional elections demonstrated, Populist voters would, under certain circumstances, support a fusion effort in races above the local level. . . . Southern Populists normally could not risk nominating an avowed Republican because the GOP was irrevocably fixed in the minds of most white southerners as the party of "Negro domination." The success of open statewide Republican-Populist fusion in North Carolina was anomalous, because North Carolina was practically the only southern state that possessed a strong Republican minority with a large native white constituency. Some Populist leaders in Texas would have liked to duplicate North Carolina's successful fusion, but the racial obstacles loomed large.

In the northern and western states Populists had reached the same conclusion that their counterparts had in Texas: They were willing to fuse with other "out" parties in order to defeat the entrenched party. In the West and North, however, the Republicans were the entrenched party, and the Democratic party was the minority party with which Populists sought to fuse. While the Republicans' use of the Bloody Shirt made fusion difficult in these nonsouthern states, in the South sectional antagonisms were compounded by the strong racial stigma that accompanied Republicanism. By 1895 many Texas Populists were beginning to fear that the strategy northern Populists had employed so successfully in their home states—fusion with the Democrats—might be attempted on the national level. The most alarming sign that such an effort might be attempted came from national Populist headquarters. Herman E. Taubeneck of Illinois, the national chairman, had displayed definite signs of favoring fusion with the Democrats in the upcoming national elections. In early 1896 Taubeneck tried to reassure Texas Populists that he favored an alliance of all reformers, as long as it could be accomplished without "the sacrifice of principle." Texas Populists could hardly argue with this statement, inasmuch as it was precisely what they had done numerous times in seeking fusion arrangements with Republicans and Independents. Satisfied for the time being, the Texas state executive committee continued to support Taubeneck. For the rest of the campaign, talk of fusion dominated political discussions in Texas. . . .

The worst fears of thousands of Texas Populists had been realized when their national convention met in July. Nearly 1,400 delegates assembled in St. Louis, knowing that the Democrats had nominated William Jennings Bryan, Nebraska's champion of free silver. The Democrats' selection of Maine's Arthur Sewall as Bryan's running mate was particularly galling to Populists because Sewell was a wealthy banker whose fidelity to silver was doubted. Representation in the Populist convention had been determined by a formula that gave each state a delegate for every senator and representative it had in Congress, plus a delegate for each two thousand Populist votes cast in any statewide election since 1891. Clearly, this formula gave disproportionate representation to heavily populated states and states in which fusion had been used successfully. The election of Nebraska's Senator William V. Allen, a strong fusionist ally of Bryan, as permanent chairman of the convention provides the best available gauge of middle-of-the-road versus fusionist sentiment; Allen defeated Maine middle-of-the roader James E. Campion by a vote of 758 to 564. With fusionists in the majority and the machinery of the convention in the hands of Allen, Bryan's nomination was accomplished. The best the middle-of-the-roaders could do was to engineer the nomination of Georgia's Thomas E. ("Tom") Watson as vice-president, keeping half the ticket in the middle of the road and possibly forcing Bryan to refuse the nomination. The Texans led the fight against Bryan, with every one of the state's 103 delegates opposing fusion to the bitter end. Dallas County's Populists reflected the attitude of the party's members in Texas. In the midst of the convention they sent their delegate, Jerome Kearby, this message: "Five hundred Populists say never surrender. Bryan means death." The Texans, embittered to the extreme, returned home to a hero's welcome and were immediately dubbed "the immortal 103" for having stayed in the middle of the road.

Texas Populists held their state convention two weeks after Bryan had been nominated in St. Louis. During the short time between the two meetings, talk of Populist-Republican fusion, which had persisted all spring, reached a fever pitch. Rumor had it that the Populists and Republicans would strike a deal whereby Populists would vote for McKinley presidential electors in return for Republican support of the Populist state ticket. The Populists officially denied any such intentions, but their anger at events in St. Louis, combined with their unceasing animosity to the Texas Democratic party, lent credence to talk of a bargain. . . .

The stridently anti-Bryan Populists understood that many rank-and-file members of the party would not accept open endorsement of the GOP presidential ticket even in return for Republican support of the Populist state candidates. The deeply felt revulsion against the Republican party in Texas would be difficult, if not impossible, for white Populists to overcome. Unlike the 1894 congressional race between Weldon and Crain, where Populists and Republicans had united behind an independent candidate, the arrangement being contemplated in 1896 would force Populists actually to cast votes for a Republican, William McKinley. . . .

The Populists again made their customary nod to blacks by electing Rayner to the executive committee, and the delegates still had to debate a number of proposed changes in the party platform. One of these planks was an eloquent "Plea For Justice," a sweeping call for black rights that had been submitted by black delegate Frank W. Thomas. The platform, as reported by the committee and adopted by the delegates, differed little from the document of 1894. Nowhere did it mention fusion. Thomas's "Plea For Justice" was one of the new additions, but the resolution had not emerged from committee unaltered. The plank as adopted read, "We are in favor of equal justice and protection under the law to all citizens without reference to race, color or nationality." The committee deleted the portion of the original proposed resolution that said: "[All men] should receive the same recognition in proportion to intelligence and capacity, and we pledge ourselves that in the execution of the law the negro shall receive his just dues, and be recognized in such positions as his capacity fits him to fill." These veiled references to black officeholding had proven too much for the white Populists. They did not want to risk alienating the white voters—as had the Republican party during Reconstruction—by supporting black officeholding. Yet the Populists wanted black support for fusion, and many of the white leaders gave every indication of sincerity in calling for "equal protection under the law" for blacks. The platform adopted at Galveston showed that the Populists had traveled further toward racial equality than the Democrats had, but even the Populists had gone only part of the way. This was about as close as southern blacks would come to equality under the law for the next sixty years.

The Populists left Galveston and began one of the most bitter campaigns in Texas history. The Democratic press followed every movement of the Populist campaign committee, which consisted of Marion Williams, Harry Tracy, and J. M. Mallett. Throughout the next two months the committee conferred on a number of occasions with Republican leaders, laying the groundwork for a fusion of all the anti-Democratic forces. However, as events at Galveston had shown, the pro-fusion Populists had to make it appear that they did not really want to support McKinley. Only by making fusion appear to be a desperate last resort forced on them by the Democrats could the Populist leaders sell fusion to the rank and file. . . .

Election day finally came amid great excitement and wide-spread fraud, intimidation, and violence. The Populist gubernatorial candidate, Jerome Kearby, lost to the Democrat Culberson by a vote of 298,568 to 238,688, and the Bryan-Sewall Democratic presidential ticket easily carried the state with 54 percent of all votes cast. Populist or fusion congressional candidates ran strong races in five districts but won none of them. The radical Populist leadership's high hopes for fusion were shattered, and the fault rested largely with the Populists themselves. In 1896 the People's party, according to the estimates of voting, continued to make inroads into Democratic ranks: 12 percent of those who supported Culberson in 1894 voted for Kearby two years later. But 28 percent of the 1894 Populists defected to the Democratic party in 1896 and voted for Culberson. In other words, in the competition for cross-party recruits, the Populists lost to the Democrats by a nearly two-to-one margin.

Some of the Populist defections from 1894 to 1896 surely can be explained by the fact that the beloved Thomas Nugent was no longer alive to carry the Populist banner. However, Jerome Kearby also enjoyed great popularity in his party; no doubt many of the approximately 42,000 Populists who defected to the Democratic party did so out of disgust over fusion. This would amount to an 84,000-vote swing, more than enough to have cost the Populists the election. It might be tempting to attribute this large-scale Populist defection to issues other than race and fusion. Were these voters simply casualties in the "battle of the standards"—i.e., men who refused to vote for McKinley because of his support for gold and who favored Bryan's pro-silver stance? Probably not. For one reason, the estimated 42,000 Populists who left the party did not just refuse to vote for McKinley; they also voted for Democratic governor Culberson, a man who only reluctantly became pro-silver. Voting for Culberson had little or nothing to do with gold versus silver—it was simply a repudiation of Populism. It cannot be seen as merely a side effect of Populists' admiration for Bryan, because such voters easily could have cast ballots for the Bryan presidential ticket and the Populist state ticket. Indeed, the state Democratic party's stance on silver was largely irrelevant. Free silver was primarily a national rather than a state issue, and the state Democratic party's reluctant support of silver clearly would not have provided sufficient incentive for thousands of Populists to vote for Culberson. The

Democratic party had appropriated several Populist planks in 1896, but the most meaningful reforms for the masses in Texas were still the exclusive property of the Populists. Dislike for McKinley's economic policies can explain why a Populist might refuse to vote for him for president, but it cannot explain why 42,000 Populists deserted the third party's gubernatorial ticket.

The racial stigma attached to Republicanism emerges as by far the most significant explanation of why white Populists forsook their party. Openly voting for "the party of the Negroes" was more than many white Populists could bear, as witnessed by the fact that only 12 percent of the 1894 Populists voted for McKinley in 1896. Ultimately, 76 percent of the eligible native-born white voters cast Bryan ballots (55 percent voting for Bryan-Sewell electors and 21 percent for the Bryan-Watson ticket). Even if all Populist Bryan-Watson voters had instead voted for McKinley and fusion, the Democratic ticket of Bryan and Sewall would still have carried the state.

The state's Republicans had, for the most part, done their best to make fusion work; about two-thirds of those who had voted for the 1894 Republican gubernatorial candidate cast ballots for Kearby in 1896. Estimates of voting by racial groups show that only 8 percent of the native white electorate cast ballots for McKinley electors, while even after fraud, almost two-thirds of the blacks supported the future Republican president. . . .

To summarize, Texas Republicans largely upheld their end of the fusion deal, notwithstanding the significant percentage of the black vote that landed in the Democratic column. Texas Populists, on the other hand, failed to deliver the white votes. Very few 1894 Populists voted for McKinley in 1896, and nearly a third of them made their apostasy complete by abandoning Kearby for Culberson. Fraud played a role, and perhaps it could explain the 60,000-vote margin between Kearby and Culberson, as some have suggested. But estimates of voting suggest that former Populists who gave their votes to Culberson accounted for a swing of approximately 84,000 votes. In evaluating the causes of the third-party defeat, this finding surely must loom as large as, if not larger than, fraud. The national convention's nomination of the Democrat William Jennings Bryan had driven Texas Populists to the desperate expedient of trying to support Republican William McKinley without appearing to do so, and that ill-fated maneuver guaranteed the destruction of Populism on the state level. . . .

In the years following 1896, white Populists accurately identified the element of race as a decisive factor in the failure of the Populist revolt. Ironically, however, those Populists mistook the nature of that racial factor. Populists increasingly blamed the blacks for the defeat of Populism, believing that fraud in areas with large black populations had been the key element in the defeats of both 1894 and 1896. Certainly there was a measure of truth in this charge. But as important as manipulation of the black vote was, it was not the most critical factor in the Populist defeat. More than fraud, the Populists owed their downfall to white southerners who were not willing to participate in a biracial coalition in order to end Democratic rule. Radicalism failed in Texas because it underestimated the power of white supremacy.

Populism in Texas declined rapidly after 1896. Many Populists dropped out of politics for varying periods of time. The more realistic or pragmatic Populists apparently returned to the Democratic party and succeeded in sweeping the "reform" wing of that party to power in 1906. But the white Populists almost entirely gave up any further attempts at a biracial coalition. The "colored brother" was "conspicuously absent" from the 1898 state Populist convention. Populists had realized that a poll tax requirement for voting would disfranchise poor whites as well as poor blacks, and prior to 1896 they had usually opposed any such measures. But even as the 1896 campaign was under way, the editor of the Populist Dallas *Southern Mercury* issued a warning to blacks about the implications of their votes being manipulated by Democrats: "The negroes are miserably to be blamed to let the democrats use them in such a way. . . . If the negro does not qualify himself to be a freeman, and act like one, the American people will become so thoroughly disgusted with this sort of thing after a while, that they may rise in their might and take the ballot away from him. Therefore, let the negro consider and be forewarned." The editor seemed oblivious to the pressures the Democrats could often put on black voters, but his warning was nonetheless prescient.

In the ensuing years many Populists made good on that warning, as they supported white primaries, the poll tax, and other disfranchisement measures that would eliminate blacks from the political equation in Texas. In 1900 a Populist editor in Milam County—a staunch old middle-of-the-roader—argued that a white man's primary would be "the solution of a long unsolved question, and one that will place the expressed will of the people in the ascendancy, thereby robbing the professional schemer and politician of his power on election day." Finally, in 1902, the state legislature placed a poll tax referendum before the voters of Texas.

Almost half (48 percent) of those who had voted Populist at the height of the party's power in the mid-1890s simply sat out the referendum. Many former Populists had given up on politics altogether or they felt so ambivalent about disfranchisement that they could not decide how to vote. However, of that remaining half of the old Populists who *did* participate in the referendum, almost three times as many supported the poll tax as opposed it. With half of them not voting, it is clear that a majority of Texas Populists did not cast votes for disfranchisement. But those Populists who returned to the Democratic party helped to inaugurate the "Progressive" era in southern politics by voting for the poll tax. As C. Vann Woodward has pointed out, it was to be Progressivism "for whites only."

Populism's Place in

United States History

Richard Hofstadter

THE FOLKLORE OF POPULISM

In 1955 Richard Hofstadter published an evaluation of Populism that
subsequently generated intense debate. He developed his highly critical
evaluation of the Populists by presenting them as adherents, among other
things, of a backward-looking movement, a conspiratorial view of history,
and anti-Semitism. He explained Populism in terms of a status revolution
that had shifted wealth and influence from the small towns and rural
areas to the urban and industrial areas. Hofstadter taught at Columbia
University for many years, and his books include *Social Darwinism in
American Thought* (1944), *The American Political Tradition* (1948), and
Anti-Intellectualism in American Life (1962).

The utopia of the Populists was in the past, not the future.
According to the agrarian myth, the health of the state was propor-
tionate to the degree to which it was dominated by the agricultural
class, and this assumption pointed to the superiority of an earlier age.
The Populists looked backward with longing to the lost agrarian
Eden, to the republican America of the early years of the nineteenth
century in which there were few millionaires and, as they saw it, no
beggars, when the laborer had excellent prospects and the farmer had
abundance, when statesmen still responded to the mood of the
people and there was no such thing as the money power. What they
meant—though they did not express themselves in such terms—was
that they would like to restore the conditions prevailing before the
development of industrialism and the commercialization of agriculture. It should not be surprising that they inherited the traditions of
Jacksonian democracy, that they revived the old Jacksonian cry:
"Equal Rights for All, Special Privileges for None," or that most of
the slogans of 1896 echoed the battle cries of 1836. . . .

Nature, as the agrarian tradition had it, was beneficent. The
United States was abundantly endowed with rich land and rich

From *The Age of Reform* by Richard Hofstadter, pp. 62–67, 70–71, 73, 77–78, 80,
82–83, 88, 90–91, 93. Copyright © 1955 by Richard Hofstadter. Reprinted by
permission of Alfred A. Knopf, Inc.

resources, and the "natural" consequence of such an endowment should be prosperity of the people. If the people failed to enjoy prosperity, it must be because of a harsh and arbitrary intrusion of human greed and error. . . . In assuming a lush natural order whose workings were being deranged by human laws, Populist writers were again drawing on the Jacksonian tradition, whose spokesmen also had pleaded for a proper obedience to "natural" laws as a prerequisite of social justice.

Somewhat akin to the notion of the beneficence of nature was the idea of a natural harmony of interests among the productive classes. To the Populist mind there was no fundamental conflict between the farmer and the worker, between the toiling people and the small businessman. While there might be corrupt individuals in any group, the underlying interests of the productive majority were the same; predatory behavior existed only because it was initiated and underwritten by a small parasitic minority in the highest places of power. As opposed to the idea that society consists of a number of different and frequently clashing interests—the social pluralism expressed, for instance, by Madison in the *Federalist*—the Populists adhered, less formally to be sure, but quite persistently, to a kind of social dualism: although they knew perfectly well that society was composed of a number of classes, for all practical purposes only one simple division need be considered. . . . "There are but two sides in the conflict that is being waged in this country today," declared a Populist manifesto. "On the one side are the allied hosts of monopolies, the money power, great trusts and railroad corporations, who seek the enactment of laws to benefit them and impoverish the people. On the other are the farmers, laborers, merchants, and all other people who produce wealth and bear the burdens of taxation. . . . Between these two there is no middle ground." . . . The people versus the interests, the public versus the plutocrats, the toiling multitude versus the money power—in various phrases this central antagonism was expressed. From this simple social classification it seemed to follow that once the techniques of misleading the people were exposed, victory over the money power ought to be easily accomplished, for in sheer numbers the people were overwhelming. . . .

The problems that faced the Populists assumed a delusive simplicity: the victory over injustice, the solution for all social ills, was concentrated in the crusade against a single, relatively small but immensely strong interest, the money power. "With the destruction of the money power," said Senator Peffer, "the death knell of gambling in grain and other commodities will be sounded; for the business of the worst men on earth will have been broken up, and the mainstay of the gamblers removed. It will be an easy matter, after the greater spoilsmen have been shorn of their power, to clip the wings of the little ones. Once get rid of the men who hold the country by the throat, the parasites can be easily removed." Since the old political parties were the primary means by which the people were kept wandering in the wilderness, the People's Party advocates insisted, only a new and independent political party could do this essential job. As the silver question became more prominent and the idea of a third party faded, the need for a monolithic solution became transmuted into another form: there was only one *issue* upon which the money power could really be beaten and this was the money issue. "When we have restored the money of the Constitution," said Bryan in his Cross of Gold speech, "all other necessary reforms will be possible; but . . . until this is done there is no other reform that can be accomplished."

While the conditions of victory were thus made to appear simple, they did not always appear easy, and it would be misleading to imply that the tone of Populistic thinking was uniformly optimistic. Often, indeed, a deep-lying vein of anxiety showed through. The very sharpness of the struggle, as the Populists experienced it, the alleged absence of compromise solutions and of intermediate groups in the body politic, the brutality and desperation that were imputed to the plutocracy—all these suggested that failure of the people to win the final contest peacefully could result only in a total victory for the plutocrats and total extinction of democratic institutions, possibly after a period of bloodshed and anarchy. "We are nearing a serious crisis," declared Weaver. "If the present strained relations between wealth owners and wealth producers continue much longer they will ripen into frightful disaster. This universal discontent must be quickly interpreted and its causes removed." "We meet," said the Populist platform of 1892, "in the midst of a nation brought to the verge of moral, political, and material ruin. Corruption dominates the ballot-box, the Legislatures, the Congress, and touches even the ermine of the bench. The people are demoralized. . . . The newspapers are largely subsidized or muzzled, public opinion silenced, business prostrated, homes covered with mortgages, labor impoverished, and the land concentrating in the hands of the capitalists. The urban workmen are denied the right to organize for self-protection, imported pauperized labor beats down their wages, a hireling standing army, unrecognized by our laws, is established to shoot them down, and they are rapidly degenerating into European conditions. The fruits of the toil of millions are boldly stolen to build up colossal fortunes for a few, unprecedented in the history of mankind; and the possessors of these, in turn, despise the Republic and endanger liberty." Such conditions foreboded "the destruction of civilization, or the establishment of an absolute despotism." . . .

✳

. . . There was something about the Populist imagination that loved the secret plot and the conspiratorial meeting. There was in fact a widespread Populist idea that all American history since the Civil War could be understood as a sustained conspiracy of the international money power.

The pervasiveness of this way of looking at things may be attributed to the common feeling that farmers and workers were not simply oppressed but oppressed deliberately, consciously, continuously, and with wanton malice by "the interests." It would of course be misleading to imply that the Populists stand alone in thinking of the events of their time as the results of a conspiracy. This kind of thinking frequently occurs when political and social antagonisms are sharp. Certain audiences are especially susceptible to it—particularly, I believe, those who have attained only a low level of education, whose access to information is poor, and who are so completely shut out from access to the centers of power that they feel themselves completely deprived of self-defense and subjected to unlimited manipulation by those who wield power. There are, moreover, certain types of popular movements of dissent that offer special opportunities to agitators with paranoid tendencies, who are able to make a vocational asset out of their psychic disturbances. Such persons have an opportunity to impose their own style of thought upon the movements they lead. It would of course be misleading to imply that there are no such things as conspiracies in history. Anything that partakes of political strategy may need, for a time at least, an element of secrecy, and is thus vulnerable to being dubbed conspiratorial. Corruption itself has the character of conspiracy. In this sense the Crédit Mobilier was a conspiracy, as was the Teapot Dome affair. If we tend to be too condescending to the Populists at this point, it may be necessary to remind ourselves that they had seen so much bribery and corruption, particularly on the part of the railroads, that they had before them a convincing model of the management of affairs through conspiratorial behavior. Indeed, what makes conspiracy theories so widely acceptable is that they usually contain a germ of truth. But there is a great difference between locating conspiracies *in* history and saying that history *is*, in effect, a conspiracy, between singling out those conspiratorial acts that do on occasion occur and weaving a vast fabric of social explanation out of nothing but skeins of evil plots. . . .

Nevertheless, when these qualifications have been taken into account, it remains true that Populist thought showed an unusually strong tendency to account for relatively impersonal events in highly personal terms. An overwhelming sense of grievance does not find satisfactory expression in impersonal explanations, except among those with a well-developed tradition of intellectualism. It is the city, after all, that is the home of intellectual complexity. The farmer lived in isolation from the great world in which his fate was actually decided. He was accused of being unusually suspicious, and certainly his situation, trying as it was, made thinking in impersonal terms difficult. Perhaps the rural middle-class leaders of Populism (this was a movement of farmers, but it was not led by farmers) had more to do than the farmer himself with the cast of Populist thinking. At any rate, Populist thought often carries one into a world in which the simple virtues and unmitigated villainies of a rural melodrama have been projected on a national and even an international scale. In Populist thought the farmer is not a speculating business-man, victimized by the risk economy of which he is a part, but rather a wounded yeoman, preyed upon by those who are alien to the life of folkish virtue. A villain was needed, marked with the unmistakable stigmata of the villains of melodrama, and the more remote he was from the familiar scene, the more plausibly his villainies could be exaggerated. . . .

One feature of the Populist conspiracy theory that has been generally overlooked is its frequent link with a kind of rhetorical anti-Semitism. The slight current of anti-Semitism that existed in the United States before the 1890's had been associated with problems of money and credit. During the closing years of the century it grew noticeably. While the jocose and rather heavy-handed anti-Semitism that can be found in Henry Adams's letters of the 1890's shows that this prejudice existed outside Populist literature, it was chiefly Populist writers who expressed that identification of the Jew with the usurer and the "international gold ring" which was the central theme of the American anti-Semitism of the age. The omnipresent symbol of Shylock can hardly be taken in itself as evidence of anti-Semitism, but the frequent references to the House of Rothschild make it clear that for many silverites the Jew was an organic part of the conspiracy theory of history. Coin Harvey's Baron Rothe was clearly meant to be Rothschild; his Rogasner (Ernest Seyd?) was a dark figure out of the coarsest anti-Semitic tradition. "You are very wise in your way," Rogasner is told at the climax of the tale, "the commercial way, inbred through generations. The politic, scheming, devious way, inbred through generations also." One of the cartoons in the effectively illustrated *Coin's Financial School* showed a map of the world dominated by the tentacles of an octopus at the site of the British Isles, labeled: "Rothschilds." In Populist demonology, anti-Semitism and Anglophobia went hand in hand. . . .

It would be easy to misstate the character of Populist anti-Semitism or to exaggerate its intensity. For Populist anti-Semitism was entirely verbal. It was a mode of expression, a rhetorical style, not a tactic or a program. It did not lead to exclusion laws, much less to riots or pogroms. There were, after all, relatively few Jews in the United States in the late 1880's and early 1890's, most of them remote from the areas of Populist strength. It is one thing, however, to say that this prejudice did not go beyond a certain symbolic usage, quite another to say that a people's choice of symbols is of no significance. Populist anti-Semitism does have its importance—chiefly as a symptom of a certain ominous credulity in the Populist mind. It is not too much to say that the Greenback-Populist tradition activated most of what we have of modern popular anti-Semitism in the United States. . . .

✳

The conspiratorial theory and the associated Anglophobic and Judophobic feelings were part of a larger complex of fear and suspicion of the stranger that haunted, and still tragically haunts, the nativist American mind. This feeling, though hardly confined to Populists and Bryanites, was nonetheless exhibited by them in a particularly virulent form. Everyone remote and alien was distrusted and hated—even Americans, if they happened to be city people. The old agrarian conception of the city as the home of moral corruption reached a new pitch. Chicago was bad; New York, which housed the Wall Street bankers, was farther away and worse; London was still farther away and still worse. This traditional distrust grew stronger as the cities grew larger, and as they were filled with immigrant aliens. As early as 1885 the Kansas preacher Josiah Strong had published *Our Country*, a book widely read in the West, in which the cities were discussed as a great problem of the future, much as though they were some kind of monstrous malignant growths on the body politic. Hamlin Garland recalled that when he first visited Chicago, in the late 1880's, having never seen a town larger than Rockford, Illinois, he naturally assumed that it swarmed with thieves. "If the city is miles across," he wondered, "how am I to get from the railway station to my hotel without being assaulted?" While such extreme fears could be quieted by some contact with the city, others were actually confirmed—especially when the farmers were confronted with city prices. Nativist prejudices were equally aroused by immigration, for which urban manufacturers, with their insatiable demand for labor, were blamed. "We have become the world's melting pot," wrote Thomas E. Watson. "The scum of creation has been dumped on us. Some of our principal cities are more foreign than American. The most dangerous and corrupting hordes of the Old World have invaded us. The vice and crime which they have planted in our midst are sickening and terrifying. What brought these Goths and Vandals to our shores? The manufacturers are mainly to blame. They wanted cheap labor: and they didn't care a curse how much harm to our future might be the consequence of their heartless policy." . . .

It is no coincidence . . . that Populism and jingoism grew concurrently in the United States during the 1890's. The rising mood of intolerant nationalism was a nationwide thing, certainly not confined to the regions of Populist strength; but among no stratum of the population was it stronger than among the Populists. Moreover it was on jingoist issues that the Populist and Bryanite sections of the country, with the aid of the yellow press and many political leaders, achieved that rapport with the masses of the cities which they never succeeded in getting on economic issues. Even conservative politicians sensed that, whatever other grounds of harmony were lacking between themselves and the populace of the hinterland, grounds for unity could be found in war. . . .

. . . The situation of the oppressed Cubans was one with which the Populist elements in the country could readily identify themselves, and they added their voice to the general cry throughout the country for an active policy of intervention. After the defeat of Bryan, popular frustration in the silver areas, blocked on domestic issues, seemed to find expression in the Cuban question. Here at last was a point at which the goldbugs could be vanquished. Neither the big business and banking community nor the Cleveland and McKinley administrations had much sympathy with the crusading fever that pervaded the country at large, and there were bitter mutual recriminations between conservative and Populist papers. Wall Street was accused of a characteristic indifference to the interests of humanity; the Populists in return were charged with favoring war as a cover under which they could smuggle in an inflationary policy. One thing seems clear: "most of the leading Congressional backers of intervention in Cuba represented southern and western states where Populism and silver were strongest." And it appears that one of the reasons why McKinley was advised by many influential Republicans to yield to the popular demand for war was the common fear, still meaningful in 1898, that the Democrats would go into the next presidential election with the irresistible slogan of Free Silver and Free Cuba as its battle cry. Jingoism was confined to no class, section, or party; but the Populist areas stood in the vanguard, and their pressure went far to bring about a needless war. . . .

As we review these aspects of Populist emotion, an odd parallel obtrudes itself. Where else in American thought during this period do we find this militancy and nationalism, these apocalyptic forebodings and drafts of world-political strategies, this hatred of big businessmen, bankers, and trusts, these fears of immigrants and urban workmen, even this occasional toying with anti-Semitic rhetoric? We find them, curiously enough, most conspicuous among a group of men who are in all obvious respects the antithesis of the Populists. During the late 1880's and the '90's there emerged in the eastern United States a small imperialist elite representing, in general, the same type that had once been Mugwumps, whose spokesmen were such solid and respectable gentlemen as Henry and Brooks Adams, Theodore Roosevelt, Henry Cabot Lodge, John Hay, and Albert J. Beveridge. . . .

Not only were the gentlemen of this imperialist elite better read and better fed than the Populists, but they despised them. This strange convergence of unlike social elements on similar ideas has its explanation, I believe, in this: both the imperialist elite and the Populists had been bypassed and humiliated by the advance of industrialism, and both were rebelling against the domination of the country by industrial and financial capitalists. The gentlemen wanted the power and status they felt due them, which had been taken away from their class and type by the *arriviste* manufacturers and railroaders and the all-too-potent banking houses. The Populists wanted a restoration of agrarian profits and popular government. Both elements found themselves impotent and deprived in an industrial culture and balked by a common enemy. On innumerable matters they disagreed, but both were strongly nationalistic, and amid the despairs and anxieties of the nineties both became ready for war if that would unseat or even embarrass the moneyed powers, or better still if it would topple the established political structure and open new opportunities for the leaders of disinherited farmers or for ambitious gentlemen. But if there seems to be in this situation any suggestion of a forerunner or analogue of modern authoritarian movements, it should by no means be exaggerated. The age was more innocent and more fortunate than ours, and by comparison with the grimmer realities of the twentieth century many of the events of the nineties take on a comic-opera quality. What came in the end was only a small war and a quick victory; when the farmers and the gentlemen finally did coalesce in politics, they produced only the genial reforms of Progressivism; and the man on the white horse turned out to be just a graduate of the Harvard boxing squad, equipped with an immense bag of platitudes, and quite willing to play the democratic game.

Lawrence Goodwyn

THE IRONY OF POPULISM

Lawrence Goodwyn's interpretation of Populism stands in sharp contrast to Hofstadter's. Goodwyn saw it as a great democratic movement that addressed fundamental problems accompanying the emergence of corporate capitalism. The Populists refused to embrace the notion that the American economic system ensured progress and prosperity. From their own experiences, they knew it did not. According to Goodwyn, Populists offered the last democratic alternative to the corporate culture that has dominated twentieth-century America.

Populism in America was not the sub-treasury plan, not the greenback heritage, not the Omaha Platform. It was not, at bottom, even the People's Party. The meaning of the agrarian revolt was its cultural assertion as a people's movement of mass democratic aspiration. Its animating essence pulsed at every level of the ambitious structure of cooperation: in the earnest probings of people bent on discovering a way to free themselves from the killing grip of the credit system ("The suballiance is a schoolroom"); in the joint-notes of the landed, given in the name of themselves and the landless ("The brotherhood stands united"); in the pride of discovery of their own legitimacy ("The merchants are listening when the County Trade Committee talks"); and in the massive and emotional effort to save the cooperative dream itself ("The Southern Exchange Shall Stand"). The democratic core of Populism was visible in the suballiance resolutions of inquiry into the patterns of economic exploitation ("find out and apply the remedy"); in the mile-long Alliance wagon trains ("The Fourth of July is Alliance Day"); in the sprawling summer encampments ("A pentecost of politics"); and, perhaps most tellingly, in the latent generosity unlocked by the culture of the movement itself, revealed in the capacity of those who had little, to empathize with those who had less ("We extend to the Knights of Labor our hearty sympathy in

Excerpted from *The Populist Moment: A Short History of the Agrarian Revolt in America* by Lawrence Goodwyn, pp. 294–310. Copyright © 1978 by Lawrence Goodwyn. Reprinted by permission of Oxford University Press, Inc.

their manly struggle against monopolistic oppression," and "The Negro people are part of the people and must be treated as such").

While each of these moments occurred in the 1890's, and have practical and symbolic meaning because they did occur, Populism in America was not an egalitarian achievement. Rather, it was an egalitarian attempt, a beginning. If it stimulated human generosity, it did not, before the movement itself was destroyed, create a settled culture of generosity. Though Populists attempted to break out of the received heritage of white supremacy, they necessarily, as white Americans, did so within the very ethos of white supremacy. At both a psychological and political level, some Populists were more successful than others in coping with the pervasive impact of the inherited caste system. Many were not successful at all. This reality extended to a number of pivotal social and political questions beside race—sectional and party loyalties, the intricacies of power relationships embedded in the monetary system, and the ways of achieving a politics supportive of popular democracy itself. In their struggle, Populists learned a great truth: cultures are hard to change. Their attempts to do so, however, provides a measure of the seriousness of their movement.

Populism thus cannot be seen as a moment of triumph, but as a moment of democratic promise. It was a spirit of egalitarian hope, expressed in the actions of two million beings—not in the prose of a platform, however creative, and not, ultimately, even in the third party, but in a self-generated culture of collective dignity and individual longing. As a movement of people, it was expansive, passionate, flawed, creative—above all, enhancing in its assertion of human striving. That was Populism in the nineteenth century.

But the agrarian revolt was more than a nineteenth-century experience. It was a demonstration of how people of a society containing a number of democratic forms could labor in pursuit of freedom, of how people could generate their own democratic culture in order to challenge the received hierarchical culture. The agrarian revolt demonstrated how intimidated people could create for themselves the psychological space to dare to aspire grandly—and to dare to be autonomous in the presence of powerful new institutions of economic concentration and cultural regimentation. The Omaha Platform gave political and symbolic substance to the people's movement, but it was the idea animating the movement itself that represents the Populist achievement. That idea—at the very heart of the movement culture—was a profoundly simple one: the Populists believed they could work together to be free individually. In their institutions of self-help, Populists developed and acted upon a crucial democratic insight: to be encouraged to surmount rigid cultural inheritances and to act with autonomy and self-confidence, individual people need the psychological support of other people. The people need to "see themselves" experimenting in new democratic forms.

In their struggle to build their cooperative commonwealth, in their "joint notes of the brotherhood," in their mass encampments, their rallies, their wagon trains, their meals for thousands, the people of Populism saw themselves. In their earnest suballiance meetings—those "unsteepled places of worship"—they saw themselves. From these places of their own came "the spirit that permeates this great reform movement." In the world they created, they fulfilled the democratic promise in the only way it can be fulfilled—by people acting in democratic ways in their daily lives. Temporary victory or defeat was never the central element, but simply human striving always was, as three epic moments of Populism vividly demonstrated in the summers of 1888, 1889, 1890. These moments were, respectively, the day to save the exchange in Texas, Alliance Day in Atlanta, when 20,000 farmers massed against the jute trust, and Alliance Day in Winfield, Kansas. Though L. L. Polk made a stirring speech to the Kansans on July 4, 1890, in Winfield, what he said was far less important than what his listeners were seeing. The wagon trains of farm families entering Cowley County from one direction alone stretched for miles. In this manner, the framers saw their own movement: the Alliance was the people, and the people were together. As a result, they dared to listen to themselves individually, and to each other, rather than passively follow the teachings of the received hierarchical culture. Their own movement was their guide. Fragile as it was, it nevertheless opened up possibilities of an autonomous democratic life. Because this happened, the substance of American Populism went beyond the political creed embedded in the People's Party, beyond the evocative images of Alliance lecturers and reform editors, beyond even the idea of freedom itself. The Populist essence was less abstract: it was an assertion of how people

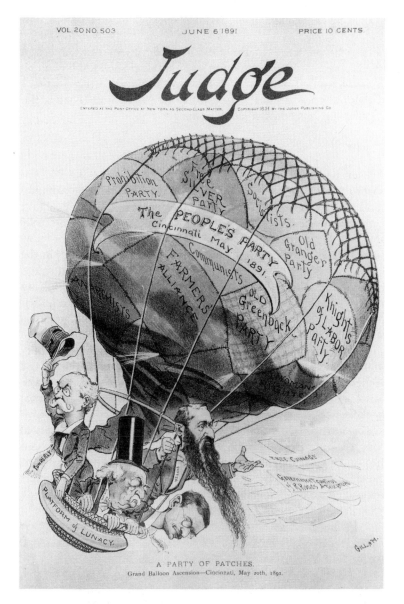

VOL. 20 NO. 503   JUNE 6 1891   PRICE 10 CENTS

"A Party of Patches. Grand Balloon Ascension, Cincinnati, May 20th, 1891." This cartoon, from the popular satirical magazine *Judge*, illustrates the eastern press' persistent attempt to belittle Populism as representing a "platform of lunacy." Among those in the balloon basket are Terence V. Powderly, "Sockless" Jerry Simpson, and William A. Peffer. Although hostile caricatures, the likenesses are recognizable. (*Kansas State Historical Society*) can *act* in the name of the idea of freedom. At root, American Populism was a demonstration of what authentic political life can be in a functioning democracy. The "brotherhood of the Alliance" attempted to address the question of how to live. That is the Populist legacy to the twentieth century.

✳

In their own time, the practical shortcoming of the Populist political effort was one the agrarian reformers did not fully comprehend: their attempt to construct a national farmer-labor coalition came before the fledgling American labor movement was internally prepared for mass insurgent politics. Alliance lecturers did not know how to reach the laboring masses in the nation's cities, and, in the 1890's, the labor movement could not effectively reach them either. Though a capacity for germane economic analysis and a growing sense of self developed in those years among American workers, their advances had not, by the time Populism arrived, been translated on a mass scale into practical political consciousness. In the 1890's, growing numbers of American workers were desperately, sometimes angrily, seeking a way out of their degradation, but the great majority of them carried their emotions with them as they voted for the major parties—or did not vote at all. By the time American industrial workers finally found a successful organizing tactic—the sit-down strike—in the 1930's, a sizable proportion of America's agricultural poor had been levered off the land and millions more had descended into numbing helplessness after generations of tenantry. Thus, when the labor movement was ready, or partly ready, the mass of farmers no longer were. That fact constitutes perhaps the single greatest irony punctuating the history of the American working class.

As for the farmers, their historical moment came in the late 1880's. They built their cooperatives, sang their songs, marched, and dreamed of a day of dignity for the "plain people."

But their movement was defeated, and the moment passed. Following the collapse of the People's Party, farm tenantry increased steadily and consistently, decade after decade, from 25 per cent in 1880, to 28 per cent in 1890, to 36 per cent in 1900, and to 38 per cent in 1910. The 180 counties in the South where at least half the farms had been tenant-operated in 1880 increased to 890 by 1935. Tenantry also spread over the fertile parts of the corn belt as an increasing amount of Midwestern farmland came to be held by mortgage companies. Some 49 per cent of Iowa farms were tenant-operated in 1935 and the land so organized amounted to 60 per cent of the farm acreage in the state. In 1940, 48 per cent of Kansas farms were tenant-operated. The comparable figure for all Southern farms was 46 per cent. But in the South, those who had avoided tenantry were scarcely in better condition than the sharecroppers. An authoritative report written by a distinguished Southern sociologist in the 1930's included the information that over half of all landowners had "short-term debts to meet current expenses on the crop." The total for both tenants and landowners shackled to the furnishing merchant reached 70 per cent of all farmers in the South. As one historian put it, the crop lien had "blanketed" the entire region. As in the Gilded Age, the system operated in a way that kept millions living literally on the wages of peonage.

✳

If the farmers of the Alliance suffered severely, what of the agrarian crusade itself? What of the National Farmers Alliance and Industrial Union, that earnest aggregation of men and women who had striven for a "cooperative commonwealth"? And what of the People's Party? Why, precisely, did it all happen, and what is its historical meaning?

As agrarian spokesmen were forever endeavoring to make clear to Americans . . . the cooperative movement taught the farmers "who and where the enemies of their interests were." The Alliancemen who learned that lesson first were the men who had been sent out by the cooperatives to make contact with the surrounding commercial world. . . . Though they possessed different political views and different sectional memories, they were altered in much the same way by the searing experience of participating in, and leading, a thwarted hope. They became desperate, defensively aggressive, angry, and creative. They reacted with boycotts, with plans for mutual self-help insurance societies, with the world's first large-scale cooperatives, and with the sub-treasury plan. The marketing and purchasing agents who learned the lessons of cooperation became both movement politicians and ideological men.

They built their cooperatives, developed new political ideas, and fashioned a democratic agenda for the nation. The destruction of the cooperatives by the American banking system was a decisive blow, for it weakened the interior structure of democracy that was the heart of the cooperative movement itself. Though, in one final burst of creativity, the agrarian radicals were able to fashion their third party, that moment in Omaha in the summer of 1892 was the movement's high tide. There was no way a political institution—a mere party—could sustain the day-to-day democratic ethos at the heart of the Alliance cooperative.

And here, among these threads woven through the tapestry of the agrarian revolt, reposes the central historical meaning of Populism. It would, perhaps, constitute a fitting epitaph for the earnest farmers of the Alliance to place these threads in relation to one another and review them a final time. For while they say much about the meaning of the agrarian revolt, they also reveal a great deal about the world Americans live in today and—most important of all—about how modern people have been culturally organized to think about that world. . . .

If the central task of democratic reform involves finding a way to oppose the received hierarchical culture with a newly created democratic culture, and if, as the Alliance experience reveals, progress toward this culminating climax necessarily must build upon prior stages of political and organizational evolution that have the effect of altering the political perspectives of millions of people, then democratic movements, to be successful, clearly require a high order of sequential achievement. Towering over all other tasks is the need to find a way to overcome deeply ingrained patterns of deference permeating the entire social order. For this to happen, individual self-respect obviously must take life on a mass scale. At the onset of this process for the Populists, small battles (the bulking of cotton) and larger battles (the war with the jute trust) needed to be fought and won so that the farmers attained the beginnings, at least, of collective self-confidence. Arrayed against these democratic dynamics was the continuing cultural authority embedded in received habits of thought, and the readily available ways that the press, the public school, and the church could refortify these inherited patterns. Against such powerful counter-influences, the only defense available to a democratic movement such as the Alliance lay within its own organizational institutions. Interior lines of communication were essential to maintain the embryonic and necessarily fragile new culture of mass self-respect engendered by the reform movement itself. In the absence of such continuing and self-generated democratic cultural influences, the organizers of popular movements inevitably face loss of control over their own destiny. They will be overwhelmed, not by their own party's politicians per se, or by passing corporate lobbies, but, more centrally, by the inherited culture itself. Their dreams will vanish into the maw of memory, as their impoverished constituencies, battered on all sides by cultural inducements to conform to received habits, gradually do precisely that. As the Alliance organizers understood, mass democratic movements, to endure, require mass democratic organization. Only in this way can individual people find the means to encourage one another through their own channels of communication—channels that are free from the specialized influences of the hierarchical society they seek to reshape.

In the years in which the National Farmers Alliance and Industrial Union created, through its cooperative crusade, the movement culture of Populism, this interior channel of communication was centered in the Alliance lecturing system. It was this instrument of self-organization that permitted the hopes of masses of farmers to be carried forward to their spokesmen and allowed the response of the same spokesmen to go back to the "industrial millions." Democratic pressure from below—from crop-mortgaged farmers desperate to escape their furnishing merchants—emboldened the early Alliance leadership to undertake the "joint-note" plan within the centralized statewide cooperative. . . .

As the farmers labored to create a workable infrastructure of mass cooperation in 1887–92, the opposition of the American banking and corporate communities gradually brought home to Alliance leaders, and to masses of farmers, the futility of the cooperative effort—in the absence of fundamental restructuring of the monetary system. The Allianceman who was forced by events to learn these lessons first—Charles Macune—was the first to brood about this dilemma, and the first to formulate a democratic solution, the sub-treasury land and loan system.

The status that the sub-treasury plan came to have in reform ranks is revealing. For, to put the matter as quietly as possible, Macune's plan was democratic. Or, to put it in archaic political terminology, it was breathtakingly radical. Under the sub-treasury, the power of private moneylenders to decide who "qualified" for crop loans and who did not would have been ended. Similarly, the enormous influence of moneylenders over interest rates would also have been circumscribed. The contracted currency, the twenty-five year decline in volume and prices, would have been ended in one abrupt—and democratic—restructuring. The prosperity levels of 1865 would have been reclaimed in one inflationary—and democratic—swoop. Most important of all, the sub-treasury addressed a problem that has largely defeated twentieth-century reformers, namely, the maldistribution of income within American society. By removing some of the more exploitive features embedded in the inherited monetary system, the sub-treasury would have achieved substantive redistribution of income from creditors to debtors. Put simply, a more democratic monetary system would have produced a more democratic sharing of the nation's total economic production. The "producing classes," no longer quite so systematically deprived of the fruits of their efforts, would have gotten a bit more of the fruits. Hierarchical forms of power and privilege in America would have undergone a significant measure of rearrangement. . . .

The shrinking parameters of twentieth-century reform thought thus help to underscore the Populist achievement. How was it that so many people in the 1890's came to associate themselves with such an inadmissible idea as the sub-treasury plan? We may be secure in the knowledge that the Populists were not "smarter" than modern Americans. Nor did it happen just because "times were hard." It happened because Populists had constructed within their own movement a specific kind of democratic environment that is not normally present in America. In the face of all the counterattacks employed by the nation's metropolitan press, culturally in step as it was with the needs of "sound-money" bankers, the sub-treasury plan was brought home to millions of Americans as a function of the movement culture of Populism. This culture was comprised of many ingredients—most visible being the infrastructure of local, county, state, and national Alliance organizations. But this was surface. More real were all of the shared experiences within the Alliance—the elaborate encampments, the wagon trains, the meals for thousands—and more real still were the years of laboring together in the suballiances to form trade committees, to negotiate with merchants, to build the cooperatives to new heights, to discuss the causes of adversity, and, in time, to come to the new movement folkway, the "Alliance Demand." The Demands took on intense practical meaning, first at Cleburne in 1886 and later as the St. Louis Platform of 1889, the Ocala Demands of 1890, and the Omaha Platform of 1892. Because these multiple methods of interior communication existed, Alliancemen found a way to believe in their own movement, rather than to respond to what the larger society said about their movement. In sum, they built insulation for themselves against the received hierarchical culture. Because they did so, the farmers of the Alliance overcame, for a time, their deference; they gained, for a time, a new plateau of self-respect that permitted autonomous democratic politics. . . .

But while these conclusions are self-evident in a political sense, and explain how the People's Party happened, they conceal an underlying organizational flaw that eventually undermined the reform movement. For while the cooperative idea awaited the enactment of a new and more democratic system of industrial commerce—the passage by a Populist Congress of the subtreasury system—the basic cooperative structure of the Alliance gradually disintegrated. . . . The underlying cause was everywhere the same: lack of access to credit. But in some places, where especially favorable circumstances temporarily bridged the credit problem, cooperatives were destroyed by raw applications of commercial power. The highly successful multi-state livestock marketing cooperative, conceived by Kansans and exported to Missouri, Nebraska, and the Dakotas, was killed by the simple decision of the Livestock Commission in Chicago to refuse to deal with the farmer cooperative. The decision was justified on the ground that the cooperative, in distributing profits to its membership, violated the "anti-rebate" rule of the commission! . . .

All important sectors of commercial America opposed the cooperative movement, not only banks and commission agencies, but grain elevator companies, railroads, mortgage companies, and, perhaps needless to add, furnishing merchants. The National Farmers Alliance itself persisted as an institution, but the cooperative purpose that sustained the personal day-to-day dedication of members to their own institution did not persist. Once the politics of the sub-treasury had been orchestrated through the lecturing system in order to bring on the new party, the lecturing system itself withered. The reason was a basic one; the lecturers no longer had anything substantive to lecture about. The Alliance could no longer save the farmers; only the new party could bring the needed structural changes in the American economic system.

"Lecturing" thus became a function of the People's Party. The new lecturers who provided the continuing internal communications link within the movement culture were the reform editors. The National Reform Press Association was to the People's Party what the lecturing system was to the Alliance, the interior adhesive of the democratic movement. The flaw in all this was the simple fact that the National Reform Press Association did not have an organized constituency, as Alliance lecturers had earlier possessed. Within the People's Party, as it organized itself, there could be no continuing democratic dialogue, no give and take of question and answer, of perceived problem and attempted solution, between rank-and-file members and elected spokesmen, such as had given genuine democratic meaning to the days of cooperative effort within the Alliance. Rather, reform editors asserted and defended the Populist vision, and their subscribers, in organizational isolation, received these views in a passive state, as it were. Such a dynamic undermines the very prospect of sustaining a democratic culture grounded—as it must be to be democratic—in individual self-respect and mass self-confidence. Individual self-respect requires self-assertion, the performance of acts, as farmers performed in their suballiance business meetings, in their country trade committees, in their statewide marketing and purchasing cooperatives. But, in vivid contrast, the passive reading of reform newspapers fortified inherited patterns of deference. Thus the democratic intensity of the People's Party declined over time, because means were not found to sustain democratic input from the mass of participating Populists. In this fundamental political sense, the movement culture of Populism was not, and could not be, as intense as the movement culture originally generated within the Alliance cooperative crusade. The people were the same, but a crucial democratic element was no longer present.

The original Alliance organizers sensed this. They labored long and hard to keep the Alliance organization intact, even after they had successfully formed the People's Party. But within the intellectual traditions of reform theory in western culture, Alliancemen found few nineteenth-century models to guide them in this organizational endeavor. . . .

. . . The self-organized people of the Alliance would serve as "a mighty base of support" for Populist candidates when they legislated democratically and a strong admonishing force when they did not. By that means the people would retain control over their own movement and not surrender it to their own politicians. While this view incorporated a sophisticated understanding of the essential ingredients of mass democracy, after the destruction of the cooperatives the organizational means to keep the Alliance alive unfortunately did not exist. The Alliance founders spoke of the continuing "educational" value of the order as a grassroots forum for political debate and they spoke of "the community" of the Alliance, sometimes in far-ranging terms that incorporated advanced ideas on women's rights and democratic human relations generally. But a community cannot persist simply because some of its members have a strong conviction that it ought to persist. A community, even one seeing itself as a "brotherhood" and "sister-hood," needs to have something fundamental to do, an organic purpose beyond "fellowship" that reaffirms the community's need to continue its collective effort. And this, after the collapse of the cooperatives, the Alliance failed to have. . . .

The era of the People's Party, therefore, may be seen as a period of gradual decline in organized democratic energy in Gilded Age politics. To be sure, there were vibrant rallies; spectacular editorials in the journalistic flagships of the Reform Press Association; moments of heady victory; and intense, colorful, and often bitter campaigns. But though all of these things were done in the name of the people's movement, it no longer, in a real sense, *was* a people's movement: the third party had no interior mass base as its core; it had only individual adherents who voted for it on election day.

In democratic terms, the structural weakness of the People's Party evolved from the failure of its organizers, in the founding convention of 1892, to understand that the third party, to be authentically democratic, had to be organized as a mass party with a mass membership. It was organized instead, like all large American parties before and since, as a representative party, with elite cadres of party regulars dominating the organizational machinery from precinct to national convention. The People's Party spoke, rather more tellingly than most American parties have ever done, in the name of the people. But in structural terms the People's Party was not made up of the people; it was comprised of party elites. Its ultimate failure, therefore, was conceptual—a failure on a theoretical level of democratic analysis.

Nevertheless, despite these necessary qualifications the People's Party was, thanks to the sheer emotional and organizational intensity that brought it into being, a political institution of unique passion and vigor in American history. There were, however, always significant gradations of participation in the movement culture. For those who had learned their cooperative lessons most thoroughly, the original Alliance dream sustained itself throughout the entire life of the third party crusade. But upon all those who had participated in these experiences in less vivid ways the pull of the received culture inexorably worked its will. And in many new Alliance states where the third party was numerically small Populism became ideologically fragile as well. In the state that led the farmers to the Alliance, Texas, and in the state that led the Alliance to the People's Party, Kansas, the agrarian dream possessed continuing, though gradually diminishing, democratic intensity. It maintained for a while an interesting thrust in Georgia, Alabama, California, and South Dakota as well. Everywhere else the democratic vision had, by 1894, begun to grow noticeably weaker and, in some places, had begun to wither with some abruptness. . . .

Long before that moment of self-destruction in 1896 the movement's organizational source, the National Farmers Alliance, having rendered its final service to farmers by creating the new party of reform in 1892, had moved into the wings of the agrarian revolt. In so doing, the Alliance transferred to the political arena the broad aims it had failed to accomplish through its cooperative crusade. The organizational boundaries of the People's Party were fixed by the previous limits of the Alliance. The greenback doctrines of the Alliance were imbibed by those who participated in the cooperative crusade, but by very few other Americans. Though several Western mining states that were not deeply affected by Alliance organizers achieved a measure of one-plank silverism, and Nebraska produced its uniquely issueless shadow movement, no American state not organized by the Alliance developed a strong

Populist presence. The fate of the parent institution and its political offspring was inextricably linked.

The largest citizen institution of nineteenth-century America, the National Farmers Alliance and Industrial Union persisted through the 1890's, defending the core doctrines of greenbackism within the People's Party and keeping to the fore the dream of a "new day for the industrial millions." Its mass roots severed by the cooperative failure at the very moment its hopes were carried forward by the People's Party, the Alliance passed from view at the end of the century. Its sole material legacy was the "Alliance warehouse" weathering in a thousand towns scattered across the American South and West. In folklore, it came to be remembered that the Alliance had been "a great movement" and that it had killed itself because it had "gone into politics." But at its zenith, it reached into forty-three states and territories and, for a moment, changed the lives and the consciousness of millions of Americans. As a mass democratic institution, the saga of the Alliance is unique in American history.

In cooperative defeat and political defeat, the farmers of the Alliance and the People's Party lost more than their movement, they lost the community they had created. They lost more than their battle on the money question, they lost their chance for a measure of autonomy. They lost more than their People's Party; they lost the hopeful, embryonic culture of generosity that their party represented. The stakes, as the Alliance founders had always known, were high, for the agrarian dream was truly a large one—a democratic society grounded in mass dignity. . . .

Bruce Palmer

A CRITIQUE FOR
INDUSTRIAL CAPITALISM

Although Bruce Palmer agreed with much of Lawrence Goodwyn's interpretation, he identified an inherent weakness in the southern Populists' ideology. They subscribed to a republican tradition that rested on the notion of a simple market economy, which encompassed a capitalist system consisting of small producers who owned their own land and businesses and reaped the profits that they derived from their labor. But by the 1890s, the United States had become a complex market economy in which most people no longer enjoyed the status of independent producers. To have developed a more viable reform program, Palmer concluded, the Populists would have had to abandon the concept of a simple market economy and have moved to a system that involved far greater state control of the economy. Professor Palmer teaches history at the University of Houston at Clear Lake City.

For all the Southern Populists . . . the proper society bore a great resemblance to the rural, agricultural communities in which most of them lived or had grown up. Farmers, or at least producers, formed its center, and nearly all its members earned their living by producing or facilitating the production and distribution of some form of tangible wealth. While individual economic competition and the market system for the most part went unchallenged, personal relationships and moral and religious precept more importantly than Adam Smith's invisible hand and the local police force appeared to delineate and guide the social and economic life of the community. The Southerners distrusted institutions and persons who dealt with intangible things such as credit, interest, and some kinds of written law, and suspected those with whom they had impersonal relationships.

The Southern Populists' ways of thinking and writing about the world they found around them, and its ideal alternative, were

Reprinted from *"Man Over Money": The Southern Populist Critique of American Capitalism* by Bruce Palmer, pp. 199–221. Copyright © 1980 by The University of North Carolina Press. Used by permission of the author and the publisher.

not only the heritage of the community in which they lived or had been raised but also reflected it. The Jeffersonian-Jacksonian metaphors dealt with and described a relatively homogeneous and harmonious rural society which knew little of railroad corporations, Andrew Carnegie, Standard Oil, or an industrial proletariat. Their religious and moral metaphors and imagery were premised on and reflected the assumption that society was best organized and governed on a personal and moral basis. The producerite metaphor, harder to pin down than these two and partaking of both of them, described a society whose most important function was the production of tangible wealth and in which the physical labor involved in producing that wealth was the most valuable and virtuous activity one could undertake. The Southern Populists used these metaphors and images which so well described their experience in a southern, rural, evangelical Protestant community to criticize another world they found developing around them—an impersonal, amoral, urban-centered, nonsouthern, industrial society—and to project their reform plans for a new social order.

. . . While [the] differences [among the reform plans of the Southern Populists] had a considerable impact on the Populists' political behavior, for the most part the differences did not affect the reformers' vision of the proper social order, because they all shared the critique of financial and industrial capitalist society which provided the impetus for their varying reform demands. All the Southern Populists, for instance, frequently and vigorously attacked cities, the home of this new society. Bringing to bear on the city the Jeffersonian, the producerite, and the religious and moral metaphors and imagery, the reformers found a number of discrepancies between it and the society they wanted. Kid-gloved, silk-hatted men lived in the city and ran politics. They did no hard work, produced no wealth, yet controlled the country. The town's dominance of the countryside, like the nonproducer's dominance of the producer, stood the proper order of society on its head because the town ultimately depended on the countryside for survival. Some Southern Populists held the failure of existing society to reflect this truth responsible for many of America's problems. An Alabama Populist pointed out that the huge land holdings of aliens and American corporations, having "driven thousands of people out of the country into towns and cities to compete with skilled labor and caused strikes, lock outs, riots, and bloodshed, and caused our nation to be filled with tramps and paupers," brought not only the decline of the countryside but unrest in the cities. . . .

Part of this hostility toward a new urban society obviously reflected the attitude of a farming population which accurately perceived a relative, and often absolute, decline of its wealth and social status. Some of their disapproval did spring from the new middle-class morality. . . . But the growing tempo of life in an increasingly impersonal and amoral industrial society was no fiction. In fact, for the Southern Populists the most serious consequence of this was not the decline of rural society but the human toll it took. The exploitation involved in nineteenth-century industrial capitalism appalled them. . . .

Charity offered no solution to the suffering; the problem lay with the system. "When plutocracy defrauds the people of this nation out of a billion dollars of value a year through the law, it is business," observed a North Carolinian. When they established soup kitchens, "it is charity." The idea of charity outraged the editor of the *Southern Mercury*. Charity, he wrote in 1895, was "the crust the robber gives back to the man he has robbed. Charity is an apology for justice, and apology will not pay the wages of the toiler, nor feed the hungry in comfort." . . . The Southern Populists often felt, in fact, that American industrial society depended on the destruction, or at least the complete degradation, of the large mass of people. It had to be reorganized and governed so that it served not just a few but the many. "If civilization is worth anything to humanity," maintained another Georgia editor, "its blessings should be extended to all . . . in proportion to their honest, earnest efforts to attain them. This is not so now." The Southern Populists could not accept industrial development at the cost of millions of poor.

The rule of thumb for correcting these abuses cut straight to the heart of the problem. As an Alabama editor wrote, "any nation that holds property rights above human rights is barbarian." A society in which the rush for gain and property exceeded acceptable limits and included the destruction of human rights the Southern Populists felt was neither proper nor decent. "Our people should be greater than our money, our commerce, or anything else in our America.". . .

The Southern Populists also revealed their recognition of the enemy in their demand that society protect the weak from the strong. It provided a focus for both their critique and their desire for a new social order. Human history, a Texas editor noted, told the story of how the strong crushed the weak "in the mad race for place and power and pelf. Over the bodies of its victims have been built the great and mighty wonders of the world.". . .

When they limited themselves to a discussion of the ideal system of production and exchange between individuals, the Southern Populists often lamented the decline of competition. Almost all of them, however, opposed using competition as a guide for humanity's wider social life and development. "Under a system where every man is for himself," wrote an Arkansas Populist, "the devil will get most of them." Few could choose consciously to accept competition if it meant that the struggle to survive destroyed most people. . . . The southern reformers agreed with the Texas Populist who wrote that the "Darwinian theory of the survival of the strongest" could no longer coexist with "the Christian theory of the survival of all," especially since the new industrial developments of the generation following the Civil War had made the effects of competition on society worse.

Obviously human need demanded a change in the system, but what would replace it? For the answer the Southern Populists drew on their Alliance heritage and expanded it to include the whole of society. "Competition forces the employer to cut down wages; he must do so or go under," reasoned an Alabama editor. "Those employers who are guided by feelings of humanity are forced out of business by competition. The system is rotten, and we toss our hat and exclaim, all hail the co-operative commonwealth!" Cooperation would once again value decency above destruction, human beings above money or property. "Each for All and All for Each" ran the motto of the *Virginia Sun*. . . .

Focusing on the human wreckage it strewed behind it, the Southern Populists grounded their criticism of the competitive order on a personal, moral analysis of society. They did not, however, question the fundamental tenets of the American economic system as they understood them—the market, supply and demand, private ownership and profit, and the beneficence of economic competition between small economic units. The only exceptions to this, the editors of the *People's Advocate* and the *Argus*, both of Austin, Texas, provided once again a striking example of the grip these ideas had on the southern reformers. These editors and their southern brethren saw the same wrongs and attributed them to the same cause, the malfunctioning of the social system. The old ideas of competition had not worked. Obviously something had to change. People had to work with and for each other. But of all the Southern Populists, only these editors accepted the logic of this position. Real cooperation, they argued, meant at least the nationalization of all monopolies and the end that this implied to the market system, private profit, and economic competition. "Socialism will set the wheels of industry in motion to satisfy the wants of every human being," insisted the editor of the *Advocate*. "It alone will give us the key to prosperity, a higher civilization." Almost all other Southern Populists rejected such a radical demand for change, although in practice they sometimes criticized the existing system more harshly than these editors. They did not follow through on the implications of their demand that American society replace economic competition with cooperation, the "cooperative commonwealth." They identified themselves as independent producers, or aspiring independent producers, within a simple market society, where economically independent individuals competed with each other while everyone, through a democratic government, owned cooperatively the major elements of distribution.

Part of the reason the Southern Populists stopped short of an attack on the market system lay in the sources to which they turned for a justification of this cooperative order. They measured the existing social order by its human refuse; they measured their cooperative society by its promise of brotherhood. An emphasis on the rights of man marked one important element in the thinking behind this metaphor, an objection to the movement away from the homogeneous, harmonious Jeffersonian ideal entailed in the growth of rigid class lines and an end to economic and social mobility. This change also involved the drift away from the concern of every person for every other, the brotherhood of men, one of the best faces of the Southern Populists' producer-centered community. The Populist party had a duty, wrote an Alabama editor, "to show to the world by its actions that there is a reality in the just and equitable relationship which, according to natures [*sic*] laws, each and every man sustains to every other man and to his Creator."

The main roots of the metaphor lay in the evangelical Protestant experience of the Southern Populists. In the idea of cooperative effort, wrote the editor of the *Virginia Sun* in early 1892, "is contained the secret to all true life and progress—the grand emancipating principle of brotherhood. A man, living to himself alone, can achieve but little. But once let him free himself from his narrow selfishness, and boldly throw himself into work for the good of all, and his share of the good of all shall be returned to him—a hundredfold more than his puny effort could ever have yielded. Thus does the spiritual law find its economic counterpart— if a man would save his life, he must first lose it." Until people realized the responsibility of each for the other, nothing would change. . . .

American society's inhumanity to most of its members seemed to the Southern Populists the most compelling reason for a change toward a new society regulated by the principle of cooperative brotherhood, where every person would be responsible for every other. The responsibility was personal, the compulsion to it moral. It was a responsibility which the Southern Populists accused the new urban industrial America of ignoring and destroying. Their Jeffersonian and Jacksonian heritage stressed the equality of all people in a relatively homogeneous, producer-oriented society; their rural experience emphasized the personal, moral connections of each person to every other; their religious background insisted on the essential equality of all people before God. All of these underlined the need for personal responsibility. On this ideal of brotherhood they built their critique of the new industrial capitalist society in America and then constructed their ideal alternative to it. It was not to be everyone for themselves but all for each other.

The irony was, of course, that they saw no particular conflict between this and the retention of a market society based on private ownership and profit, the same base on which rested the industrial and financial capitalist society they opposed. None of their sources for the ideal of brotherhood and responsibility in a cooperative society suggested any problem. And when their experience did, the Southern Populists proposed as a solution a simple market society within a cooperative national economy. This resolution became untenable only when they turned to dealing with the benefits of America's existing industrial structure, benefits they wished to retain.

By no means did the Southern Populists reject industrial society. Their exposure to some aspects of it in America, particularly the social suffering it caused, resulted in only an apparent repudiation; they actually responded far differently. They disliked not industrial development but its impact on American society. The New South and railroads attracted them precisely because they promised economic improvement and even industrial expansion. . . .

While the Southern Populists . . . often called for a restoration of Jeffersonian and Jacksonian politics, they consciously designed their specific reforms to meet the needs of a new society. The allusions to older forms most often referred only to general principles of government. America needed to return to earlier forms, maintained a North Carolina Allianceman, to regain a government which protected all Americans rather than a special few, a government "founded upon the principle of justice and equality to the whole people," a government "restored to its primitive parity." Neither Jeffersonian nor Jacksonian politics produced specific demands for a subtreasury, for legal tender irredeemable fiat paper money, for government ownership of the railroads, for an increase in the effort of the national government to guarantee the well-being of all the members of society. Only their standards did the Southern Populists discover in the past. Like any thoughtful and creative reform group, they tried to make use of their heritage without allowing themselves to be limited by it, to recreate with new policies a society of equal rights for all and special privileges to none.

But what of the times southern reformers seemed to be calling for, a return not just to the principles but the reality of a pre–Civil War America? In most of these cases the reformers did not specifically reject post–Civil War American society, although they appeared at times to imply it. In part these implications disclosed again the Southern Populists' failure to realize what their reform vision might mean for the continued economic development they wanted to retain. The harmonious, homogeneous, producer-oriented society—Jeffersonian America—had little to do with the reality of industrial America. The Southern Populists who made these apparent rejections of late nineteenth-century America, however, did not consciously reject industrial society. . . .

. . . The Southern Populists proposed their reforms not to end industrial development but to stimulate it while making its benefits available to a much greater number. They wanted to alter the system in which this change had occurred in order to make it more responsive to human needs, to reduce the suffering it had so far produced. They did not consider such reforms incompatible with the continued, even increased, tempo of industrial expansion as they variously understood it.

Not all the ideas the Southern Populists held about American industrial society derived from older notions. Continued exposure to it made them, like many other Americans of their generation, more aware of and attuned to its realities. Their acceptance of the fruits of the new order and its physical manifestations—railroads, factories, steam and electric power—testified to the effect of contemporary experience. So did their attitude toward self-sufficient farming, which directly contradicted important elements in their Jeffersonian heritage.

Their opponents constantly told the Southern Populists that they could solve all their economic problems by diversifying their agriculture and raising on the farm all of what they needed. Some Southern Populists did admit that until social and economic conditions improved a degree of self-sufficiency might be warranted. But self-sufficiency as an ideal they rejected almost completely. . . .

A system of regional interchange also complemented the Southern Populists' ideas for a simple market society within a cooperative rather than a competitive national social and economic system. When each section, because of transportation at cost, could produce what its soil grew best and exchange it for things other sections could produce more cheaply, posited James Murdock, the whole nation would become "like one vast community making their exchanges to an advantage." No panics could occur and no one suffer biting poverty. With people freezing and starving, a policy of economic self-sufficiency for the farmer made no sense. Besides being against all notions of economic and social progress, a policy of "hog and hominy" also would reduce the quality of life for the farmers and all those whom their products benefited. This perception took into account changes from an earlier society and economy and accepted their significance and value while rejecting the use to which they had so far been put.

The new industrial America also affected the Southern Populists at a deeper level. As the country moved from a primarily agricultural society to an industrial one, the meaning of words common to both often altered significantly. The Southern Populists' use of words like "industry," "manufacturing," and "capital" demonstrated their halfway position between two worlds and illustrated their efforts, conscious and unconscious, to come to terms with a new and strange form of social organization without rejecting the whole of it.

The southern reformers' use of the word "industry" generally reflected an older definition of the word, referring primarily to diligent physical labor which resulted in a tangible product. . . . The word also retained older moral loadings of the virtue of physical labor as opposed to the evils of sloth and laziness. The great evils of existing society, stated a North Carolina Allianceman, all sprang from the privileged aristocracy's ability to live high off the products of the "industrial classes," those people who worked for a living by producing tangible goods.

This particular use of the word also revealed the Southern Populists' peculiar class position, the source of many of the inconsistencies in their approach to industrial America, especially their effort to combine a simple market society for small independent producers with the nationalization of distribution facilities. Being landowners or aspiring landowners and having little experience or knowledge of urban industrial America, the Southern Populists overlooked the growth of huge manufacturing complexes like Standard Oil and Carnegie Steel as well as the new classes created by them. For the reformers the most significant alignments in society did not parallel the division between employer and employee or wage laborer and owner, but ran along lines demarked by the kind of work people did, between those who by their physical effort produced tangible goods and those who did not. That put farmers and laborers together in what the Southern Populists considered the most important "class" in society, the "industrial" class. The Southern Populists intended to reform society in their interest. . . .

Some things, however, suggested the massive changes in American society had begun to affect the Southern Populists. Their use of the word "industry" did not always reflect clearly either the past or the future. It did not when an Alabama editor referred to the last thirty years of American history as "a period of productive energy and industrial development without a parallel." He could have been speaking as easily of an increase in the ability of the individual producer to create tangible wealth with the aid of new machinery as to the development of industrial capitalism in this country after the Civil War. . . .

The use of the word "capital," and its other forms, "capitalist" and "capitalism," showed the same double meaning that "industry" did. For some of the Southern Populists "capital" and "capitalist" remained synonomous with access to and possession of large amounts of money. Capitalists put their money to use through a financial system which they controlled and which allowed them to rob the producer. By contracting the money supply the capitalists exploited the producer by assuring the dominance of money over humanity.

But however unnecessary capitalists and their immense monetary wealth might be in a simple market society of independent producers, of American industrial society they constituted a very necessary part, and a few Southern Populists realized it. Some argued, for instance, that capital needed labor and labor needed capital. "It is not the object of the People's party," wrote a Georgia Populist, "to array labor against capital, as has been charged, but to secure by legislation such harmony that will do away with that friction." At least part of this idea of interdependence grew from the reformers' greenback inheritance—their desire for a harmonious, cooperative society—and their experience as farmers needing credit. Acceptance of the idea, however, showed other sources, for it often forced the Populists to choose between their contention that "wealth belongs to him who creates it" and their commitment to private property, profit, and the market system. The two might coexist in a simple market society where no market in labor occurred, but in an industrial capitalist America the two were mutually exclusive. If the laborers had a right to all the wealth they created, none would be left over for the investor, the capitalist. Averse to tinkering with what they perceived to be the basic foundations of America's economic system and eager for the benefits the new industrial order promised, the more perceptive Southern Populists sometimes had to acknowledge the importance of capital, and in doing so tended to change their definition of the term. . . .

The notion that capital equaled money accumulated in the hands of one person, the capitalist as moneylender or usurer, remained strong, but alongside it appeared the more modern notion that expanded production required capital, the concept of capitalist as investor and aid to the producer. In support of capital investment in agriculture a Georgia Populist maintained that it increased production more per dollar invested than capital invested in "manufactories." Others were not so partial to the farmers. A Virginia Populist arguing for an increase in the circulating currency claimed that "it requires capital to develop production and main-tain the commerce and industries of a country, as well as for financial purposes." The editor of the *Texas Advance* opposed a suggested tax on the net income of corporations because it "would tend to deter men of moderate means from taking stock, thus hampering every industry requiring a combination of capital, while the millionaires would go free." The tax should fall on the millionaires who produced nothing, built up no industry, provided no one with employment. However accurate his notion of how the millionaires acquired or spent their wealth, this Populist distin-guished between invested and idle capital, the former being necessary to economic development. An idea of the importance of investment capital, while not common, appeared often enough among Southern Populists to demonstrate their effort to deal—consciously sometimes, but often unconsciously—with American industrial capitalism in terms of that society's needs and their own aspirations within it.

Perhaps more than anything else, however, the noticeable occurrence of a machine image in their language illustrated the impact of industrial America on the Southern Populists. A North Carolina editor defended the farmers' lack of starched collars with the assertion that despite the fact, the farmers were "the driving wheel of the nation." . . .

The machine image, and newly defined terms like "capital" and "industry," represented the entering wedge not only of a new understanding of American industrial society, but a new way of thinking. The earliest definition of industry referred to the individual activity necessary to produce some particular and tangible product. Capital as money, associated with those who did no work and lived by preying directly off those who did, the Southern Populists rejected as distinctly amoral. The newer use of the term "industry" no longer referred much to some particularly personal enterprise but to a whole complex of social and economic arrangements which had little immediate reference to any chiefly concrete or discreet human activity. Capital retained its impersonality and intangibility, its essential amorality, and the reformers accepted it as such as an aid to labor in a harmonious society where they could retain the market place along with industrial expansion.

Almost all of the southern reformers had enough experience with industrial society to realize the great potential of machines for improving human life. They turned to machine images and metaphors because those they had inherited—Jeffersonian, producerite, and religious and moral—proved inadequate for describing and interpreting a modern industrial society. They lacked enough experience, however, to realize the implications of what they did. Except for perhaps the editor of the *Southern Mercury*, they had no idea of how the very impersonality, inhumanity, and amorality of the industrial and financial capitalism at which they aimed their severest criticisms could creep into their thinking anyway, a product of their increased experience with the manifestations of that society and their requirement that its material benefits be retained along with the essentials of the economic system in which it grew. Their class position made it impossible for them to understand that in the very process of accepting, either from ignorance or necessity, some of the adjuncts to industrial development in a market-oriented, private enterprise, capitalist economy, they paved the way for a vitiation of their criticism of that society, a criticism which they based on their personal and moral judgment of the needs of a decent and human America.

Once again, . . . as in the case of how far reform of the economic structure of the country should go, as in the case of the degree to which the government should be involved in the social and economic life of the country, as in the case of how rigorously they should define landownership by use, the Southern Populists ran afoul of contradictions within their own beliefs and demands. . . . They wanted to prohibit really large-scale landholding and speculation without threatening their position as landlords or potential landlords. They wanted the subtreasury system and government ownership of the railroad, telegraph, and telephone systems while retaining a small economic government. They wanted to eliminate harmful competition and spread the benefits of industrialization more widely, but do it while preserving in the form of a simple market society the very competitive, private ownership, profit-oriented market economy and social order which they criticized for seriously breaking down. They wanted a personal, moral society while retaining the industrial system which bred an America characterized by the very opposite of these qualities. An inadequate understanding of the operation of an industrial capitalist society led to an ineffective effort to reform it. . . .

. . .[A]mong the Southern Populists . . . the commitment to private profit and property and some sort of competitive market economy remained quite strong, even in 1896. Their equivocating on the land issue, their ideas about the cooperation of capital and labor for industrial growth, and their advocacy of the simple market society of independent producers all suggested how far even the radical Populists had to go to reach a position from which to build a more viable alternative to American capitalism, one which avoided the problems of trying to alter the very nature of the system while retaining its most basic elements. But their ease with the idea of socialism, their advocacy of the precedence of human rights over those of property, and the *Mercury*'s realization that machinery when owned by a few could be used to exploit workers as well as increase the benefits of industrial society for farmers, indicated that the antimonopoly greenbackers were headed in the right direction.

But the radical Southern Populists did not move far enough fast enough. They had neither sufficient time nor analysis to build by 1896 a viable political movement outside the two major parties. By that year large numbers of Americans had already begun to make other arrangements for their future. The "full dinner pail" promised by William McKinley and his backers in 1896 proved more appealing, and more promising, than the hazy class politics of the radical Populists.

For financial reform Southern Populists the dream did not fail, but their analysis did, and they joined Bryan in what proved to be an empty crusade. But then the radicals could not yet offer a very clear alternative, much less explain it even to a majority of their own Populist brethren. The radicals had traveled only a bit further down the line than many of those Southern Populists who joined Bryan. They did not yet sufficiently comprehend the workings of American industrial and financial capitalism and could not prevent Bryan from speaking for many of those Americans yet unwilling to join their fellows in accepting the corporate state in exchange for the American Way of Life.

Ironically, even indications of a greater understanding of that society suggest that it, too, would not have sufficed. The Southern Populists' movements toward understanding that system well may have been at the expense of the very qualities upon which they based their demands for change. The inability to understand adequately the industrial system they sought to retain contributed considerably to their immediate failure in 1896. The long-range loss, however, may not have been the machine metaphor but older notions of a just and decent America. The Southern Populists lost in 1896 because they retained too much of what the rest of the nation lost in McKinley's victory. For these reasons 1896 marked the demise of the last large-scale threat to the values and ideals of our contemporary capitalist society. . . .

The Southern Populists did not generally come from or speak much for the mudsill of their society, the tenant farmers black and white, although they obviously, and with good reason, feared their decline into it. They did number, however, among those who suffered from and helped pay for, economically and socially, the expansion of American industrial capitalism in the thirty-five years following the Civil War. They were only the last in a line of rural movements protesting this situation.

Their ambiguous position in their own community, neither top nor bottom but losing ground rapidly, very probably had a great deal to do with the peculiar duality of much of their response to a new America. Their acceptance and rejection of the new order, their acceptance and rejection of their own experience and past, accounted for much of the complexity of their thought. On balance, however, the ideal social order which the Southern Populists wanted to create, and even more the critique they made of the existing order, came out of their experience living in a personal, intimate, relatively simple, tangible, homogeneous, and moral community. This world was supported and described by their inherited ways of interpreting and understanding the world around them. . . . They found themselves in the 1880s and 1890s increasingly threatened by collapse into economic servitude and social dependency while a world of cities, vast industrial developments, a complicated and stratified social organization, a world of impersonality, important intangibles, complexity and distance, and amoral in the traditional, personal sense of morality, destroyed the community and values they knew and understood and in which they believed.

While they learned to understand the intimate connection between the destruction of their personal lives and communities and the growth of that new world, literally every Southern Populist wanted to retain the material benefits of industrial development. They rejected only the social consequences which followed in the wake of America's particular organization of that expansion. The acceptance of the new order involved in deliberately choosing the benefits of American industrial capitalism had begun already before 1896 to change their view of the ideal society in important ways, but not enough. They did not really comprehend the new order. They did not really know how it worked. Their background and experience did not equip them to understand industrial capitalist society and its manifestations—cities, proletariats, factories, concentrated wealth, and capital. . . .

So the Southern Populist lost in 1896, but so did a whole range of values which produced a distinctive and valid criticism of American industrial and financial capitalism based on that society's inability to serve all the members of the community. For all their provincialism, narrow-mindedness, and confusion, the Southern Populists, at their best and from their own particular standpoint, realized that a social order which set every person against every other, each group or class in society against every other, the Devil taking the hindmost, represented only exploitation to most of its members and would very likely destroy itself eventually. They never denied the benefits of industrial development, but unless these could be attained within the context of a more decent, responsible, and human social order, in which all benefited according to their contribution, this development could not be considered progress, or even very worthwhile by most of the people it affected. . . .

Robert W. Cherny

POPULISTS, PROGRESSIVES, AND THE TRANSFORMATION OF NEBRASKA POLITICS

Robert W. Cherny presented Populism as a grass-roots movement that profoundly altered Nebraska politics. Prior to the 1890s, Nebraska politics had been highly amateurish and tended to form along ethnic lines relating to the prohibition issue. Populism shattered that system by uniting farmers along economic lines as well as across ethnic lines. After the Populist era, Nebraska politics remained more issue oriented. When Cherny compared Populism and progressivism, he found more differences than similarities. In reaching that conclusion, he confirmed a point that other scholars have made over the past quarter century: Populism was quite different from twentieth-century liberalism. Robert Cherny's publications include *A Righteous Cause: The Life of William Jennings Bryan* (1985).

What . . . was the relationship between the Populist and progressive movements in Nebraska? Were they, as a historian in the progressive tradition put it, "the same ideas traveling in the same direction, with new leaders, new vitality, and new weapons, against the old forces of privilege and corruption"? Or were they, as Hofstadter and others have argued, somewhat similar in their proposals but quite different in their essential natures, with Populism nostalgic, simplistic, even paranoid, and progressivism more complex and sophisticated in its analysis of problems, led by men "who suffered from the events of their time not through a shrinkage in their means but through the changed pattern in the distribution of deference and power"? Or were the two movements totally different, with Populism . . . basically humanitarian and protosocialist and progressivism . . . the "victory of big businessmen in achieving the rationalization of the economy that only the federal government could provide"? We may

Reprinted from *Populism, Progressivism, and the Transformation of Nebraska Politics, 1885–1915* by Robert W. Cherny, pp. 151–152, 154, 157–166, by permission of the University of Nebraska Press. Copyright © 1981 by the University of Nebraska Press.

begin to approach these questions by comparing the two movements in Nebraska along three dimensions: voting behavior, political leadership, and policies. . . .

[Voting analysis] suggests (*a*) that economic distress is the factor that links voting for Populism with voting for Norris–La Follette Republicans or Clark Democrats; (*b*) that former Populists did not, by any means, form a cohesive voting bloc; and (*c*) that some candidates widely described as "progressive" had very different sources of voter support, not related to agricultural economics. . . .

A comparison of the collective profiles of the leaders of Populism with those of the progressive movement reveals more differences than similarities. Populist leaders are most different with regard to the various measures of socioeconomic standing and occupation. Only about 5 to 7 percent of the Populist leaders belonged to the high-status Masonic lodge, compared with 20 percent of the progressive Democratic leaders and nearly half of the progressive Republican leaders. Only a third of the Populist leaders had attended college; the same proportion of Republican progressive leaders had attended graduate or professional school. Nearly three-fourths of all Populist leaders were farmers; only a third of the Democrats and a quarter of the progressive Republicans were engaged in agriculture. Only 16 percent of the Populist leaders were professionals, compared with 30 percent of the Democrats and well over half of the most prominent Republican progressives.

These comparisons suggest that the Populist and progressive leadership groups were not drawn from the same, or even from similar, socioeconomic groups. The typical Populist leader was a farmer whose education and associations marked him as lower middle class. He was not, to be sure, typical of most farmers—as indicated by the fact that a third of all Populist leaders had attended college; he was very likely held in esteem by his rural neighbors for his learning or abilities, and he very probably had filled such neighborhood offices as road supervisor, school board member, or justice of the peace. Even among the fifty-four most prominent Populist leaders of the 1890s, 46 percent were farmers. Among progressive political leaders, by contrast, only about 25 percent were farmers, and the most common occupations were professional, especially the law. Progressive leaders tended to have more formal education than Populists and at more distinguished institutions; their membership in socially prestigious fraternal associations like the Masons put them in the upper socioeconomic levels of their communities. . . .

At the level of policy or policy proposals, the two movements were also more different than similar. For the Populists, the origin of most of their grievances could be traced to the emergence of industrialism: giant industrial corporations, allied with corrupt and extravagant officeholders, were making it impossible for farmers and workers to achieve the good life. Farmers suffered most from deflation, moneylenders, railroads, land monopolists, and taxes; workers suffered from exploitation by unfeeling employers, competition with convict labor, the use of Pinkertons, and inability to negotiate with their employers on the basis of equality. The solution to these problems was to be found in the use of government to restrict special privilege and to contain monopoly power. Populist spokesmen extended the labor theory of value to its logical conclusion and advocated the cooperative commonwealth. Nebraska Populist platforms reflected this in arguing that the people, through the government, should own and operate the most essential systems that transferred, but did not create, value—transportation, communication, banking—plus industries that provided public necessities (e.g., coal) and municipal utilities. Labor should be made equal to capital by forcing the arbitration of labor grievances, and laws should alleviate the conditions of the workingman. For this massive redistribution of economic wealth and power to be effective, it was essential that the people improve their control over the medium of redistribution, the government, through direct elections, a secret ballot, and the initiative and referendum. Underlying all Populist proposals was an economic framework based upon the labor theory of value plus a strong faith in the people's inherent virtue and ability to make the correct decisions when given the facts.

Progressives, for the most part, proposed neither reordering of social values nor redistribution of economic power. Few progressives—no Republican progressives—would have been comfortable with the Populist dogma that "wealth belongs to him who creates it." The closest approach the Republican progressives of Nebraska made to such a concept was their suggestion, in 1912, that "all honest labor and toil should be justly compensated." Few progressive proposals—and *no* progressive enactments—posed a serious threat to capital investments. Where Populists had proposed the redistribution of economic power and wealth, progressives proposed regulation. The progressive Republican platform of 1912 echoed Roosevelt in giving first priority to demands for a "permanent non-partisan tariff commission" and "non-partisan industrial commission." Coupled to these demands for regulation, especially among Republican progressives, was a clear admiration for efficiency and businesslike methods in public administration; beginning in 1907, Republican platforms and pronouncements fairly bristled with praise for Republican administrators as demonstrating "business sagacity," "businesslike administration," and "a high standard of efficiency." . . .

In one area Populists and progressives seem in basic agreement: both favored restructuring the political process with the ostensible objective of increasing the role of the people. Populists, in the 1892s, favored the direct election of all officials, the initiative and referendum, the secret ballot, and the extension of the civil service. Republican progressives, too, favored the initiative and referendum, direct election of United States senators (although they opposed the Oregon Pledge Law), and extension of the civil service principle in state government, and they added the recall, the direct primary, a nationwide presidential primary, the short ballot, a nonpartisan board of control for state institutions, and placing post offices under civil service. Democrats endorsed all of these except the nationwide presidential primary, the short ballot and the placing post offices under civil service and added municipal home rule for Omaha and South Omaha, a nonpartisan judiciary (opposed by Republicans), the nonpartisan election of school superintendents, and equitable legislative apportionment.

Democratic progressivism did not emerge suddenly, as did the Republican variety in 1906; Nebraska Democrats did not falter from the path they chose in 1894, continuing to endorse some Populist proposals and to add to them. To be sure, Democratic progressives did not embrace the cooperative commonwealth, but their policy proposals place them somewhere between Republican progressives and Populists in the area of economics. They endorsed Republican regulation schemes but typically demanded more power for the regulating agency, including, in 1907, the licensing of corporations, and also called for legal distinction "between the natural man and the artificial person, called a corporation." They demanded a national income tax and a national inheritance tax plus careful study of the state tax system to make it as equitable as possible. Perhaps the most publicized Democratic accomplishment was the creation of the state bank deposit guaranty system, which required state-chartered banks (and allowed federally chartered banks) to contribute to an insurance fund to be used to reimburse depositors of a failed bank. The 1913 Democratic legislature also fulfilled a long-standing Democratic promise by passing a workmen's compensation law. Democrats also consistently favored the eight-hour day and some system of conciliation in labor disputes that would allow the state to investigate and publicize but would not include binding arbitration. Other Democratic accomplishments included the Oregon Pledge Law, the initiative and referendum, the state board of control, and nonpartisan election of judicial and educational officials. Some Democratic progressives also continued to promote the cause of public ownership of the railroads.

This survey of policy and policy proposals suggests the Populists and Republican progressives were quite different. Populists advocated a reordering of social values and a redistribution of wealth and economic power. Republican progressives favored no such radical change, proposing regulation but never redistribution. For Populists, regulation was only an interim measure; for Republican progressives it became an end in itself. Democratic progressives fell somewhere between, committed to some redistributive measures—the income and inheritance taxes, designed to reduce "swollen fortunes"; the bank guaranty law, taxing banks in the interests of depositors; workmen's compensation and employer liability; and, at least among some Democratic progressives, government ownership of railroads.

Contemporaries of the two movements in Nebraska tended to ignore the sometimes subtle—but often incredibly obvious—distinctions between Populism and progressivism and to emphasize the extent to which, in William Allen White's words, the progressives "caught the Populists in swimming and stole all of their clothing except the frayed underdrawers of free silver." Albert Watkins, anti-Populist and antisilver in the 1890s but later a progressive Democrat, titled the section of his 1913 state history dealing with the progressive period "Return of the Republican

Prodigal—His Conversion to Populism." The *Nebraska State Journal*, Republican and progressive, suggested in 1912 under the title, "Populism Triumphant," . . . "the work the populist party set out to do has been done, though by other hands, or is about to be done by other hands that once scorned its proposals." The Populists themselves took a similar view in their 1911 state platform: "The people's independent party of Nebraska . . . rejoices because the principles that it announced twenty years ago . . . have now been accepted in greater or less degree by all parties and all right-thinking men." Although the principles of greater popular participation in politics and government were widely accepted during the progressive years and given wider rhetorical praise than formerly, the heart of the Populist program—government ownership and operation of transportation, communication, banking, and other such services—was never accepted by the progressive movement, nor were Populist proposals for the direct election of the president. For the Populists of 1911 to claim that their "principles" had been universally accepted was a self-congratulatory delusion.

✳

Before the Populist prairie fire raged across the Nebraska plains, politics revolved almost entirely upon a single axis and was largely symbolic. The axis of politics was, of course, ethnic—pitting Catholics and conservative Lutherans, Germans, Czechs, Irish, and Poles, against old-stock Protestants and pietistic immigrants, around a series of issues such as woman suffrage and school attendance laws, but more than anything else around the issue of alcohol. Such single-axis politics, dividing along the lines of ethnoreligious values, were not new to the 1880s; such alignments could be found to the east before Nebraska Territory was even opened to permanent settlement.

Economic issues were either absent or very secondary to the vast majority of voters. Few—if any—of the voters took a burning interest in the tariff rate or railroad subsidies unless, of course, subsidy might mean a transcontinental trunk line in one's own community, bringing growth, new jobs, and prosperity. In the absence of economic *issues*, politics tended to focus upon economic *distribution*—using government to give things in order to bring growth.

The things distributed might vary from year to year and from state to federal levels. At the state level, the government could distribute such "things" as normal schools and state hospitals, subsidies for mineral discoveries or for particular crops, or subsidies for railroad construction. At a federal level the "things" included tariff protection and land grants. In the absence of economic issues, distribution of such favors and the distribution of patronage were the major functions of state government. Distribution was politically easy, for coalitions among representatives of communities would typically bargain over the distribution of favors until at least a majority of the representatives felt they had something to take back to the community. If a community's representative failed, it was usually not of great moment, for he did not have a strong stake in being reelected and might even view his service rather grudgingly in the first place.

The ethnic, single-dimension politics of the pre-Populist period was highly conducive to a politics of symbols and to a high degree of party loyalty. Politics in the 1880s seemed to revolve largely around symbols—ritual invocations of party saints and dogmas, ritual exorcisms of the opposing party. Fervor was as high in politics as in church—not surprisingly, given the close connection between the two. The voter's ethnic group identity, religion, and party affiliation were bound together, mutually reinforcing one another. Party loyalty was consequently intense and was vividly displayed during campaigns, when symbols and relics were displayed and invoked and the faithful were exhorted to do battle with the foe. Political leadership was but a part of the larger symbolism. The specific candidate mattered little to Republicans or Democrats; what mattered more was his symbolic nature. In 1888 both parties seemed to achieve the ultimate in this sort of symbolism. The Republican candidate for governor, John Milton Thayer, was born in Massachusetts, graduated from Brown University, came to Nebraska Territory in 1854, became a general in the territorial militia in 1855, practiced law and engaged in territorial politics as an opponent of slavery, volunteered when war broke out in 1861 and left the military as a brigadier general, was elected to the United States Senate in 1867 and sided with the Radical Republicans against Johnson, failed of reelection in 1871, served as governor of Wyoming Territory from 1875 to 1879, returned to Nebraska, was elected state GAR [Grand Army of the Republic] commander in

1886, was elected governor for the first time the same year, and was elected to his second term in 1888. The Democrats nominated John A. McShane, born in Ohio, Catholic and of Irish parentage, educated only through the common schools. He came to Omaha in 1874 and immediately plunged into business ventures and Democratic politics, investing in lumbering, ironworks, and real estate and becoming president of the Union Stock Yards in 1884 and president of the Union Stock Yards Bank in 1887; he was elected to the state legislature in 1880, 1882, and 1884 and to Congress in 1886 when Edward Rosewater bolted the Republican nominee. Both Thayer, the Yankee abolitionist and Civil War veteran, and McShane, the Irish Catholic Omaha businessman and politician, were almost stereotypes of the images their parties projected to the voters. Nominations for office and officeholding itself were largely symbolic exercises; state government actually did very little throughout the period beyond the distributive functions already described. Officeholding was a duty for a few honored party members, and officeholders were amateurs, filling an office for a short period and expecting—sometimes clearly longing—to return to their "normal" life and activities. Symbolic politics with a high degree of party loyalty produced symbolic leadership, amateur leadership, a high degree of turnover in officeholders, and minimal intraparty disputes over issues.

Voter initiative in the early 1890s, in the form of Populism, irrevocably altered this single-dimension, symbolic, amateur political system. Populism sprang from the grass roots; Alliance members led their state leadership into politics, rather than vice versa. Populism was an economic and occupational movement, uniting marginal farmers across ethnic lines of division. Politics became something more than symbolic invocations; politics became a fire, an obsession, a revolution. Politics became mass rallies, excited speeches, singing. Old party lines shattered, new ones formed. The new lines, however, formed not along one dimension, but along two. Economics became as important a determinant of voting as ethnicity. The Populists became the party of marginal farmers, regardless of ethnicity. The Democrats, without the less prosperous of their erstwhile adherents, became a party of more prosperous anti-prohibitionists. Republicans, also losing their less prosperous adherents, became concentrated in the towns and in those more prosperous rural areas peopled by old-stock Protestants.

The next crucial step, the coalition of Populists and Democrats, also came as a result of voter initiative. Democratic voters far preceded their party leaders in embracing the new party. Bryan, the most charismatic of a new crop of Democratic leaders, led the party in the same direction Democratic voters had already moved. In the process, the Democratic party made a sharp break with the leadership of the past. Leadership within the Democratic party became tied to economic issues to a far greater extent than formerly. The emergence of Populism not only marked the emergence of a multiple-issue politics with crosscutting lines of cleavage, it also precipitated conversion and schism within the Democratic party, as party leaders fought bitterly over the attitude their party ought take on a range of economic issues. A similar conversion and schism took place within the Republican party, although with less bitterness and with only a small minority aligning themselves with the Populists. Disputes over economic issues, intra-party wrangling and schism, and the weakening of party loyalties all served to focus special attention upon those new party leaders who seemed capable of bringing order from the chaos. Personality became a far more important political force than ever before; Bryan was only the most successful of a field of new faces. Within Bryan's party, the same upheaval produced a host of other leaders . . . who would ultimately develop followings of their own rivaling that of the Commoner. The process was much slower within the Republican party, probably because of its greater stability at the grass roots. Republican voters, after the initial losses of 1890, were not moving to the new party; quite the reverse was true, as Republicans recovered the loyalty of some former adherents through the early 1890s.

The end result of this was a new political system. The continuation of multiple, crosscutting determinants of voting behavior made for a system in which party loyalties were permanently weaker, at least among those voters most subject to cross-pressures. The presence of a body of voters receptive to issues and prone to ticket-scratching made for an emphasis on the issues that attracted those votes and for an emphasis on personality as a way of securing votes without issues. The continuation of intense intraparty disputes over nominations (e.g., any of the fusion conventions, the Republican senatorial election of 1900, or the Republican nomination for the United States Senate in 1904) helped move the party leaders to accept a new means of resolving such disputes without creating the schisms characteristic of the 1890s. The new device was the direct primary, which removed the process of nomination from the arena of bargaining (a convention) and placed it instead in the arena of campaigning. Some party leaders sought to capitalize on weakened party loyalties by promoting nonpartisanship; the most prominent example is the creation of the nonpartisan judiciary, which many saw as a way of securing the votes of those with weak loyalties to a party without imposing the barrier of a party label. Certain other divisive issues were dealt with in a similar fashion, through the creation of a nonpartisan regulatory commission, the ultimate solution to the problem of the railroads after the failure in the 1890s of so many efforts to legislate rates. Regulation removed the problem from the arena of political bargaining (in this case, the legislature) and turned it over to nonpartisan commissioners elected directly by the people.

The creation of the new political system was initiated by the voters, in three distinct steps. The emergence of a complex socio-economic structure, in which the fortunes of Nebraska farmers were tied to decisions by railroad boards of directors and grain exchange brokers, imperiled the self-sufficiency of a simpler past well within the memory of many. The emergence of these economic forces gave rise to demands to control them, and voters initiated the new, multiple-issue politics by creating a new party. Established leaders sought to contain this voter impulse within the old party structure (e.g., the 1890 Republican antimonopoly convention, or the reluctance of Alliance leaders to call an independent political convention), but they failed. The voters' demands were too strong, and the old party structures were shaken or shattered. The new party sought to use the power of government in a way it had never been used before. The new party favored government ownership of the railroads and as an interim measure sought, in both the 1891 and 1893 legislative sessions, to use the power of government to set railroad rates directly, through law. The second step at which voters took the initiative was in the creation of the Democratic-Populist coalition. Many old party leaders sought to prevent this coalition, even to the point of encouraging party schism. The coalition, preceded by the actions of voters, nonetheless came into existence and dominated state politics for six years. Its aftereffects could be seen within the Democratic party even after the Populist party ended as a significant independent political force. The third step, for which voter initiative was also crucial, was the emergence of a seemingly permanent situation in which multiple-issue politics produced weakened party loyalties and increased emphasis on both issue-oriented politics and the politics of personality. Once again party leaders sought to contain this development through such devices as the direct primary, the initiative and referendum, the nonpartisan judiciary, and the nonpartisan regulatory commission. These efforts were successful in deflecting the major thrust of the voters in marginal agricultural areas, a thrust that, throughout the period from 1890 through at least the 1912 election, was in the direction not of regulation, but of government ownership. Although the thrust was deflected, the tension remained and continued to influence state politics at least until World War II, producing the Non-Partisan League party of 1920, which drew nearly a quarter of the vote, the Progressive party of 1922 and 1924, strong support for George W. Norris throughout the 1920s and 1930s, and a base for "Brother Charley" Bryan's gubernatorial victories of 1922, 1930, and 1932. This tension was finally reduced about the time of World War II, apparently by a combination of assimilation and the final elimination of large numbers of marginal farmers. Both Norris and Bryan lost their last campaigns for office in 1942.

✳

The farmers who drove their wagons in the Alliance parades of 1890 had hoped they were initiating a new political system. And a new political system did emerge in Nebraska. But the new system was not what the farmers of 1890 had sought. The goal of their most optimistic leaders—the cooperative commonwealth—would never be realized. Their enemies—the corporations, the bankers, the railroads—would never come under public ownership, although they would yield to varying degrees of regulation. The status of the farmer improved markedly during the late 1890s and early twentieth century, but the improvement was only temporary. Agricultural depression reappeared after World War I and seemed to become permanent, yielding only when massive numbers of farm families left their land for the cities and those who survived brought a section, two sections, or more together as a single farm unit. Land that had once supported ten families now appeared inadequate to support one. While collecting Nebraska folk songs in the 1930s, Federal Writers' Project researchers found one by Luna E. Kellie, who was secretary of the state Farmers' Alliance through the late 1890s:

> There's a dear old homestead on Nebraska's fertile plain
>> Where I toiled my manhood's strength away;
> All that labor now is lost to me, but it is Shylock's gain,
>> For that dear old home he claims today.
>
> *Chorus*
> Ah, my dear prairie home! Nevermore in years to come
>> Can I call what I made by toil my own;
> The railroads and banks combined, the lawyers paid to find
>> Out a way to rob me of my home.
>
> It was many years ago that I first saw through this scheme,
>> And I struggled from their meshes to get free;
> But my neighbors all around me then were in a party dream,
>> And they voted to rob my home from me.
>
> *Chorus*
> Now their homes are gone as well as mine, and they're awake at last,
>> And they now see the great injustice done;
> While some few their homes may save, yet the greater part, alas!
>> Must be homeless for all time to come.
>
> *Chorus*
> We must now the robbers pay for a chance to till the soil,
>> And when God calls us over the great range,
> All heaven will be owned, I suppose, by men who never toil,
>> So I doubt if we notice the exchange.

Another Writers' Project Song, this one anonymous, was more humorous, but no less resigned:

> Of all the years since I began
>> To mix in politics,
> The one that tries my inner man is
>> Eighteen Ninety-six;
> And as this aching void I feel,
>> I cast a wishful glance,
> And count them all from hip to heel,
>> These patches on my pants.

Worth Robert Miller

THE REPUBLICAN TRADITION

By viewing Populism within the context of the republican tradition—
which holds that government's major role is to promote the God-given
right of self-fulfillment—Worth Robert Miller situates his work within a
strong trend in Populist historiography. According to this view, the
Populists clashed with the prevailing ethos of the Gilded Age, which
elevated property rights to the level of human rights. Its proponents
were system oriented and believed that the plight of some hapless
individuals was a small price to pay for the great advances that the
nation had experienced. Had the Populists prevailed, they would have
continued to debate America's commitment to the kind of industrial
capitalism that became so strong in the Gilded Age. In addition to his
work on Oklahoma Populism, Professor Miller is the author of "Building
a Progressive Coalition in Texas: The Populist-Reform Democratic
Rapprochement, 1900–1907," *Journal of Southern History* 52 (May
1986) : 163–182.

The Populist Revolt was the product of the still-vital neorepublican
mind of the late nineteenth century as it evaluated the results of the
economic, political, and social revolutions of Gilded Age America.
Throughout the late nineteenth century, spokesmen representing a
series of egalitarian third-party movements put forth an apocalyptic
critique of the Gilded Age's cosmopolitan ethos that was rooted in
the ideology of the founding fathers. Third-party agitators were
especially successful in mobilizing a following where economic and
political conditions had discredited major-party spokesmen, as on
the Great Plains and in the cotton-belt South during the late 1880s
and 1890s.

Whether the course of late-nineteenth-century development
constituted an advance of civilization or a degeneration toward barbarism became a major point of contention in America with the
coming of the Populist revolt. Cosmopolitan elements looked back

From *Oklahoma Populism: A History of the People's Party in the Oklahoma Territory*
by Worth Robert Miller, pp. 181–184, 186–189. Copyright © 1987 by the
University of Oklahoma Press.

to the pronouncements of John Locke, who elevated property rights to an equal place beside human rights, for inspiration in judging contemporary events. These men pointed to such material factors as increased wealth, expanded production, and a proliferation of services as signs of the nation's advance. They were, in essence, system-oriented. They saw the plight of individual victims as a small price to pay for the significant advances of the nation as a whole.

The republican ideal of the founding fathers, which informed the Populists' assessment of late-nineteenth-century events, viewed the protection of individual liberties as the ultimate goal of society. The role of government was to promote social conditions that would aid the individual's God-given right to self-fulfillment. This humanistic orientation was moral in nature and based upon precepts of justice to the individual. It dictated the rejection of any social development that encouraged the debasement of any human. Such a viewpoint naturally had special appeal to those who saw themselves as victims of the contemporary system.

When railroads first appeared in a region, the almost universal response was enthusiasm for the new commercial and industrial world. Farmers and merchants alike wanted to believe that they were on the brink of the sustained prosperity that the philosophies of laissez-faire capitalism and social Darwinism promised. The more aggressive farmers bought machinery, fertilizer, and more land, all on credit, and quickly discovered that they were the most efficient producers of the age. Their agricultural production vastly outpaced the purchasing capacity of other Americans and even the world. Prices for agricultural commodities naturally plummeted. Railroad operators and other middlemen, however, took their profits regardless of the farmers' plight. In site of this, commercial elements proclaimed the emerging economic system just and laid the blame for agrarian problems on the farmer. He overproduced, they claimed. A crisis in agriculture occurred when mortgages were numerous, credit was tight, and transportation costs were more expensive.

As the economy of the Plains and the South worsened, farmers turned to their elected officials for aid. Government had provided tariffs to protect manufacturers, land grants to aid railroads, and deflation to help creditors. But when farmers put forth their claims upon the political process, they received little more than the worn-out slogans of laissez-faire. The inadequate response of the Gilded

Age's political elite to the plight of the farmer produced a political crisis in these outlying regions of the nation.

Many southern and western farmers had never completely committed themselves to the panaceas of Gilded Age enterprise. Although they had entered the world of commercial agriculture, they were primarily family farmers, not agribusinessmen. By the 1890s their operations often were only marginally profitable. Diversification, however, saved them from the worst effects of the late nineteenth century's agricultural crisis. This reaffirmed their commitment to the more traditional agrarian ethos. In the darkest days of the depression of the 1890s, many who had committed themselves to the dominant ideology of the era began to have second thoughts about their new commitment and searched for new answers. Frequently they found the ideology of the People's party more rewarding.

The cyclical interpretation of social development that late-nineteenth-century egalitarians inherited from the founding fathers lent positive connotations to the simplicity, equality, industriousness, and frugality of the developing society and a negative attitude to the hedonism, luxury, venality, and exploitation of a developed nation. Their Whiggish orientation caused them to see the latter as a triumph of power over liberty. . . .

Late-nineteenth-century egalitarians believed that the principles handed down by the founding fathers were universal truths, valid for all times and conditions. Many of the economic and social developments of the Gilded Age, furthermore, appeared to be consistent with the inherited warnings of social degeneration. Lawmakers seemed to abdicate their responsibility for monetary policy to America's, and, worse yet, England's, banker elite. Government policies, such as the protective tariff and land grants to railroads, promoted the ultimate consolidation of wealth and power—monopoly. The gap between the rich and the poor widened distinctly. The process also destroyed the independent family farmer, the bulwark of liberty in a republic. Rather than using the power of government to stem this spreading cancer, Populists believed that America's Gilded Age political elite aided the process through unneeded extravagance, financed by bonding schemes likely to force future generations into economic dependence.

To return America to the path charted at the nation's founding, late-nineteenth-century egalitarians devised a series of remedies that, when combined, formed the Omaha platform of 1892. With the exception of the Alliance's subtreasury plan, each demand cataloged in the document had appeared in previous third-party manifestos. The People's party was only the largest and most successful of a series of late-nineteenth-century egalitarian movements that shared a common spirit rooted in the republican ideology of the American Revolution. . . .

In the national arena Populists looked to an active government as the salvation of the nation. They called for elected representatives to restore monetary policy to popular control and then to reverse the trend toward concentrated wealth with the graduated income tax. Populists called for greenbacks to reflate the currency and provide needed credit in outlying regions of the nation. They favored postal-savings banks to secure the deposits of average citizens, who often lost everything through the speculations of bankers. Populist spokesmen also called for government ownership of the railroads, telephones, and telegraphs. They reasoned that such monopolies concentrated too much wealth and power in the hands of the few. Although this solution seemed to contradict the Populists' antipathy toward the proliferation of offices, returning the American people to their egalitarian heritage and popular control would make active government acceptable. To facilitate the return of popular control, Populists also advocated direct democracy through the initiative and referendum, plus popular election of the president and senators. Where Adam Smith had feared the power of the government, Populists feared the power of the few and saw popular control of an active government as their savior. . . .

Populist antielitism also manifested itself in other ways. Third-party legislators generally opposed bills to professionalize what today are called the "professions." They believed that such preference amounted to granting a special franchise or establishing an aristocracy. More important, however, Populists wished to deny the Gilded Age elite's claim to special status. Such men were seen as wanting the government to grant them monopoly status because of their superior advantages, namely a better education. . . .

How well most Populists understood the workings of the modern industrial economy can be questioned. Some third-party advocates clearly realized that many of the undesirable events in a modern industrial society resulted from the impersonal workings of a complex economic system rather than from conspiracies. Many others did not. Using the conspiracy metaphor, however, Populists could label their opposition immoral, which provided a stronger motivation for action than did appeals not invested with moral overtones. Still, Populists were not unique in their conspiracy-mindedness. The so-called anarchist plots associated with the agrarian and labor troubles of the late nineteenth century played an equally important role in the minds of their cosmopolitan rivals, who might have been expected to know better. Industrialism was in its infancy, and most people struggled to understand the meaning of its impact. In large part, accusations of conspiracy were simply the level upon which politics was played in the 1890s.

Although Populists chose economic policy as their battlefield, morality was their cause. They looked backward to an earlier moral order for their inspiration. Populists did recognize, however, that commercial and industrial society was a permanent part of the American landscape. Instead of engaging in a frenzy of Luddite retrogression, they attempted to address problems within the context of their morally based mind-set. They accepted industrialism but demanded that it be made humane. The adoption of many of their solutions in the twentieth century attests to the practicality of their reforms. Populists wanted both the benefits of industrialization and a moral social order.

Various scholars have noted the almost religious fervor of the Populist appeal. For many, the People's party replaced the church as a vehicle for moral expression. The apocalyptic vision of Populism, however, encouraged a drive for quick victory. Third-party disciples believed that the crisis of the age was upon them in 1896. The result would be either civilization or barbarism. Desperation caused many of Populism's oldest and most noted leaders to temporize their positions and accept the pragmatism of fusion with Democrats. Those not disheartened by this transition from justice to expediency finally lost heart upon the defeat of William Jennings Bryan.

The nomination of Bryan for president in 1896 saved the Democratic party from going the way of the Whigs. Three major parties vied for the allegiance of the American electorate in the 1890s. If men like Grover Cleveland had controlled the Democratic party in 1896, the People's party could well have replaced it as the GOP's major rival. If the People's party had survived as a major force in the political life of the nation, the American electorate would have been presented with a continuing debate over its commitment to capitalism. Instead, the great political debate of twentieth-century America has been over how best to save capitalism.

SUGGESTIONS FOR ADDITIONAL READING

General Histories. The publication of John D. Hicks's *The Populist Revolt: A History of the Farmers' Alliance and the People's Party* (1931) marked the first inclusive history of the movement, and it remains an important starting point for students of the movement. For a retrospective review of that book see Martin Ridge, " Populism Redux: John D. Hicks and *The Populist Revolt*," *Reviews in American History* (March, 1985). The second detailed history of the movement appeared forty-five years after Hicks's publication when Lawrence Goodwyn published *Democratic Promise: The Populist Movement in America* (1976). For a shorter version of that book see *The Populist Moment: A Short History of the Agrarian Revolt in America* (1978). Goodwyn's passionately argued work offers fresh perspective and stands as one of the most important books on the movement. For critical assessments of Goodwyn see David Montgomery, "On Goodwyn's Populists," *Marxist Perspectives* (Summer, 1978); Robert W. Cherny, "Lawrence Goodwyn and Nebraska Populism: A Review Essay," *Great Plains Quarterly* (Summer, 1981); Stanley B. Parsons et al., "The Role of Cooperatives in the Movement Culture of Populism," *Journal of American History* (March, 1983).

Two short histories of American Populism recently appeared: Gene Clanton, *Populism: The Humane Preference in America, 1890–1900* (1991) and Robert C. McMath, Jr., *American Populism: A Social History, 1977–1898* (1993). McMath has written an unusually insightful, concise history of the movement. Originally written in 1899 and republished in 1992, William A. Peffer's *Populism, Its Rise and Fall* represents a valuable history written by a person who played a major role in the People's party. Basing his work on textual analyses of major Populist spokesmen, Normal Pollack discussed the movement's ideology in two books: *The Just Polity: Populism, Law, and Human Welfare* (1987) and *The Humane Economy: Populism, Capitalism, and Democracy* (1990). In *American Radicalism, 1865–1901* (1946), Chester McArthur Destler examined Populist ideology within the context of earlier reforms and explored the attempt to forge a Populist-labor coalition in Illinois.

Other general accounts that warrent consideration include James M. Youngsdale, *Populsim: A Psychohistorical Perspective* (1975) and James Turner, "Understanding the Populists," *Journal of American History* (September, 1980).

Henry C. Dethloff and Robert W. Miller, eds., *A List of References for the History of the Farmers' Alliance and Populist Party* (1989) offers the most inclusive bibliography. For a critical assessment of Populist scholarship since 1970 see William F. Holmes, "Populism: In Search of Context," *Agricultural History* (Fall, 1990).

Background. For studies examining agricultural and economic development in the West that contributed to the rise of Populism see Fred A. Shannon, *The Farmers' Last Frontier, 1865–1900* (1945); Gilbert C. Fite, *The Farmers' Frontier, 1865–1900* (1966); Allan Bogue, *Money at Interest: The Farm Mortgage on the Middle Boarder* (1955); Bogue, *From Prairie to Corn Belt: Farming on the Illinois and Iowa Prairies in the Nineteenth Century* (1963); Roy Vernon Scott, *The Agrarian Movement in Illinois, 1880–1896* (1962); Craig Miner, *West of Wichita: Settling the High Plains of Kansas, 1865–1900* (1986); and Anne Mayhew, "A Reappraisal of the Causes of Farm Protest in the United States, 1870-1900," *Journal of Economic History* (June, 1972).

Developments in the South are discussed in C. Vann Woodward, *Origins of the New South, 1877–1913* (1951); Theodore Saloutos, *Farmer Movements in the South, 1865–1933* (1960); Gavin Wright, *Old South, New South: Revolutions in the Southern Economy Since the Civil War* (1986); and Lacy C. Ford, "Rednecks and Merchants: Economic Development and Social Tensions in the South Carolina Upcountry, 1865–1900," *Journal of American History* (September, 1984).

In *The Roots of Southern Populism: Yeomen Farmers and the Transformation of the Georgia Upcountry* (1983) Steven Hahn explained Populism as a response to the change that the upcountry experienced between 1850 and 1890 as it moved from a precapitalist to a capitalist society. A pivotal issue in Hahn's interpretation involves the opposition of the small farmer class to the implementation of fence laws that restricted their livestock from foraging in the woods and open range. The *Journal of Southern History* (May, 1993) published a stimulating exchange of that issue: Shawn

Everett Kantor and J. Morgan Kousser, "Common Sense or Commonwealth? The Fence Law and Institutonal Change in the Postbellum South;" Steven Hahn, "A Response: Common Cents or Historical Sense?"; and Kanton and Kousser, "A Rejoinder: Two Visions of History."

Agricultural Organizations. The history of the Patrons of Husbandry is discussed in Solon J. Buck, *The Granger Movement* (1913); D. Sven Nordin, *Rich Harvest: A History of the Grange, 1867–1900* (1974); and Thomas A. Woods, *Knights of the Plow: Oliver H. Kelley and the Origins of the Grange in Republican Ideology* (1991). The starting point for understanding the Southern Alliance is Robert C. McMath's *Populist Vanguard: A History of the Southern Farmers' Alliance* (1974). See also McMath's "Sandy Land and Hogs 'n the Timber: (Agri)cultural Origins of the Farmers' Alliance in Texas," in Steven Hahn and Jonathan Prude, eds., *Countryside in the Age of Capitalist Transformation: Essays in the Social History of Rural America* (1985). Two sociologists have written important studies of the Alliance: Michael Schwartz, *Radical Protest and Social Structure: The Southern Farmers' Alliance and Cotton Tenancy, 1880–1890* (1976); and Donna A. Barnes, *Farmers in Rebellion: The Rise and Fall of the Southern Farmers' Alliance and People's Party in Texas* (1984). Other studies that address the Southern Alliance include Lala Carr Steelman, "The Role of Elias Carr in the North Carolina Farmers' Alliance," *North Carolina Historical Review* (Spring, 1980); Steelman, *The North Carolina Farmers' Alliance: A Political History, 1887–1893* (1985); Theodore R. Mitchell, *Political Education in the Southern Farmers' Alliance, 1887–1900* (1987); William F. Holmes, "The Southern Farmers' Alliance and the Georgia Senatorial Election of 1890," *Journal of Southern History* (May, 1984); and Holmes "The Southern Farmers' Alliance and the Jute Cartel," *Journal of Southern History* (February, 1994). For information on the Northern Alliance see Roy V. Scott, "Milton George and the Farmers' Alliance Movement," *Mississippi Valley Historical Review* (June, 1958).

Historiography of the 1950s and 1960s. Much of the work that appeared during these decades can be considered as part of a distinct school, because it related to a debate between those who viewed Populism as a movement harboring dangerous tendencies and those who viewed it as a constructive reform. For studies that present Populism as a negative force see Richard Hofstadter, *The Age of Reform: From Bryan to F.D.R.* (1955); Victor C. Ferkiss, "Populist Influences on Amercian Fascism," *Western Political Quarterly* (June, 1957); Peter Viereck, "The Revolt Against the Elite," in Daniel Bell, ed., *The Radical Right: The New Amercian Right* (1964); Seymour M. Lipset, "The Sources of the Radical Right," *ibid.*, and Oscar Handlin, "Reconsidering the Populists," *Agricultural History* (April, 1965).

For works that present Populism as a positive force see C. Vann Woodward, "The Populist Heritage and the Intellectual," *American Scholar* (Winter, 1959); Norman Pollack, "Hofstadter on Populism: A Critique of the *Age of Reform*," *Journal of Southern History* (November, 1960); Pollack, *The Populist Response to Industrial America* (1962); Pollack, "The Myth of Populist Anti-Semitism," *American Historical Review* (October, 1962); Walter T. K. Nugent, *The Tolerant Populists: Kansas Populism and Nativism* (1963); and Michael Paul Rogin, *The Intellectuals and McCarthy: The Radical Specter* (1967).

Hofstadter's work received illuminating analysis in Alan Brinkley, "Richard Hofstadter's *The Age of Reform:* A Reconsideration," *Reviews in American History* (September, 1985) and Richard M. Collins, "The Originality Trap: Richard Hofstadter on Populism," *Journal of American History* (June, 1989).

Populism in the Western Plains. Arthur F. Bentley's *The Conditions of the Western Farmer as Illustrated by the Ecomonic History of a Nebraska Township* (1893) was one of the earliest scholarly studies that examined the conditions that gave rise to Populism. Important studies of Nebraska Populism that appeared more recently include Frederick C. Luebke, "Mainstreet and the Countryside: Patterns of Voting in Nebraska during the Populist Era," *Nebraska History* (Fall, 1969); Stanley B. Parsons, *The Populist Context: Rural vs. Urban Power on a Great Plains Frontier* (1973); and Robert W. Cherny, *Populism, Progressivism, and the Transformation of Nebraska Politics, 1885–1915* (1981). Whereas Parsons presented Populism as a movement without great staying power, Cherny found that it enjoyed strong grass roots support and that it influenced Nebraska politics well into the twentieth century.

Able studies of Kansas Populism include Gene Clanton, *Kansas Populism: Ideas and Men* (1969); Peter H. Argersinger, *Populism and Politics: William Alfred Peffer and the People's Party* (1974); and Scott G. McNail, *The Road to Rebellion: Class Formation and Kansas Populism, 1865–1900* (1988).

Other studies that warrant attention include Peter H. Argersinger, "Ideology and Behavior: Legislative Politics and Western Populism," *Agricultural History* (January, 1984); Argersinger, "Populists in Power; Public Policy and Legislative Behavior," *Journal of Interdisciplinary History* (Summer, 1987); John Dibbern, "Who Were the Populists? A Study of Grass Roots Alliancemen in Dakota," *Agricultural History* (October, 1982); Martin Ridge, *Ignatius Donnelly: The Portrait of a Politician* (1962); Worth Robert Miller, *Oklahoma Populism: A History of the People's Party in the Oklahoma Territory* (1987); Roger F. Wyman, "Agrarian or Working-Class Radicalism? The Electorial Basis of Populism in Wisconsin," *Political Science Quarterly* (Winter, 1974–1975); and Karl D. Bicha, *Western Populism: Studies in Ambivalent Conservatism* (1976).

Populism in the Rocky Mountains and on the West Coast. Mary Ellen Glass, *Silver and Politics in Nevada, 1892–1902* (1969); Thomas Clich, *Urban Populism and Free Silver in Montana: A Narrative of Ideology in Political Action* (1972); James Edward Wright, *The Politics of Populism: Dissent in Colorado* (1974); Robert W. Larson, *New Mexico Populism: A Study of Radical Protest in a Western Territory* (1974); Larson, *Populism in the Mountain West* (1986); Carlos A. Schwantes, *Radical Heritage: Labor, Socialism and Reform in Washington and British Columbia, 1885–1917* (1979); John R. Morris, *Davis Waite: The Ideology of a Western Populist* (1981); John T. McGreevy, "Farmers, Nationalists, and the Origins of California Populism," *Pacific Historical Review* (November, 1989); and William Joseph Gaboury, *Dissension in the Rockies: A History of Idaho Populism* (1988).

Southern Populism. Roscoe Martin, *The People's Party in Texas* (1933); C. Vann Woodward, *Tom Watson: Agrarian Rebel* (1938); William I. Hair, *Bourbonism and Agrarian Protest: Louisiana Politics, 1877–1900* (1969); Sheldon Hackney, *Populism to Progressivism in Alabama* (1969); William Warren Rogers, *The*

One-Gallused Rebellion: Agrarianism in Alabama, 1865–1896 (1970); Frederick A. Bode, "Religion and Class Hegemony: A Populist Critique in North Carolina, " *Journal of Southern History* (August, 1971); Carl N. Degler, *The Other South: Southern Dissenters in the Nineteenth Century* (1974); Roger Louis Hart, *Redeemers, Bourbons, and Populists: Tennessee, 1870-1896* (1975); Bruce Palmer, *"Man over Money": The Southern Populist Critique of American Capitalism* (1980); Dwight B. Billings, Jr., *Planters and the Making of a "New South": Class, Politics, and Development in North Carolina, 1865–1900* (1983); Barton C. Shaw, *The Wool-Hat Boys: Georgia's Populist Party* (1984); Paul D. Escott, *Many Excellent People: Power and Privilege in North Carolina* (1985); James L. Hunt, "The Making of a Populist: Marion Butler, 1863–1895," *North Carolina Historical Review* (January, April, July, 1985); Charles L. Flynn, Jr., "Procrustean Bedfellows and Populists: An Alternative Hypothesis," in Jeffrey J. Crow et al., eds., *Race, Class, and Politics in Southern History: Essays in Honor of Robert Durden* (1989); and Eric Anderson, "The Populists and Capitalist America: The Case of Edgecombe County, North Carolina," *ibid.* For an insightful treatment of southern Populism that synthesizes much of the recent literature, see Edward L. Ayers, *The Promise of the New South: Life After Reconstruction* (1992).

Populism and Race. C. Vann Woodward initiated the argument that the Populists offered an alternative to the harsh racism that swept across the South in the 1890s. See Woodward's *Strange Career of Jim Crow* (1955, 1974). Woodward's position received strong support in Lawrence Goodwyn's "Populist Dreams and Negro Rights: East Texas as a Case Study," *American Historical Review* (December, 1971). Although he does not directly address the issue of the Populists offering an alternative to harsher forms of racism, J. Morgan Kousser's *The Shaping of Southern Politics: Suffrage Restriction and the Establishment of the One-Party South, 1880–1910* (1974) lends support to Woodward's position. Historians who have argued that the southern Populists treated African Americans more or less like southern Democrats treated them include Robert Saunders, "Southern Populists and the Negro, 1893–1895," *Journal of Negro History* (July, 1969); Charles Crowe, "Tom Watson, Populists, and Blacks Reconsidered," *idid.,* (April, 1970); Gerald H. Gaither, *Blacks and the Populist Revolt:*

Ballots and Bigotry in the "New South" (1977); Barton C. Shaw, *The Wool Hat Boys: Georgia's Populist Party* (1984); Worth Robert Miller, "Building a Progressive Coalition in Texas: The Populist-Reform Democratic Rapprochement, 1900–1907," *Journal of Southern History* (May, 1986); Gregg Cantrell and D. Scott Barton, "Texas Populists and the Failure of Biracial Politics," *ibid.* (November, 1989).

For other studies that address the issue of Populism and race see William H. Chafe, "The Negro and Populism: A Kansas Case Study," *Journal of Southern History* (August, 1968); Floyd J. Miller, "Black Protest and White Leadership: A Note on the Colored Farmers' Alliance," *Phylon* (Summer, 1972); Martin Dunn, "Black Populism: A Study of the Colored Farmers' Alliance through 1891," *Journal of Ethnic Studies* (Fall, 1974); and William F. Holmes, "The Demise of the Southern Farmers' Alliance," *Journal of Southern History* (May, 1975).

Gender and Populism. Although no one has yet published an in-depth work on the role of women in the movement, the following are helpful: Annie L. Diggs, "The Women of the Alliance Movement," *Arena* (July, 1892); Julie Roy Jeffrey, "Women in the Southern Farmers' Alliance: A Reconsideration of the Role and Status of Women in the Late-Nineteenth-Century South," *Feminist Studies* (Fall, 1975); Mari Jo Buhle, *Women and American Socialism, 1870–1920* (1981); Ruth Borden, *Women and Temperance: The Quest for Power and Liberty, 1873–1900* (1981); Marilyn Dell Brady; "Populism and Feminism in a Newspaper by and for Women of the Kansas Farmers' Alliance, 1891–1894," *Kansas History* (Winter, 1984–1985).

Political Developments of the 1890s. Paul Glad, *The Trumpet Soundeth: William Jennings Bryan and His Democracy, 1896–1912* (1960); Stanley L. Jones, *The Presidential Election of 1896* (1964); Gilbert C. Fite, "Republican Strategy and the Farm Vote in the Presidential Campaign of 1896," *Mississippi Valley Historical Review* (July, 1959); Carl N. Degler, "American Political Parties and the Rise of the City," *Journal of American History* (June, 1964); Robert Durden, *The Climax of Populism: The Election of 1896* (1966); Paul Kleppner, *The Cross of Culture: a Social Analysis of Midwestern Politics, 1850–1900* (1970); Richard Jensen, *The Winning of the Midwest: Social and Political Conflict,*

1888–1896 (1971); and Peter H. Argersinger, " 'A Place on the Ballot': Fusion, Politics and Antifusion Laws," *American Historical Review* (April, 1980).

Populism, Progressivism, and Socialism. For earlier works that argued for a close relation between Populism and Progressivism see John D. Hicks, "The Legacy of Populism in the Middle West," *Agricultural History* (October, 1949). However, Sheldon Hackney, *Populism to Progressivism in Alabama* (1969) argued that the two movements were quite distinct. Scholars who have come to similar conclusions include Gene Clanton, "Populism, Progressivism, and Equality: The Kansas Paradigm," *Agricultural History* (July, 1977) and Robert W. Cherny, *Populism, Progressivism, and the Transformation of Nebraska Politics* (1981). Historians who recently have found continuity between Populism and Progressivism include Jeffrey J. Crow, " 'Populism to Progressivism' in North Carolina: Governor Daniel Russell and His War on the Southern Railway Company," *Historian* (August, 1975); Worth Robert Miller, "Building a Progressive Coalition in Texas: The Populist-Reform Democratic Rapproachement, 1900–1907," *Journal of Southern History* (May, 1986); Sam Webb, "From Independents to Populists to Progressive Republicans: The Case of Chilton County, Alabama, 1880–1920," *ibid.* (November, 1993). James R. Green has explored the relation between Populism and socialism: *Grass Roots Socialism in the Southwest, 1895–1943* (1978) and "Populism, Socialism, and the Promise of Democracy," *Radical History* (Fall, 1980).